The Black Towns

NORMAN L. CROCKETT

THE REGENTS PRESS OF KANSAS

Lawrence

Bur
E
185.6
.C93

Library of Congress Cataloging in Publication Data
Crockett, Norman L
    The Black towns.
    Bibliography: p.
    Includes index.
    1. Afro-Americans—History—1877-1964.
2. Black nationalism—United States—History.
3. Cities and towns—United States—History.
4. Afro-American—Segregation. I. Title.
E185.6.C93   973'.04'96073   78-15099
ISBN 0-7006-0185-6

THE BLACK TOWNS

ANARCHY

TO

FOUR BEAUTIFUL PEOPLE

Norman, Jr.
Scott
Denise
Colleen

Contents

List of Illustrations

Preface

FROM APPOMATTOX TO WORLD WAR I, blacks continued their quest for a secure position in the American system. The problem was how to be both black and American. That is, how could people with dark skin find acceptance, or even toleration, in a society in which the boundaries of normative behavior, the values, and the very definition of what it meant to be an American were determined and enforced by whites? At every turn, white and American seemed to be synonymous. Blacks learned, as immigrants discovered soon after their arrival on American shores, that the melting pot only melted those individuals with light complexions who were willing to renounce their cultural or ethnic identity. Dark-skinned people, and those immigrants who refused to forsake their heritage, quickly felt the full force of white American prejudice and violence. Yet, whether they were the products of slavery and the plantation system or of the discrimination and segregation of a northern city, most blacks during the immediate postbellum years considered the United States as their home. Their cultural identity as a people, although at times vague, was clearly rooted in the American past.

Reducing the strategies to their simplest terms, black leaders followed four basic approaches in attempting to solve the black-American dichotomy: political action inside the framework of the Republican party; concentration on economic self-help, moral uplift, and racial solidarity; direct and open confrontation with all forms of social injustice; and exodus to Canada, Africa, or some other country. Some black spokesmen shifted from one position to another, while the philosophy of any individual might contain a combination of several proposals. Nothing worked. As blacks groped for the correct formula, or a combination of formulas, violence against them increased while social practice and legislative statute drove the race deeper and deeper into segregation and poverty.

A few black leaders proposed a fifth approach—self-segregation inside the United States within the protective confines of an all-black community. Precedent existed for such an idea. Several black settlements formed during the post-Revolutionary era, and by the late antebellum years a number of such towns dotted the East and the Middle West. Since most of the residents of these early communities isolated themselves, sought only to be left alone, and farmed small plots of marginal land, whites usually ignored them. Many of the people moving to such settlements were uneducated former slaves who lacked the ability or inclination to articulate the practical or ideological reasons underlying their migration to a separate community.

The black-town idea reached its peak in the fifty years after the Civil War. The dearth of extant records prohibits an exact enumeration of them, but at least sixty black communities were settled between 1865 and 1915. With more than twenty, Oklahoma led all other states. Unfortunately, little is known about many of the black towns. We know little of the aspirations, fears, and everyday lives of people living in such places as Blackdom, New Mexico; Hobson City, Alabama; Allensworth, California; and Rentiesville, Oklahoma, because residents failed to record their experiences and whites were not interested in preserving and collecting material on the black towns.

This study concentrates on the formation, growth, and failure of five such communities. Comparison with fragmentary records available on other black towns indicates that these five represent a typical picture of black-town life in other communities of a similar size and type during the same time period. The towns and the date of their settlement are: Nicodemus, Kansas (1879), established at the time of the black exodus from the South; Mound Bayou, Mississippi (1887), perhaps the most prominent black town because of its close ties to Booker T. Washington and Tuskegee Institute; Langston, Oklahoma (1891), plotted after the run into the Unassigned Lands and visualized by one of its promoters as the nucleus for the creation of an all-black state in the West; and Clearview (1903) and Boley (1904), in Oklahoma, twin communities in the Creek Nation which offer the opportunity to observe certain aspects of Indian-black relations in one area. As used here, the term "black town" refers to a separate community containing a population at least 90 percent black in which the residents attempted to determine their own political destiny.

The rhetoric and behavior of blacks—isolated from the domination of whites and freed from the daily reinforcement of their subordinate rank in the larger society—inside the limits of their own community provide the chance to observe in microcosm black attitudes about many aspects of American life. The role of blacks in town promotion and settlement, long a neglected area in western and urban history, can also be examined. Moreover, the black-town experiment clearly indicates the ambiguities in black thought between integration and separation, and perception and reality, and also illustrates the impact of isolation on individuals and groups. The black-town ideology, in large part formulated and expounded by promoters, sought to combine economic self-help and moral uplift with an intense pride in race, while at the same time encouraging an active role in county and state politics. Unlike those who migrated thousands of miles to Africa, some people who entered the towns as settlers saw the community as a temporary expedient. Integration into the mainstream of American life constituted their ultimate goal.

The dream of the black town as an agricultural service center, growing in population and filling with small stores and manufacturing plants hiring local labor, ran counter to the economic realities of the time. Such a vision, consistent with the appeal of the Republican party in the North during the late 1850's, disregarded the development of large-scale enterprise and the drive for industrial concentration around the turn of the century. Although discrimination and the lack of capital played a part in their demise, the black towns' failure must also be attributed to the many forces at work in the local, regional, and national economies. The onslaught of modernization destroyed thousands of small towns, unhampered by racial prejudice, during the same period. Yet, lacking money and education, and unaccustomed to guiding their own political affairs, poor blacks from the rural South responded to the call of promoters to join them in a racial and town-building experiment.

Most scholars in the social and genetic sciences have discarded the use of race as a meaningful category in attempting to understand human differences. In the pages that follow, the terms "race" and "racial" are employed only in the context in which they were used by white and black alike around the turn of the century.

I am indebted to the personnel of many libraries, manuscript collections, and county repositories, but the fear that one who helped might be overlooked prohibits the naming and thanking of each individual. In a general way, however, I would like to express my appreciation to the staff of the Library of Congress, Kansas State Historical Society, Hampton Institute, Mississippi Department of Archives and History, and the Oklahoma Historical Society. Valuable assistance was rendered by many people employed in the county courthouses in Cleveland, Mississippi, and Hill City, Kansas, and in Okemah and Guthrie, Oklahoma. My thanks also to Mrs. Ora Switzer and Mrs. Margaret Moore for sharing their knowledge of Nicodemus and Hill City, Kansas. Larry Christensen, H. Wayne Morgan, Henry Tobias, William Savage, Jr., and Philip Vaughan read all or portions of the manuscript and offered constructive advice. Of course, I do not expect them to share the blame for any mistakes. The patience of my wife, De Crockett, while reading and re-reading revised drafts of the same chapter and then posing important ideas and questions, and her understanding while I mentally walked the streets of the black towns can hardly be repaid with a simple thank you, but I extend it anyway. Grants from The University of Oklahoma Research Council and funds from the Department of History helped in large part to finance this study.

1

Promoters
and Settlers

IT WAS MID-AFTERNOON and Willianna Hickman was
exhausted. Nearly three weeks had passed since she, her
husband, Daniel, and their six children had left Payne Station, Kentucky, bound for Nicodemus, Kansas. The Hickman family had joined a party of approximately three
hundred people leaving in May, 1878, and it seemed to her
they had been homeless for months. It had taken only two
days to reach Ellis, Kansas, by rail, but en route an epidemic
of measles had spread through the children in the group,
killing several. She felt fortunate that the members of her
family had been spared, but they were all ill, tired, or irrita-
ble, and the two weeks spent recuperating in a crowded
tent pitched near Ellis had failed to raise her spirits. Now
after a full day and a morning in a bumpy wagon they were
finally nearing Nicodemus. The barren and treeless land-
scape in the area seemed uninviting—so unlike northern
Kentucky—but she could at least look forward to a settled
existence in a new house. As they neared their destination
others in the party began shouting and singing. But Willianna could not see the town site. Then, she recalled years
later, "my husband pointed out various smokes coming out

1

of the ground and said, that is Nicodemus. The families lived in dugouts . . . and I began to cry."[1]

The idea for the establishment of Nicodemus—the name the early black colonists chose for their new town—belonged originally to William Smith and Thomas Harris, two black ministers from Clarksville, Tennessee, who traveled west in the spring of 1877 in search of land. Smith and Harris, joined by W. R. Hill, a Kansas land speculator, returned to the South to promote the town in Tennessee and Kentucky. Hill spread the proposal for the establishment of a black settlement by speaking before the congregations of rural churches. Although he was white, Hill met some success in the little Baptist church at Georgetown, a few miles north of Lexington, and his audience was soon captivated by stories of a western paradise filled with abundant game, wild horses, and soil so fertile that a minimum of labor yielded bountiful harvests. Eventually a colonization society was organized in Lexington to formulate plans for a departure from that city in the summer or fall. The area described in such colorful detail lay in the heart of the Great Plains on the South Solomon River in what was soon to become Graham County in northwestern Kansas.[2]

Hill had emigrated from Indiana to Kansas in 1876 at the age of twenty-six, attracted there by the opportunities for speculation in land and the fees homesteaders were willing to pay for locating and filing claims. Plans for a black town constituted only one of his colonization schemes. In December of 1877, for example, he journeyed from Ellis to eastern Kansas to organize a group of white settlers to migrate to the western half of the state, and in January of the following year he located them near the present site of Stockton. Hill's major promotional venture, however, was the founding of Hill City in 1878, a town he named after himself and which he hoped in time would become the seat of Graham County.[3]

Hill's activities soon attracted the attention of James P. Pomeroy, an Atchison coal dealer and land speculator. Following a meeting between the two in Atchison, Pomeroy

W. R. Hill, founder of Nicodemus and Hill City, Kansas.
Courtesy Kansas State Historical Society.

apparently agreed to finance the promotion of Hill City as
the county seat. Millbrook had been named the temporary
county seat of Graham County, but Pomeroy offered to
donate a courthouse, costing at least $10,000, and the land on
which to build it if voters would agree to move the seat of
government. During the early 1880's, Pomeroy continued to
fund Hill City's "boom," invested in approximately eighty
thousand acres of land in Graham, Norton, and Trego counties, and hired Hill as his agent. Hill's close relationship

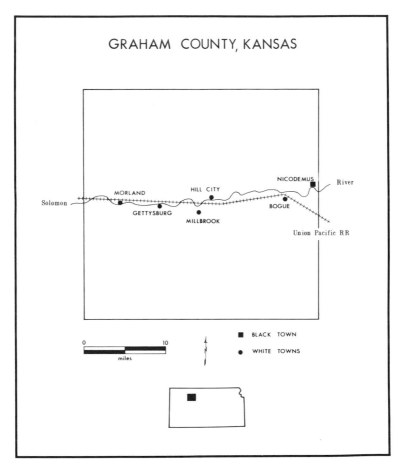

GRAHAM COUNTY, KANSAS

with Pomeroy, along with his later activities, convinced some whites in western Kansas that the creation and settlement of Nicodemus was a plot Hill perpetuated to further his own political ambitions and to ensure the location of the county seat at Hill City.[4]

It was against this setting that the first band of potential Nicodemus recruits, numbering some sixty men, women, and children, arrived in Kansas in June, 1877. They were not alone. Those bound for the new town mingled with the

NICODEMUS,

THE GATE CITY OF GRAHAM COUNTY

has had no unhealthy boom, but has kept steady pace with the development of the surrounding country.

Nicodemus has excellent water, enterprising citizens, good schools, churches and is surrounded by farming lands that surpass any in the beautiful South Solomon Valley.

If you are looking for safe investments, sure profits and a home where the people are wide awake take advantage of the cheap rates, pack your grip and steer your bark for Nicodemus. Don't wait, delay will prove dangerous.

Promotional advertisement for Nicodemus. From *Western Cyclone*.

flood of black immigrants pouring out of the South into Kansas in the late 1870's. Driven out of Mississippi, Louisiana, and other states along the Mississippi River by crop failures, fever, and outrages against their race, and lured northward by the promotional literature and lectures of Benjamin "Pap" Singleton, an ex-slave and self-professed "Black Moses," the blacks inundated the populations of Leavenworth, Wyandotte, Kansas City, and Topeka. Although Singleton's stories and speeches of a haven for blacks in Kansas no doubt intensified the desire for migration and colonization throughout the South, there is no indication that settlers bound for Nicodemus were a part of the exodus or that Singleton was in any way connected with the settlement in Graham County.[5]

The first contingent of settlers reached the Nicodemus town site in July, 1877. Those who had paid $5 in advance were entitled to select a town lot, while other staked out farm claims within the quarter-mile section filed on by the town site company headed by Harris and managed by Hill. In addition to the individuals and families who joined the colony from time to time, four other organized groups, two from Kentucky and one each from Tennessee and Mississippi, arrived within the first three years. By 1879, the Nicodemus colony numbered approximately seven hundred persons scattered over a seventy-two–square-mile area, while inside the town limits stood thirty-five houses, two churches, and one store, most constructed from the sod of the Kansas prairie.[6]

Nicodemus may have been touted as a Utopia where southern blacks could find freedom from want, but life for many early residents became almost unbearable. Those living in dugouts quickly found swarms of fleas demanding equal occupancy, and, lacking pesticides, settlers met only partial success in exterminating the parasites by throwing hot ashes on the dirt floors. In addition to the fleas, coyotes, rattlesnakes, and tarantulas infested the countryside. Life's precarious existence posed further problems for the very

All Colored People

THAT WANT TO

GO TO KANSAS,

On September 5th, 1877,

Can do so for $5.00

IMMIGRATION.

WHEREAS, We, the colored people of Lexington, Ky,. knowing that there is an abundance of choice lands now belonging to the Government, have assembled ourselves together for the purpose of locating on said lands. Therefore,

BE IT RESOLVED, That we do now organize ourselves into a Colony, as follows:— Any person wishing to become a member of this Colony can do so by paying the sum of one dollar ($1.00), and this money is to be paid by the first of September, 1877, in instalments of twenty-five cents at a time, or otherwise as may be desired.

RESOLVED, That this Colony has agreed to consolidate itself with the Nicodemus Towns, Solomon Valley, Graham County, Kansas, and can only do so by entering the vacant lands now in their midst, which costs $5.00.

RESOLVED, That this Colony shall consist of seven officers—President, Vice-President, Secretary, Treasurer, and three Trustees. President—M. M. Bell; Vice-President —Isaac Talbott; Secretary—W. J. Niles; Treasurer—Daniel Clarke; Trustees—Jerry Lee, William Jones, and Abner Webster.

RESOLVED, That this Colony shall have from one to two hundred militia, more or less, as the case may require, to keep peace and order, and any member failing to pay in his dues, as aforesaid, or failing to comply with the above rules in any particular, will not be recognized or protected by the Colony.

Kansas immigration circular. Courtesy Kansas State Historical
Society.

young. In order to protect their babies from the ravages of prairie fires, mothers wrapped them in wet blankets and placed them in the deep holes being dug for wells.

Despite these and other hardships, at least one businessman remained optimistic concerning the town's future. Z. T. Fletcher, one of the earliest settlers, opened a general store in the first building constructed completely above ground level, but one customer later recalled that in the beginning cornmeal and syrup constituted the total inventory. For several months, then, settlers from the colony could be seen walking the thirty-five miles to and from Ellis for provisions. Five teams of harness animals were shared by all those who wished to farm, and travelers in wagon trains passing westward were sometimes offered lodging in exchange for a few days' use of their animals and plows. Those lacking horses or oxen struggled to turn the heavy sod with shovels, hoes, or other hand tools. To provide hungry families with a diet of more than rabbits and birds, men of the settlement walked to Ellis and surrounding towns seeking work, and a few roamed as far as eastern Colorado. The women and children who remained at home collected dried bones from the prairie for sale to dealers who shipped them east to be ground into fertilizer. But even with all these efforts, there was not enough money for subsistence.[7]

In an attempt to aid the destitute, two Nicodemus ministers, Silas Lee and S. P. Roundtree, journeyed to nearby white communities to solicit food and clothing, but the resentment they encountered there against blacks prompted them to search for aid in eastern Kansas and in states farther north.[8] Economic prosperity came slowly. Stephen Lilly, enumerator for the Kansas state census in 1885, reported that Nicodemus township contained "no libraries, no manufactories, no mines . . . no newspapers" and that 40 percent of the year's wheat crop had been destroyed by severe winter weather.[9] Understandably, some residents returned to the South, others moved on west, but most remained. Very soon, they believed, the railroad would arrive and Nicodemus would boom.

The train gradually picked up speed and moved north toward Vicksburg. Isaiah T. Montgomery, his cousin Benjamin T. Green, and seven other men stood near the track staring at the wilderness before them. This was to be the new Canaan for blacks in the Mississippi Delta, this overgrown, swampy land bordered by the Yazoo and Mississippi rivers—the home of the mosquito, periodic floods, wild animals, and fever—where no person had previously been induced to settle. Montgomery had secretly been here twice before, once staying for a month, before deciding reluctantly to accept an offer from the Louisville, New Orleans, and Texas Railroad for land divided into small tracts for black farmers and the right to cut and sell the timber. Now, in the

Isaiah T. Montgomery, founder of Mound Bayou, Mississippi. Courtesy Mississippi Department of Archives and History.

summer of 1886, he had returned with Green and the others to commence clearing the land for the first group of black settlers scheduled to arrive the following February.[10]

Montgomery, a medium-sized and muscular man who kept his own counsel, was no stranger to hard work and adversity. Born a slave in 1847 on Mississippi's Hurricane Plantation and owned by Joseph Davis (brother of Jefferson Davis), Isaiah entered the Davis household at the age of nine as a servant and filing clerk. Taught to read and write by George Stewart, another slave, he later became Joseph's private secretary and office attendant, handling plantation records and sorting and filing correspondence. At the outbreak of the Civil War, most of the Davis slaves were moved into Alabama, but Isaiah remained with his father at Hurricane to look after the plantation. Taken aboard the Union gunboat *Benton* on the Mississippi River, he became seriously ill while serving as a cabin boy and gunner's mate and was taken north and released from the service in late 1863 in Mound City, Illinois. During the next two years he worked as a carpenter and in a canal boat dockyard near Cumminsville, Ohio.[11]

With his father, Benjamin, and brother, William, Montgomery returned to the South at the close of the war. The three men signed agreements to operate the combined plantations of Joseph and Jefferson Davis with the ultimate intention of purchasing the land. The settlement there, composed primarily of blacks who had been slaves in the immediate locality, thrived for seven years; and in time Montgomery and Sons became the third largest cotton-producing concern in Mississippi. But recurring floods, a fire, falling prices, and the possibility of lengthy court litigations with some of the Davis heirs convinced Montgomery to abandon the project.[12]

In addition, the Kansas exodus in the late 1870's seriously threatened Montgomery's farming operations. During March, 1879, twenty families—comprising seventy men, women, and children—suddenly left the Davis plantations bound for the Promised Land of Kansas. After arriving in Wyandotte, some of the disappointed "exodusters" sought Montgomery's assistance in returning south. Responding to their pleas, he left for Kansas on April 22. He discovered that eight or ten had died en route, and the remaining refugees were short of food and living in makeshift shanties, in boxcars, or in tents pitched along the levee. Unaccustomed to the climate, several had contracted pneumonia or suffered from severe cases of diarrhea from drinking the water of the Missouri River. For those who wished to return, Montgomery booked passage on the next steamboat bound for St. Louis. He then journeyed on to determine the whereabouts of others. In Lawrence he found nine families from the Davis plantations who wanted to remain in Kansas, and it was there he conceived the idea for the creation of a settlement composed of people coming from the same part of Mississippi. Montgomery proposed the plan to the Kansas Freedmen's Relief Association, purchased a section of land, and helped to locate the emigrants in what was called the Wabaunsee Colony fifty miles west of Topeka. He then returned to Mississippi and wrote to the governor of Kansas explaining his actions.[13]

Montgomery personally favored the exodus, although he harbored some doubts concerning its practicability; even the scene of suffering and despair he first encountered near the river at Wyandotte failed to alter his opinion. After visiting Kansas, talking to some of the people there, and witnessing the attempts to aid members of his race, he felt that with proper organization and leadership migration to the West offered industrious blacks an opportunity to better their condition. Upon his return to Mississippi, he was besieged with questions regarding the exodus, and he admitted to Kansas Governor John St. John that he spoke to blacks and whites differently on the subject. Since any favorable comment would spread like wildfire and might initiate a new wave of emigration, Montgomery carefully concealed his true feelings as well as his activities in aiding refugees, although he continued to dispatch seed and supplies to those he had helped settle at Wabaunsee. To inquiring whites he said that the state was unequipped to handle a wholesale influx of blacks, that much suffering existed, and that Kansans did not understand the "proper management of colored people."[14] This pleased them. If St. John responded to his letter, Montgomery warned him not to affix a return address on the outside of the envelope because in Mississippi it had been a "custom of a century or more to ransack the mails to prevent the circulation of documents breathing the spirit of freedom."[15]

After closing out the operation of the Davis plantations, Montgomery moved to Vicksburg and in 1885 opened a small mercantile firm near the present site of the national cemetery. It was there that George W. McGinnis, land commissioner for the Louisville, New Orleans, and Texas Railroad, first approached him proposing the opening of company lands in Bolivar County to black farmers. The L.N.O. and T., owned by Collis P. Huntington and R. T. Wilson, received the land grant in the mid-1880's. It was hoped that the sale of granted land would help defray some of the costs of construction, as well as quickly build settlement along the line. But railroad officials found farmers reluctant to enter the area because of the climate and the danger of malaria. McGinnis, believing that blacks were immune to the diseases of the Delta and unaffected by the high humidity and intense heat, first approached James Hill, a railroad employee and prominent black politician in Vicksburg, for assistance. Hill, knowing of the previous settlement on the Davis plantations, referred him to Montgomery. In addition to receiving the timber rights and permission to locate the new town halfway between Memphis and Vicksburg, Montgomery was assured that the railroad would never completely cancel a contract with a black settler as long as any hope of success remained. If and when a farmer failed, Montgomery agreed to put another person on the land.[16]

Isaiah contacted his thirty-two–year-old cousin Benja-

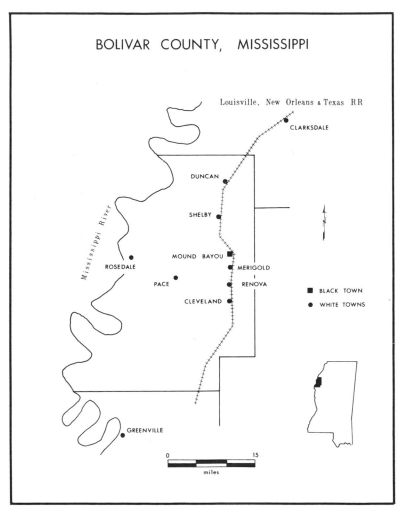

BOLIVAR COUNTY, MISSISSIPPI

Louisville, New Orleans & Texas RR

CLARKSDALE

DUNCAN

SHELBY

Mississippi River

MOUND BAYOU

ROSEDALE

MERIGOLD

PACE

RENOVA

CLEVELAND

■ BLACK TOWN
● WHITE TOWNS

GREENVILLE

0   15
miles

min T. Green, a merchant in Newton, Mississippi, who had previously worked for the Montgomerys, and persuaded him to join in purchasing 840 acres, clearing the land, and laying out the new town. By the fall of 1886, despite swarms of mosquitoes, Montgomery, Green, and their seven companions had managed to clear ninety acres and, with the aid

13

of a crude sawmill, had cut and stacked enough lumber for several houses. An Indian burial mound lying to the east and the presence of several small bayous that traversed the area inspired Montgomery to name the forty-acre town site Mound Bayou. With the preliminary work completed, the party returned to Vicksburg to marshal the first group of settlers.[17]

Although much of their labor was lost that first winter when high water wrecked the sawmill and swept away much of the lumber, forty-seven people entered Bolivar County to settle Mound Bayou in February, 1888. They came in family groups, and several had previously been associated with Montgomery and Sons at the close of the Civil War. Later, these original settlers were joined by refugees who fled to the town to escape the terror of "whitecappers" who roamed the southern counties of the state threatening blacks and driving them from their homes. One victim was told he could remain on his farm if he did not sell any of his land to other blacks or rent it to them on a sharecropping basis, attempt to expand operations, or employ his own children as laborers. He left.[18]

Within the first year, Green and Montgomery added another seven hundred acres to their original 840. Immigrants who wished to farm bought plots as small as forty acres in size at a selling price of $7 to $8 an acre, paying $1 per acre down and the balance in five equal installments. And to ensure development of the tract, Montgomery spent much of his time during the first two years traveling and delivering speeches to advertise the town. Although the railroad provided him with a surveyor and constructed a depot there, the company declined to invest additional capital in the venture. To provide necessities, Green formed a partnership with M. R. Montgomery, Isaiah's uncle, and the pair opened a general store, added a gin, and traded in cotton and lumber. To raise cash, the settlers turned to the only exploitable natural resource, timber, and within three years they had cut and sold nearly $9,000 worth of railroad ties and barrel staves. With a population of 183 in 1898, the town sought incorporation from the state, and Montgomery was appointed the first mayor. By 1904, Mound Bayou had grown to four hundred inhabitants, with an additional 2,500 farmers scattered over the township.[19]

Despite rapid growth of the town, life there remained difficult and food scarce. Entire families took to the fields, clearing the trees and heavy undergrowth in order to plant cotton, corn, and other crops. Of necessity, house-raisings and work-sharing became common practices. During the first year, Montgomery taught the younger children to read and write in his cabin in the evening. At harvest time, the women and children of the settlement sought work picking cotton at fifty cents per hundred pounds at Shelby and the other towns of the Yazoo Delta.[20] One settler who brought his family to Mound Bayou in 1888 later remembered that "many times we had only bread to eat and water to drink. Grease for use in the preparation of our scanty meals . . . was a rarity, and we often made along without it sometimes for two and three months in succession."[21]

Benjamin Green, a practical man who disliked whites, occasionally argued with the idealistic Montgomery over the future of the settlement.[22] Green envisioned little more than a permanent sawmill and gin, commercial houses, and an economic concentration on the sale of cotton and lumber to outside markets. Montgomery, on the other hand, hoped to create the ideal agrarian community free of class conflict or competition for wealth and with a social order based on brotherly love, all revolving around family life, schools, and churches.[23] His plan, he wrote Booker T. Washington in May, 1904, was to teach "high class farming, improvement of homes, thrift, saving, and abandonment of the mortgage systems; and add to urban life sufficient attractions to hold younger people."[24] Using Mound Bayou as his base for capital and credit, Montgomery hoped to expand black influence to the surrounding towns of Clarksdale and Greenville.[25]

It was August, 1882, and eastern Kansas was hot and humid. The Republican state convention was meeting in Leavenworth, and as the voting for auditor proceeded one delegate moved that the rules be suspended and that McCabe be nominated by acclamation. The motion failed, but a majority of the four hundred delegates nominated him on the fifth ballot. When the chair finally announced the nominee, the convention hall rocked with shouts and applause. Edward Preston McCabe, soon to be elected auditor of Kansas, was black.[26]

In just six years McCabe had moved from organizing local Republican clubs in Chicago during the Hayes-Tilden campaign to become the nominee of his party for state office. Born in Troy, New York, in 1850 and orphaned at an early age, he worked at various jobs in Maine, Massachusetts, and Rhode Island before moving to Illinois in 1875 and entering local politics there. He briefly worked as a timekeeper for Potter Palmer, the hotel and restaurant owner, and then moved into the Cook County treasurer's office to accept a clerkship. McCabe, described by one who knew him as "Indian color with straight black hair, . . . dressy and a good talker,"[27] decided to move farther west in 1878. In April of that year he arrived in Leavenworth, where he joined his friend Abram T. Hall, a thirty-one–year-old native of Illinois who had worked as a reporter on newspapers in Indianapolis, Chicago, St. Paul, Memphis, and Detroit.[28]

Hall had originally intended to proceed to a colony established by Benjamin Singleton in Hodgeman County, but by chance he overheard a conversation in a restaurant concerning Nicodemus. He and McCabe sought out John W. Niles, an agent for the settlement who was in Leavenworth to guide a party of immigrants to the town site and to pick up a shipment of relief supplies donated and sent there by the people of Topeka. The pair signed on with the group bound for Graham County. Moving first by train and then transferring to wagons, they arrived in Nicodemus in early May, 1878. Hall, who detested Kansas and thought it

Edward P. McCabe, promoter of Langston, Oklahoma. Courtesy Western History Collections, University of Oklahoma Library.

too much like a desert, had his initial encounter with rattle-snakes, chewed wild garlic to quench his thirst, and cooked with dried cow chips during the two-day journey overland. McCabe, he later remembered, found it impossible to eat food prepared so close to such unique fuel, and he sat in nauseated silence while Hall and others consumed a hearty meal the first evening.[29]

Hall and McCabe shared a sod house for a time while

17

they were employed as government surveyors and locators on public lands. Politics soon beckoned to both, however, and the white reaction to their activities was immediate. A group of businessmen in Gettysburg, a small town a few miles west of Nicodemus, formally petitioned Governor St. John in November, 1879, warning that the appointment of Hall to take the first county census would "cause a feeling against the colored people that will be detrimental," as well as strengthen a rumor current in the eastern half of the state that a majority of the population of Graham County was black.[30] Since Nicodemus township would soon be legally organized, John H. Currie, the editor of the Gettysburg *Lever,* feared that if Hall were made enumerator he might report that the area fell short of the required population of fifteen hundred, thereby defeating county formation and leaving the town of Nicodemus the virtual county seat for an indefinite period.[31] At about the same time, John S. Henry, representative of the Baptist Home Mission Board for northwestern Kansas, cautioned the governor that "the feeling against the first office of the county being given to a Col[ored] man is intense," and reminded him that the appointment would bring Hall "in contact with every excited man in the Co."[32] Despite such pressure, St. John awarded Hall the post that same month. Within one year, Hall sold all his holdings to McCabe and returned east, first to Missouri, then Illinois, eventually serving thirty-one years as a reporter and columnist for the *Pittsburgh Sunday Press.*[33]

McCabe, meanwhile, sought the county clerkship. In March, 1880, he wrote to the governor expressing fear that designing whites had used his name on county seat petitions without his consent in order to garner votes among his race. Although he and Hall had met privately with St. John during January of the previous year hoping to have Nicodemus named as the temporary county seat, and while they were still secretly working toward that goal, McCabe publicly endorsed Hill City. In response to support from both Nicodemus and Hill City, the governor appointed McCabe Graham County clerk in April, 1880.[34]

McCabe's nomination and subsequent election as auditor in November, 1882, marked the first time a black had held such a high state political office in Kansas. Support for him was far from unanimous. Upon hearing the news of the nomination at Leavenworth in August, T. J. Pickett, editor of the *Kirwin Chief*, launched into a tirade over the party's action. Perhaps illustrating his racial attitudes rather than his personal acquaintance with McCabe, the editor characterized him as a "shrewd, unscrupulous, impudent fellow, without character or moral standing."[35] McCabe had been placed on the Republican ticket, he argued, by the anti–St. John faction in the convention to embarrass the governor and to force him to keep his past promises to blacks. The *Parsons Eclipse* implicitly questioned McCabe's honesty, pointing out to its readers that the "auditor has access to the treasury at all times and admission to the money vaults when he sees fit to do so." And along with woman suffrage, prohibition, and railroad legislation, the liability of a black candidate gave the party a heavy burden to carry until November.[36]

McCabe lived in Topeka with his wife, Sarah, and their daughter, Edwina, during his four years as state auditor. Since he had won a second term in 1884 by a large margin, he had every reason to expect that his tenure in that office would continue for at least two more years. Kansas Republicans chose Topeka for the site of the 1886 state convention. In his acceptance speech for a second term as governor, John A. Martin told the assembled delegates that this was the last time he would seek the office because he felt it improper for a public servant to aspire to a third term. The insinuation was clear to the convention and to Edward McCabe. With no possibility of winning renomination, he withdrew his name from contention on July 7. The party chose Tim McCarthy as its nominee for auditor, thus essentially ending McCabe's political career in Kansas.[37]

Extant records fail to reveal all of McCabe's activities during the two years following his resignation as auditor in late 1886, but in September of that year he visited Nicodemus to speak at the ninth anniversary celebration of the town's founding. At that time, rumors circulated that he would accept a position with the Santa Fe railroad when his term of office expired. His political ambitions evidently continued, because in May, 1888, the *Nicodemus Cyclone* openly endorsed him as a candidate for delegate-at-large to the Republican National Convention soon to meet in Chicago.[38]

With the news that settlers could legally enter the Unassigned Lands in Oklahoma on March 22, 1889, McCabe formulated plans to leave Kansas and begin a new life farther south. Traveling with two white friends, he arrived in Guthrie the first day of the land rush amid the frenzied confusion generated by thousands of homeseekers. McCabe then searched for opportunities. In early 1890 he began to promote the black town of Langston, forty miles northeast of Oklahoma City. The new town, located on a hill near the Cimarron River, was named after John Mercer Langston, a prominent Howard University scholar and representative from Virginia to the fifty-first Congress.[39]

The Langston tract was subdivided into town lots, and within two years seventeen hundred of them had been sold at prices ranging from $10 to $50. To ensure sufficient room for future expansion, an additional 160 acres were added and divided into small plots suitable for farming. Operating out of his Guthrie real estate office on Oklahoma Street, McCabe founded the *Langston City Herald* in October, 1890, a newspaper designed to promote the settlement. Its circulation soon reached six hundred subscribers. Armed with weekly issues of the *Herald*, as much an advertising brochure as a newspaper, and with land contracts containing provisions for installment payments, McCabe's agents in the South solicited buyers for Langston real estate. A contract with the McCabe Townsite Company entitled its holder to a

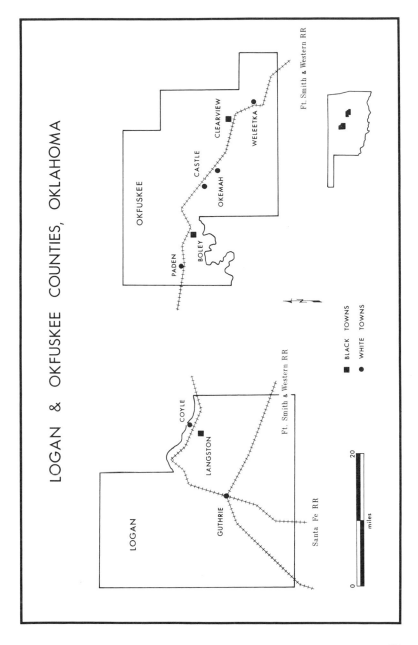

LOGAN & OKFUSKEE COUNTIES, OKLAHOMA

OKFUSKEE

PADEN

BOLEY

CASTLE

OKEMAH

CLEARVIEW

WELEETKA

Ft. Smith & Western RR

LOGAN

GUTHRIE

COYLE

LANGSTON

Ft. Smith & Western RR

Santa Fe RR

BLACK TOWNS
WHITE TOWNS

0   20
miles

railroad ticket to Guthrie, twelve miles away, and the choice of available lots.[40]

Promise and reality sometimes differed. Potential settlers were enticed to Langston by illustrations appearing in early editions of the *Herald* picturing massive buildings and

Black family on a claim near Guthrie, about 1889. Courtesy Western History Collections, University of Oklahoma Library.

broad streets—McCabe's vision of the future. Upon arrival, however, they encountered one general store and a small cluster of wooden shacks surrounded by a tent city whose residents impatiently awaited the construction of houses. Realizing the deception, several returned to the South. Although McCabe warned those contemplating relocation in Oklahoma to come prepared, not all were as fortunate as one early settler who came from Missouri with three teams of horses and enough money to support his family until a meager crop of corn and cotton could be harvested. In April, 1891, a correspondent for the *New York Times* found two hundred people living in Langston, some destitute and owning nothing except their own clothing. In order to feed the hungry, eighty-three acres of land had recently been plowed for use as a cooperative garden plot for the entire community.[41]

Despite the hardships, black families and all their

household belongings continued to pour out of the packed day coaches periodically arriving at the Guthrie depot. Others traveled by wagon, and some even walked. It was this rapid influx of black farmers from Arkansas, Texas, and other southern states that intensified the racial antagonism seething just beneath the surface ever since the territory opened. And the advertisements for Langston convinced a number of whites that the black immigrants who continued to fill the road from Guthrie to the new town represented the advance guard of a much larger invasion force.[42] McCabe had made no secret of his plan to use Langston as the nucleus of an all-black state with himself as governor.

For varying reasons, the idea of a separate territory or state set aside for the exclusive occupancy of blacks found supporters during the antebellum years, and similar proposals persisted well into the twentieth century. McCabe's scheme, however, appears to be the first systematic plan to bring the dream of a black state to fruition. In early March, 1890, he traveled to the nation's capital intent upon convincing President Benjamin Harrison that the Unassigned Lands represented an ideal geographic location for an all-black state and proposed that he be named governor as soon as the new territory was officially organized. Removal to the new lands in Oklahoma, he argued in a letter to the president, would free members of the race from the degradation of the southern caste system, thus providing them the opportunity to prove to the people of the United States their capabilities for social and economic advancement and self-government.[43] No record remains indicating Harrison's personal opinion on the matter or of his response, if any, to McCabe, but many whites in Oklahoma and elsewhere immediately feared the very worst.

Rumors circulated in newspapers that thousands of poverty-stricken blacks from all over the South were laying plans to converge on Oklahoma. During March and April, 1890, correspondents for the *St. Louis Globe-Democrat* and other newspapers reported the departure of a carload of emigrants from Helena, Arkansas, composed of the "lowest of the negro element," possessing just enough money for the expenses of the trip north; the arrival in Little Rock of five hundred blacks from Jefferson County bound for the new territory, although "completely destitute and without money"; and growing concern among the residents of Memphis that farms in the surrounding area would be completely depopulated if all those who contemplated moving to Oklahoma should leave. Some newspapers predicted violence against McCabe and the race. A white settler in Oklahoma told a reporter for the *Kansas City Evening News* that he "would not give five cents for his [McCabe's] life," if he was appointed governor and that if "the negroes attempt to capture that territory they will have to fight for it." The *New York Times* quoted an individual who had just returned from Oklahoma in February, 1890, to the effect that if Harrison appointed McCabe governor, the black leader would be assassinated within a week after he entered the territory.[44]

Unaffected by these and other threats, McCabe moved forward with his plans, hoping to congregate a large number of blacks in a majority of the senatorial and representative districts before a statehood bill could reach Congress. In September, 1891, the same month Langston was incorporated, the federal government opened the Iowa, Sac and Fox, and Shawnee and Pottawatomie reservations to settlers. For several weeks McCabe's southern agents had advertised the town as the logical gathering point for those blacks wishing to make the run because of its close proximity to the new lands. In late September the *Norman Transcript*, well known for its hostility toward blacks, reported that the town site was totally covered with immigrants' tents and that open conflict seemed inevitable because a group of couriers from the encampment had recently gone to Oklahoma City and "purchased twenty carbines and hastened back to the front."[45] Such acts, concluded the *Transcript*, placed the public land office in Oklahoma City in jeopardy. Some of the fifteen hundred men and women who awaited the opening gun at

Langston on September 22 had previously attempted to join other settlers along the starting line farther north, but fled to the protection of the town in an effort to escape the potential violence of armed whites.[46]

Claiming credit for the settlement of one thousand black families in Oklahoma during 1891, R. Emmett Stewart, new editor of the *Langston City Herald,* issued the call in November, 1892, for members of the race living in the South to begin preparations for the land rush into the Cherokee Outlet the following year. While cautioning possible settlers neither to expect a picnic nor to come unless capable of self-support for one year, the *Herald* optimistically proclaimed that freedom in Oklahoma costs only "a winchester, a frying pan, and $15.00 to file."[47]

While continuing to boost Langston from his Guthrie office, McCabe also turned his attention to the Cherokee Outlet. He entered the outlet a few days after the formal opening and, after working out a financial arrangement for some land on a Cherokee allotment, he began plotting the black town of Liberty. In September, 1893, the Santa Fe railroad commenced construction of a small depot there, while he supervised the building of several cottages, proposing to sell them to emigrants from the South on an installment basis. Liberty, however, was stillborn. The violent reaction of the white residents of Perry, three miles to the south, convinced McCabe of both the danger and hopelessness of the project.[48]

Newspaper stories of charge and denial concerning McCabe's actions, plus arguments over the exact number of blacks in Oklahoma, remained unabated during the 1890's. McCabe, meanwhile, continued to build his political future. He seemed to be everywhere—organizing local political clubs, serving as a delegate to the National Republican League, and secretary of the Republican Central Committee of Guthrie, working on campaign programs, and serving as Logan County treasurer and secretary to the Territorial Republican League. His work for the party evidently bore fruit, because in July, 1897, Governor Cassius Barnes appointed him assistant territorial auditor. Earlier that same year, the legislature gave McCabe's town a boost by creating the Colored Agricultural and Normal University locating it at Langston.[49]

By this time, however, it was obvious to most observers that McCabe and others had failed to attract a sufficient number of blacks to build a separate state somewhere in the territory. Blacks never accounted for more than 10 percent of the total population at any time during the decade of the nineties. The dream of a black state was dying, but with McCabe in office, the new university, and the Republicans in control of the territorial legislature, Langston might still become a haven from discrimination and the black cultural center of the Southwest.

Early March issues of the local newspaper had predicted that the 1911 meeting of the Farmers' Conference at Clearview, although the first such gathering there, would be well attended by people from the neighboring towns in Okfuskee County. The size of the turnout no doubt disappointed its sponsors, but James E. Thompson, a fifty-two–year-old ex-slave, had patiently waited through a morning and afternoon of talks on farming and the virtues of rural life. One after another, a succession of speakers had offered practical advice on truck farming and raising chickens, horses, and hogs, on diversified crops and the relationship between farmer and merchant. Finally, the evening session opened and it was Thompson's turn to deliver a formal lecture on town building.

Pacing back and forth on the stage in front of his audience of time-worn and weather-beaten men and women, he began slowly, mixing serious thoughts with occasional humor. These were his people, and Clearview was his home. Where better to test the initial reaction to his plan? He complimented himself upon the good fortune of this opportunity to address the Farmers' Conference and spoke of the pressing need for similar organizations in other areas. Specifically, he mentioned the Patriarchs of America, a secret fraternal order he had organized only a few weeks earlier. With little transition or warning, Thompson shifted subjects. Our plan, he said, is

> to have the government set apart some territory in some part of the United States, for the colonization of the Negroes; to have the government appraise and buy this land with government bonds which will run for a long term of years and to sell it to the Negroes in small tracts at its appraised value; the principal and interest on this land, to be collected annually in the form of a tax. . . .[50]

James E. Thompson, the wealthiest resident in the black town of Clearview, Oklahoma, hoped to revive the demand for a separate state for his race.

In many respects, Clearview was similar to the other twenty-odd black settlements in Indian Territory. Most were spawned by the easy access to cheap land made available to those coming in from the outside to take part in a series of runs, auctions, and lotteries or through the acquisition of farms granted to former Indian slaves. Also, a growing racial animosity between Indians and blacks, coupled with attempts by southern whites to impose a rigid system of segregation, constituted strong reasons for the formation of such a large number of separate communities there.

Although definitive statements concerning the treatment of Indian slaves by each of the Five Civilized Tribes must await further research, current studies indicate that through their ability to articulate and negotiate Indian demands to the federal government, some blacks rose to positions of prominence within the Seminole and Creek tribes, while many slaves enjoyed a social and economic status unheard of in the ante-bellum South. Several married into Indian families. Thinking they could escape the antagonism of whites and find a more hospitable environment, a number of blacks from the North and South illegally filtered into Indian Territory during the early 1880's. As early as 1881, James Milton Turner, a black St. Louis lawyer and former consul general to Liberia, organized the Freedmen's Oklahoma Association, which promised 160 acres of public land to any freedman who would settle there.[51] By 1898, Congress had legalized the recommendations of the Dawes Commission, which in effect succeeded in dissolving tribal autonomy as well as opening Indian lands to settlement. Thus, Creek freedmen, many of whom held allotments and were listed on tribal rolls, were quickly joined by a host of black homesteaders from surrounding states.

What followed was a curious admixture of red, black, and white racial ideologies. At first, the Creek freedmen objected to the arrival of what they called "Watchina," or "State Negroes," looking upon them as inferior and a threat to their prestige and position. One Creek freedman later remembered that he had refused to mix with the newcomers because, as he put it, "I was eating out the same pot with the Indians . . . while they was still licking the master's boots in Texas."[52] The intrusion of white racial attitudes from the South helped to intensify and solidify the barriers already present between those who claimed to be full-blood Indians and freedmen. In time most full bloods drew no distinction between Watchina and their former slaves. Freedmen were quick to blame the immigrants for the new caste system which classified freedmen as black rather than Indian, especially pointing to the willingness of some southern blacks to accommodate to white demands. One Creek freedman argued that it was the bowing and scraping of "those state niggers from Texas that ruined it for us," while another added that if "the Southern Negro didn't Uncle Tom so much they never would have drawed the line between the races."[53] What had once been local option became law when the school board of the Creek Nation ruled in 1904 that all blacks, whether tribal members or new arrivals, would attend separate schools.

Three blacks, Lemuel Jackson, James Roper, and John Grayson, plotted the Clearview town site in June, 1903, locating it near the Fort Smith and Western Railroad, midway between Guthrie, Oklahoma Territory, and Fort Smith, Arkansas. Jackson, a Creek freedman who later received an allotment a few miles south of Okmulgee, came with his parents to the Clearview area at the age of ten. Years later he remembered that there was "no particular reason for their moving here—[we] just got tired of the last place."[54] Roper, a native of East Tennessee, spent his youth in Arkansas and later served as postmaster at the small community of Surrounded Hill. He came to the Creek Nation in 1889 to accept a position as instructor of Indian freedmen at Tallahassee College. Very active in Republican politics in the territory, Roper was appointed postmaster at Okmulgee where he served five years before settling near Clearview around the turn of the century. Later "called" to the ministry of the Missionary Baptist Church, John Grayson was born in the vicinity of the town site and, in addition to numerous business investments, operated a 480-acre sheep and cattle ranch. To attract settlers and to advertise the community, the trio formed the Lincoln Townsite Company, hoping to sell residential lots measuring 50 by 140 feet for $18 in cash or on the installment plan.[55]

From the beginning, Grayson and Roper dominated Clearview commercial life. Grayson became president and Roper secretary of the Abe Lincoln Trading Company, a corporate venture they organized to operate a general store, deal in farm produce, and buy and sell real estate. With a total capitalization of only $2,500, the officers sold stock in the enterprise to the general public at $25 per share, offering to sell partial shares in denominations small enough to attract any interested investor. Grayson also held part interest in the town's newspaper, operated a meat market, and served as Clearview's first postmaster. In addition to promoting the town site and trading companies and lending money on land, Roper owned a sawmill and lumberyard. By August, 1904,

Clearview's leaders claimed a population of 250 served by one school, two churches, and seven businesses. Within seven years, Jackson and Roper sold out their holdings and moved to Okmulgee. Grayson disposed of most of his investments in Clearview, but he remained in the area to operate his ranch and to buy and sell farm real estate.[56]

In a few years most blacks in eastern Oklahoma considered Clearview a "solid State Colored Town," with no Indian freedmen living within its limits. The early editions of the *Lincoln Tribune*, however, sometimes subtly hinted at the earlier conflict between "state" immigrants and the original black residents of the Creek Nation. In a long article in October, 1904, editor Ernest Lynwood attempted to identify two major types of black pioneers who had settled in the West. Fortunately, he argued, few people in Clearview resembled what he labeled the "Americanized Negro," who, regardless of how black, was neither conscious of his color nor his race. Lacking any feelings of racial solidarity, this group had migrated primarily from the North where they had been indoctrinated in white schools. According to Lynwood, the major stumbling block impeding the progress of the race, however, was the heavy concentration of the "educated Southern Negro," who believed in black inferiority and was white in everything but skin tone. Because an individual in this class sought only to be a "good Negro," he or she reinforced the white image of the race, but under no circumstances would he stand up to a white and defend the rights of other blacks.[57]

To Lynwood, the Creeks seemed blind to the realities of politics, and were, therefore, easily duped by whites. In editorials he sometimes blended sympathy with sarcasm. In biblical prose Lynwood wrote: "And it came to pass that the Creek Indians had a pay day at Okmulgee, which was likened unto a bunco game, where the government done the boosting while the business men worked the shell; and there was great rejoicing amongst the people of the tribe, who came to town broke and went away busted."[58]

About the time that James Roper and Lemuel Jackson departed Clearview, James E. Thompson moved to the town site from Anadarko, a small community southwest of Oklahoma City. Using profits gleaned from an earlier coal-mining investment, Thompson began buying Clearview town lots and purchasing or leasing surrounding farms. By the time of the 1914 meeting of the National Negro Business League in Muskogee, Oklahoma, he could proudly announce to Booker T. Washington and the assembled delegates that he owned or managed a total of 5,800 acres of land in Okfuskee County. Thompson, heavy-set and with a large moustache and piercing eyes, was frequently interrupted by applause from the convention as he detailed his successes as a cotton, grain, and livestock farmer and merchant. Owning eighteen hundred acres, he rented most of the additional four thousand acres under his control to black farmers in the area. Renters either paid him in cash or worked on a share-cropping basis, with Thompson providing houses for tenants and their families.[59]

In January, 1911, he organized the Patriarchs of America, a fraternal lodge with headquarters at Clearview. The membership, open to all persons of African descent above the age of one, paid annual dues of $1.50 for adults and fifty cents for children. The lodge sought to attract both sexes. Although women attended Patriarch meetings and actively participated in programs by reading papers and leading discussion groups, Thompson's wife, Neva, was instrumental in forming a ladies' auxiliary called the Sisters of Ethiopia. At the first organizational meeting, Thompson was elected Supreme Patriarch, and L. W. Warren, another Clearview resident and former editor of the *Boley Progress*, Supreme Shepherd. In June, Warren assumed editorship of the *Clearview Patriarch*, the local newspaper financed by Thompson and heralded as the official organ of the new fraternity.[60]

The specific aims of the Patriarchs of America remained vague during the first few months of the organization's existence. Newspaper claims that the fraternal order would help

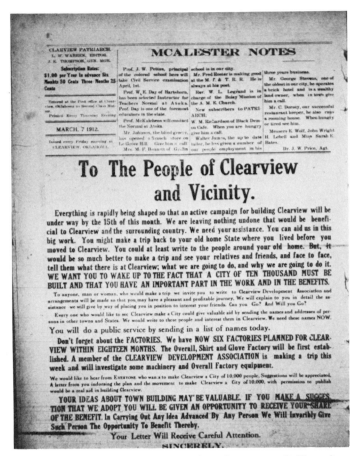

Newspaper advertisement promoting the town of Clearview.
From *Clearview Patriarch.*

"widows, orphans, and the helpless" or would "do for the
negro what Masonry has done for the civilized world" suggested that in structure and intent the Patriarchs would
resemble any one of a hundred other black benevolent societies in the United States.[61] Evidently, Thompson shared his

plans with only a few confidants prior to his address to the Clearview Farmers' Conference in May, 1911. In addition to a government bond issue to buy land for the race, he also proposed the complete separation of black and white governments in the new territory or state. Any whites currently living in the designated area would be compensated for their immediate relocation into selected cities. All legal matters involving blacks would be handled by a system of federal courts established there. To ensure elimination of legal discrimination, any black charged with a crime in a white-controlled city could receive an automatic change of venue to one of the new federal courts.[62]

Thompson's organization of the Patriarchs and his proposed solution for the race problem in part stemmed from his earlier experience in county politics. In August, 1907, the credentials committee of the Okfuskee County Republican Convention was asked to choose between contesting black and white delegations from Paden and Weleetka. In an attempt to solve a bitter dispute, both delegations were seated, with each delegate allowed to cast one-half vote. After the convention chose a black permanent chairman, most of the white delegates walked out, formed a rump convention, and picked a second slate of nominees. The remaining fifty-eight black and twenty-four white delegates nominated Thompson for county commissioner.[63]

Racial tensions increased during the primary, with most of the county newspapers supporting the Republican bolters. The editor of the *Paden Times*, for example, praised those who refused to remain, charging that "the white man has no rights in a Republican convention which a nigger is bound to respect." The defeat of Thompson for county office prompted Edwin W. James, the *Weleetka American* editor, to report, "In this commissioner's district George P. Greer defeated the Clearview nigger by a safe majority."[64]

Thompson never again sought political office, and concluded in 1912 that amalgamation offered the only lasting solution to the vexing race issue. But since white attitudes made this impossible in the foreseeable future, physical separation seemed the logical alternative. In July, 1912, the Patriarchs elected Thompson their representative to travel to the nation's capital to outline the colonization scheme to Congress. Upon his return, he optimistically reported the creation of a permanent committee in Washington to lobby for the plan. Both he and Warren continued to travel throughout the South—lecturing, organizing local Patriarch lodges, selling real estate, and boosting Clearview's inherent destiny as the industrial hub of black enterprise in the United States.[65]

Ralph W. Tyler, roving organizer for the National Negro Business League (NNBL), found traveling in Oklahoma in 1913 exasperating, and he sometimes wondered if his monthly salary of $135 plus expenses provided adequate compensation for his troubles. On several occasions, poor passenger service on railroads operating in the state forced him to waste a full day moving a distance of one hundred miles or less, and since restaurant accommodations for blacks were usually lacking, he frequently endured long hours without food. Slow trains, Jim Crow coaches, and missed meals were only three of several irritations. Although he was gratified to receive the support shown the NNBL by most blacks, he bitterly complained to Emmett Scott, Booker T. Washington's private secretary, that a number of Methodist ministers he had encountered were poor allies for the league because they refused to assist in any movement that might take even a small donation away from the church.[66] Tyler had previously been auditor of the United States Navy, and although he seemed easily riled by such attitudes and inconveniences, his new duties in organizing local leagues and speaking to various business groups provided him with an opportunity to observe the economic progress of his race in all sections of the country.

The National Negro Business League planned to meet

in Muskogee in 1914, and Booker T. Washington was eager to form a number of chapters in the state prior to the opening of the August convention. Thus, at the insistence of Washington and the urging of T. J. Elliott, a prominent black business and political leader in Muskogee, Tyler entered Oklahoma in November, 1913, armed with an itinerary calling for one-day stops in the major cities and most of the black towns. By Christmas day, Tyler had visited Guthrie, McAlester, Oklahoma City, Muskogee, and Tulsa, describing the latter as "a regular Monte Carlo."[67]

With the possible exception of his recent visit to Mound Bayou, Mississippi, Tyler received his most enthusiastic reception at Boley, a black town approximately twenty miles northwest of Clearview and also located near the Fort Smith and Western Railroad. At the time of his arrival, the town's boosters claimed a population of three thousand, and Tyler was immediately impressed with the amount of commercial activity there plus the high degree of business expertise he encountered. Tyler later wrote Washington comparing Boley to much larger white towns. After delivering his speech in Boley's new $35,000 Masonic Temple, Tyler was the honored guest at a banquet held by the local business league. At this gathering, Boley businessmen formally invited Washington and all the delegates attending the national meeting in Muskogee to visit the town by special train in August. Tyler departed from Boley with nothing but praise for the people there, claiming that Oklahoma possessed wonderful possibilities for blacks and that a "more loyal, royal, and progressive lot of Negroes are not to be found in any state."[68]

According to a frequently repeated story, Boley, Oklahoma, resulted from an argument at Weleetka between Lake Moore, an attorney, and another white man over the black potential for self-government. The existence of such a debate, although unsubstantiated by available records, seems plausible; but more pragmatic reasons accounted for the creation of the town. In 1903, the Fort Smith and Western

Railroad crews were laying track west from Fort Smith, Arkansas, toward Guthrie. The new line passed through the allotment of Abigail Barnett, a young Choctaw freedwoman. Since Abigail's land was of marginal value for agricultural use, her father, James, recognized that its market price could be enhanced through the formation of a town site. Moore, Barnett, and W. H. Boley, the F. S. and W. roadmaster, joined in a scheme to form a town site company to develop the tract. Since blacks were to constitute the potential customers for the sale of lots in the new town and farms in the hinterland, the group persuaded Thomas M. Haynes, a black farmer from Paris, Texas, to join them as manager. Haynes had migrated into the area sometime in the late 1890's and had become well acquainted with Boley and the other railroad construction workers. Of necessity, the track crews occasionally spent the night in or near Haynes' home located a mile or two from the railroad right-of-way rather than make the long trip to a nearby town after a hard day's work. The Fort Smith and Western initially aided in the project by building a spur, constructing a $1,350 depot, employing a black station agent, and stopping four trains a day at the new town named in honor of W. H. Boley.[69]

Boley was officially opened on September 22, 1904, and in May of the following year a charter of incorporation was granted. Meanwhile Haynes, possessing little formal education, searched for money to develop the community and settlers to fill it. He gained an important ally in his town-building venture in 1904 with the arrival of David J. Turner, a druggist. Working separately and in partnership, Turner and Haynes concentrated their resources and skills on the promotion of business enterprises. Turner opened a drug store in 1905, and since he owned the only safe in town, as a favor to his customers he often held their savings. Hence, he soon collected much of the town's available capital. Later that year Haynes formed a commercial club composed of most of Boley's business and professional men, which in turn sponsored the opening of the Farmers and Merchants' Bank

Farmers and Merchants' Bank, Boley, with David J. Turner standing in front. Courtesy Oklahoma Historical Society.

with Turner as cashier and Haynes vice-president. In addition to their individual speculations, the Haynes and Turner Real Estate Company was formed to buy and sell town lots and area farms. Turner promoted Boley's first telephone system and, in partnership with Haynes, purchased the physical plant for the town's newspaper. Railroad leaders joined in the project when they gave Boley preferential treatment over Clearview. In late 1904, for example, Hilliard Taylor, a cotton buyer and lumber dealer in Okfuskee County, purchased a $6,000 gin in Houston, Texas, planning to install it in Clearview in time to process the 1905 crop. The Fort Smith and Western, however, refused to stop in Clearview to unload the consignment, offering instead to haul it on to Boley free of charge. As a consequence, an advertisement of the H. Taylor Gin Company appeared in the first issue of the *Boley Progress.*[70]

With backing from the commercial club he had organized, Haynes employed all the standard techniques to entice settlers to Boley. Special circulars, along with thousands of copies of a booster edition of the newspaper, were mailed out detailing the unrestrained privileges and unmatched opportunities awaiting the industrious.[71] Haynes hired agents to tour the southern states, while those in Boley were urged to write ministers and family friends in the South seeking their assistance in advertising the new town. In April, 1905, O. H. Bradley, editor of the *Boley Progress,* announced the coming of a week-long summer carnival to begin June 19. Those attending could expect concerts by a black band, Indian ball games between Creek and Seminole teams, mule races, bronco busting, and free refreshments. And, of course, the once-in-a-lifetime chance to purchase town lots at the reduced price of $35 and up, with only one-third down and the balance due in five months. Unimproved land was offered during carnival week for $10 to $15 per acre. For those farmers preferring to rent, land could be obtained for twenty-five to thirty cents per acre on a five-year lease. To reduce transportation costs for prospective visitors, the Fort Smith and Western offered special tourist rates and excursion fares from Little Rock and other towns.[72]

People came from all over the South. The editor of the *Progress,* never one to underestimate the size of a crowd, placed the number in attendance at five thousand and noted that farm leases and town lots sold like "soda or ice cream on a hot day."[73] During the first year after the carnival, a steady stream of immigrants continued to arrive at the Boley depot, usually met there by a self-appointed committee of townspeople who welcomed newcomers. Sometimes eight to ten families would alight from the same train, their luggage and household belongings covering the freight platform and forming a pyramid six to seven feet high. Entire communities moved. Such was the case when the black residents of Rusk, southeast of Dallas, Texas, migrated en masse to form a settlement of the same name three miles southwest of Boley.[74]

New hopes for continued population growth came in March, 1905, when H. B. Lewis, head of the American Colony Company of Atlanta, Georgia, signed an agreement with the town site officials to locate the organization's headquarters in Boley. Lewis hoped to collect and transport two thousand settlers to the town, ultimately creating a black county by the time the territory sought statehood. Paranoia quickly struck whites in the area, and as Boley's population increased, rumors circulated in the towns along the Fort Smith and Western that blacks in the Boley area were quietly offering white farmers more for their land than it was worth in order to "Africanize Okfuskee County."[75]

Early arrivals in Boley found clear water, abundant trees, and fertile soil. Housing, however, was less plentiful. For almost a year, the Turner and Haynes two-story real estate office towered above the hundreds of tents dotting the thirty-six–square-mile township. A few families who came unprepared for the rigors of camping were boarded on the second floor of the frame building. Moses J. Jones, assistant town site manager and later city attorney, lived above the real estate office with his bride of two weeks while trees were cleared from their lots to permit construction of what Mrs. Jones described as a "two-room shot-gun house with openings for three windows and two doors, into which we moved minus the doors."[76]

Much of the land on which the town of Boley rested had previously been owned by Creek freedmen, but a proclamation issued by President Theodore Roosevelt in April, 1904, permitted them to sell their allotment holdings on the open market. The conflict between ex-slaves and incoming black immigrants from the South, so evident during early territorial days, led to armed clashes in Boley. Some of the freedmen, or "Natives," as the residents of Boley called them, frequently broke up church services and other public gatherings with gunfire and periodically amused themselves by riding through the town late at night shooting out windows. Mrs. Moses J. Jones remembered that "a burning light in a house served as their target," and therefore her family spent many sleepless and fearful nights sitting in a dark house.[77] A few people on both sides were wounded or killed during such skirmishes, but in time overt violence soon subsided and the hostility between the two groups took the milder form of complete social separation. Although conflict with both freedmen and whites continued, Boley residents basked in an economic and political freedom unknown in their previous environment.

Promoters such as Haynes, Hill, McCabe, Thompson, Montgomery, and a few others who joined them shortly saw clearly from the beginning the opportunity for economic rewards through the formation and development of a separate black community. To be sure, they advanced their personal fortunes through forming town sites. Whether their ultimate intention was to gain riches or to aid those less fortunate than themselves remains a mystery. Many individuals, regardless of color, in other times and places in American history have found little difficulty in rationalizing the wedding of high principle with the acquisition of wealth. And as is still the case, some believed that the many should labor for the benefit of a few. The underlying reasons prompting many black families to move themselves and their belongings hundreds of miles to one of the new towns are also unknown. Poverty and racism have been and remain intertwined in American society. Some settlers may have sincerely thought that the accumulation of personal property represented the first step toward a solution to the race problem. But, for whatever reasons—social, economic, political, personal, or racial—most black-town immigrants came with an incredible optimism concerning the correctness of what they were about. The hopes, fears, and aspirations of groups are often reflected in their music. Although residents in all five of the black towns might not have agreed with it, one stanza of a song sung by the early settlers of Boley communicated their pride in the community and their absolute certainty concerning the future: "Be courageous, brother, and forget the past—the great and mighty problem of race has been solved at last."

2
Image and Ideology

BLACK-TOWN NEWSPAPER EDITORS, promoters, and their agents employed the tactics common to most town propagandists in the American West and South to entice settlers. Boosters candidly admitted that words were inadequate to describe fully the natural advantages of each community and its hinterland. Most tried, however. In 1888 the editor at Nicodemus apologized for a pen unable to do the town justice, but assured his readers that residents there enjoyed a climate representing a healthy median between the "malaria of the lowland and the intense cold of the north," inspiring long life, good appetite, and prodigious energy. The countryside around Langston in 1892 was "as fertile as ever was moistened by nature's falling tears, or kissed by heaven's sunshine." With such soil and climate it was little wonder that crops were always bountiful and on occasion yielded valuable by-products, reflected in the case of a farmer near Langston in 1895 whose corn stalks were "almost large enough for house logs."[1]

Only the absence of settlers prevented the transformation of nature's masterpiece into the garden spot of the continent. To attract those settlers, promoters formed immigration societies, gave away town lots, sponsored celebrations, arranged excursion tours, dispatched traveling agents, and mailed out booster literature, all aimed at extolling the virtues of the area and coaxing the cautious or disbelieving into the new Eden. Those who came were sometimes forewarned. The editor of the Clearview paper in 1904 cautioned people contemplating their first visit to that town that after beholding it with the naked eye leaving might be difficult. Therefore, he instructed them to "bring your trunk when you come."[2]

Sometimes booster literature was aimed directly at those who might consider leaving rather than at the prospective buyer. Blacks were frequently warned of the inhumanity found in the white-dominated world just beyond the town limits. And although life might seem difficult, residents of the black town could rest assured that economic prosperity would eventually come to the patient and industrious who stuck it out. Quitters faced certain disaster. Those who grumbled about high prices, a heavy tax burden, or poor services were labeled "town knockers" and admonished to mend their ways and remain silent. "If you can't boost, don't knock," counseled the *Clearview Patriarch* in May, 1912.[3] Editors stereotyped those who complained as lazy, shiftless malcontents lacking initiative and jealous of the success of others.

To counteract unfavorable internal comments and the possible appeal of other towns, newspapers occasionally ran stories on the high cost of living in other areas. M. C. Inlow, editor of the *Nicodemus Cyclone*, advised Nicodemus readers in November, 1887, that "the people of Graham County and western Kansas need not think for a single moment that hard times are confined principally in their midst. . . . The tightness of money is universal." The following spring, the *Cyclone* interviewed a visitor who reported high land prices and living expenses in the West, convincing the editor that northwest Kansas offered "greater advantages to a poor man than Cal[ifornia]." In 1908 the *Boley Beacon* attacked those opposing a new school building, because taxes in Boley were supposedly much lower than in other states.[4]

Those who criticized and those who departed were branded as traitors to the race, and black-town boosters continually played upon the guilt and fear of racial members living in the South in order to attract them to the new communities and to hold them once they arrived. Stories disclosing atrocities against the race dotted the columns of most black newspapers throughout the United States. Black-town leaders, however, used such incidents as a promotional device. Promoters in Nicodemus and the three Oklahoma towns ridiculed those who seemed content to live in terror in the South, unable to protect themselves or families from white insults, discrimination, and physical harm. The black-town press detailed and embroidered upon accounts of racial injustice and violence in southern states and printed verbatim speeches containing racial slurs by prominent politicians such as James K. Vardaman, governor of Mississippi. These stories usually prompted editorial comment inviting the abused to move to a black town where people enjoyed the full benefits of political freedom and economic security. "Langston City," argued the *Herald* editor in August, 1894, was "the negro's refuge from lynching, burning at the stake and other lawlessness." In early 1906, the *Boley Progress* equated moving there with the Pilgrim's search for freedom.[5]

The maintenance of true manhood, argued the promoters, demanded an immediate exodus from a hostile environment. B. Kernan Bruce, editor at Clearview in 1904, seemed convinced that in time the "best element of the race" would depart the South while the "chicken-hearted and ignorant Negro will stay there and become a shy beast." Bruce urged those who were determined to remain in Alabama to visit the local graveyard to call on Ham's mother. Some editors followed the approach of the *Langston City Herald*, suggesting that a subscription to the newspaper provided concerned blacks with the opportunity to keep abreast of the latest brutality against the race in southern states.[6]

A deep sense of urgency permeated the propaganda issued by most black-town boosters. Much of the argument for haste, however, reflected nothing more than the "Come! Rush! Boom!" mentality of all American land speculators and real estate agents from the colonial period to the present. Each day of hesitation, according to their pronouncements, jeopardized chances to get in on the beginning of a marvelous investment where possibilities for quick wealth loomed just over the horizon. Town newspapers heralded the weekly arrival of new families who always found the surrounding countryside a wonder to behold. Nicodemus was full of "strangers looking for homes in this new Garden of Eden," according to the *Western Cyclone* in 1887, while the great influx of newcomers into Boley in December, 1905, had forced developers there to open several new additions to the town site just to accommodate them. Surprises were also possible. In 1912, potential Clearview settlers were cautioned to expect the unusual; those who purchased land for farming might later discover that they also owned "a coal bed or an oil pool." To the boosters, increased population and rising land values meant a spurt in economic prosperity for all and unlimited growth in the future. Usually eager to elaborate on any subject at great length, Hugh K. Lightfoot, the Nicodemus editor, found one word adequate to describe the phenomenal activity in his town during March, 1887: "Boom! Boom!! BOOM!!!"[7]

Promoters felt that appeals to racial pride were an effective drawing device, and many of their booster campaigns centered upon the white belief in black inferiority. Segregated and isolated from white society, blacks could disprove current racial theories as well as bolster the validity of their demands for political and economic equality, activity which would ultimately eliminate white prejudice. In March, 1905, the *Boley Progress* appealed to blacks to "come and help to prove to the caucasian race . . . that the Negro is a law-making and law-abiding citizen and help solve the great racial problem before us." And in April of the following year, the *Western Age* proudly announced that the "Negroes of Langston are daily demonstrating to the world that the race can form a municipal government and conduct its official machinery as good as other races."[8]

Boomer literature also warned blacks that the new towns perhaps represented their last opportunity to acquire a home or farm of their own. Furthermore, the promoters insisted that ownership of property, and especially land, constituted the first step toward full citizenship. As long as blacks remained mobile and lacked property, political freedom would continue to elude them, relegating the race to a continuing life of poverty and discrimination. As the *Boley Progress* phrased it in March, 1905, "if you will come here now and get a good location . . . we will be able to demand our rights." Pointing out that two-thirds of the black voters of Logan County in 1906 earned their living farming, S. Douglas Russell, editor of the *Western Age* at Langston, concluded, "they are indeed free men, the bosses can't touch them." Blacks who purchased land also blocked the encroachment of whites who, it was claimed, were pouring into the area and buying up choice farms. In the spring of 1906, the *Boley Progress* reported on the tide of white homeseekers entering Indian Territory, cautioning the race that if the available lands fell into the "possession of the white people the hope for the Negro is gone."[9]

Those seeking settlers for the black towns also called upon members of the race to sacrifice now for the benefit of future generations. Blacks alone must and could solve the race issue once and for all, they argued, and its leaders now held the solution within their grasp if only the black population of the country recognized the need for solidarity through colonization in segregated communities. "Your children's children will call you blessed if you take advantage of this wonderful opportunity," argued the *Boley Progress* in 1905. And in a speech to the first colony of Mound Bayou settlers, Isaiah T. Montgomery exhorted them not to stagger at the difficulties they faced. Calling upon them to think of the past while looking to the future, Montgomery asked, "Have you not for centuries braved the miasma and hewed down forests like these at the behest of a Master? Can you not do it now for yourselves and your children unto successive generations?" Even if financial rewards failed to come to the living, to the promoters the black town represented more than just another incorporated community. In an advertisement appealing to southern farmers in 1906, Thomas M. Haynes, Boley's promoter, compared his town to the pyramids of Egypt, "an imperishable attestation of the power, might and intellectual genius of a race."[10]

In short, black-town developers tried to convince potential settlers that the success of their community would eliminate poverty and racial prejudice, prompting whites to extend to blacks the full rights of American citizenship.

Several settlers who articulated reasons for moving to black towns mentioned the desire to escape from white discrimination as a major reason prompting relocation. According to one early resident of an Oklahoma town, people moved there because they wanted to be free and "they was tired of the way white folks was treating them," while an ex-slave who came to Indian Territory with her father claimed blacks "came in searchin' for education and freedom. I mean they come here lookin' for de same things lots of Negroes is goin' North for now." To several, leaving the South meant gaining self-respect and personal dignity. A farmer recalled that living in Texas required having to "bow down and grin to all the poor white folks. I even had to call little poor white boys 'Mister,' " but in Langston, "no matter how little you be here, you can still be a man." While outside Boley, asserted one of its settlers, "you always have that prejudice to contend with," but inside the town limits "everybody can be somebody."[11]

Proving that blacks possessed the ability to incorporate a town and govern it without white knowledge or supervision ranked especially high with some settlers. One man who moved from Texas to Langston in 1892 at the age of twelve remembered that in its formative years people there displayed an intense pride in the community because "everybody wanted to prove to the world that colored folks could run a town without white folks." And although Langston businessmen claimed they earned few profits in some years they continued to operate just to demonstrate "that the colored man was capable of running his own business." The practice of attempting to exclude whites tended to unify divergent groups which sometimes clashed over municipal policies and regulations. One black-town resident argued that "we might have fought among ourselves because we didn't know nothing about organizing a town, but we was hellbent on keeping whites out."[12]

In addition to race pride and escaping to freedom, the quest for economic security also attracted blacks to the new communities. The attitudes and actions of R. B. Scruggs, born in the South in 1861, exemplified many black-town residents. Scruggs, who described himself at the time of his departure from the South as "just an old green boy, never away from home," moved to Nicodemus in 1878 because he thought migration represented his one "chance to own a real piece of land." Upon his arrival in Kansas, Scruggs realized that the abundant game and fertile soil promised by W. R. Hill and other promoters constituted nothing but a cruel hoax designed to attract settlers. Nevertheless, he filed on a claim near Nicodemus and then accepted part-time employment—in livery barns in Stockton and Ellsworth, odd jobs in Bunker Hill, and railroad work near Salina—in order to support his family. In time, Scruggs built up his holdings to a total of 720 acres. Asked about the hardships of the early years, he later remembered, "no matter how bad it got . . . we was just so proud of the land."[13]

Nicodemus drew other early settlers primarily from the Upper South. Of the original 149 families, a majority came from approximately the same geographic location, the area north of Lexington, Kentucky. Although most of the first families came from the South, others arrived from Rhode

47

Island, Massachusetts, New Hampshire, New York, Ohio, and Vermont. A scattering of settlers from Sweden, Italy, France, and England could also be counted among the first arrivals. The average family size in early Nicodemus consisted of from four to five members with an adult median age of forty-four.[14] The editor of the *Ellis Standard* described a party of eighty individuals bound for Nicodemus who passed through his town during the fall of 1877 as "not advanced beyond middle age and seemingly in robust health."[15] Convinced that a new life would come through the ownership and cultivation of the land, these poor rural blacks first responded to the booster literature and speeches of Nicodemus promoters. Professionals and those who later came to occupy positions of social, economic, and political prominence and power in the town migrated from the northern states.[16]

A somewhat different pattern of settlement and leadership developed farther south in Mound Bayou. Settlers from the South, a majority in their mid-thirties, moved to the new town during the 1890's. More than half of the original fifty were from Mississippi, with one coming from as far away as the West Indies. At Mound Bayou's inception it seemed only natural that Isaiah T. Montgomery should exert leadership since Montgomery had plotted the town site and migrated there with several of his former laborers. As development continued, however, economically prosperous blacks from biracial communities in the state soon became the major decision makers. Indicative of this trend was Charles Banks. Before moving to Mound Bayou in 1903, he had operated a successful mercantile business in Clarksdale, Mississippi. After organizing the Bank of Mound Bayou the following year he became the town's most prominent figure as well as one of Mississippi's most politically active Republicans.

From the very beginning, promoters in Boley, Langston, and Clearview appealed to blacks living in the South while expending little time or money to attract people residing in other regions. Most of the black settlers who entered these towns, therefore, came from the Deep South and the border states of Tennessee, Kentucky, and Missouri. A majority of the first settlers in the three Oklahoma towns were share-croppers or laborers drawn to the area by the possibility of acquiring farms in Indian Territory or in the Unassigned Lands. In all three cases, black professionals trained in the South arrived later and assumed leadership positions in the new communities.[17]

Aside from the skin color and mutual poverty of their residents, Nicodemus, Mound Bayou, Clearview, Boley, and Langston possessed several common characteristics which differentiated them from white communities of similar size during the initial stages of development. A large number of residents lived inside the town limits but earned their liveli-hood during the day by farming land they owned or rented in the surrounding countryside. Also, rapid population growth frequently resulted from the efforts of town boosters or their agents who were able to lure large family groups, with strong kinship ties inside each family, from the same geographic area. Individual settlers continued to trickle into the towns, but population during the early years usually in-creased in spurts with as many as one hundred immigrants arriving at the same time. Many persons of each town were acquainted with, if indeed not distantly related to, one another before they arrived. This mutual background of shared friends and family no doubt helped to ensure group cohesiveness and mitigate conflict. Rather than the typical pattern of development of most small agricultural communi-ties in the West and South—that is, the arrival of the farmer, then the merchant, the artisan, and later the professional—in some of the black towns all these economic and social groups arrived at approximately the same time. Finally, although black and white settlers alike shared the hardships of the frontier environment and the difficulty of attempting to build a rural community at a time when all national indices pointed in the opposite direction, because of their lack of capital, the absence of skills, inadequate farm machinery, and racial prejudice, blacks migrating there suffered deprivations unknown to the typical white settler.

As in all young communities, the black-town press maintained a constant chatter of optimistic predictions of future growth and prosperity. Black-town editors, however, went further. The new towns offered a controlled environment, isolated from the dominant white society, permitting the economic and moral uplift of the race. The addition of each new business, church, street, lodge, or person ensured the continued economic success of the venture and also illustrated the potential capabilities of blacks in general. Boosters tried to convince residents that pride in the race and pride in the community were synonymous, and each day the town continued to exist reinforced the argument that blacks could improve if given the opportunity. This double mission of boosterism and race pride added an extra optimism and an ideological orientation to black-town newspapers seldom found in their white counterparts.

The racial ideology in part explains the type of local news which filled the columns of the black-town press. Starting with so little, any growth seemed monumental. Editors frequently launched into lengthy discussions on any event, from the program of a Sunday school to the construction of a house, indicating town growth or the economic and moral uplift of the race. As he had done with similar meetings in the past, the editor of the *Western Age* at Langston pointed to a gathering at the New Hope Baptist Church in July, 1908, as indicative of "mental, moral and intellectual improvement."[18]

Black-town leaders blamed the race for many of its problems, and editors played upon the theme of racial inferiority to attract settlers, neutralize internal dissension, and to promote unity and pride in the town. Black inferiority, they argued, resulted from bad habits developed during years of dependence and bondage, imitation of whites, lack of equal opportunity, and white exploitation, rather than innate differences. In the environment of a segregated community, blacks could uplift themselves morally, accumulate capital, acquire business and trade skills, and learn self-government. This would convince even the most doubting members of white society that they deserved acceptance as equals. Self-help, moral uplift, and racial solidarity, as those terms were employed by Booker T. Washington, comprised the formula, the isolated black town the laboratory.

Since skin color, poverty, and uplifting the race to the point of white acceptance constituted the common bonds in black towns, few similarities existed between them and the various utopian communities established in the United States during the nineteenth and early twentieth centuries.[19] In many cases those who joined in the utopian experiments rejected the values of the larger society and sought to withdraw from its real and imagined evils. Although a few black-town settlers mentioned moving there in order to protect their children from white discrimination, from their arrival they generally accepted the capitalist system and the Protestant ethic. Like the Booker T. Washington philosophy, the black-town ideology contained an implicit assumption that at some time in the future the race would be accepted into the mainstream of American life. In the case of the black town that meant that ultimately it would cease to exist. Boosters either failed to recognize the internal contradiction in their own argument or simply ignored it as a reasonable possibility in the foreseeable future. If the town succeeded as a racial experiment, it failed as a viable community, thereby spelling economic disaster for those with investments there.

If black-town editors praised those who pursued endeavors consistent with racial uplift, they also attempted to set the moral tone of the community and to regulate social behavior by strongly condemning individual and group activity thought to be antisocial or detrimental to the image of the town and race. Editorials and local news items sometimes warned citizens that bad habits and conduct might discourage potential settlers, adversely influence women and young children, and discredit blacks in the eyes of whites living in nearby towns. Although they seldom did it, editors continually threatened to ridicule publicly those people who misbehaved by printing their names in the newspaper. Some editors possessed more than moral suasion. In May, 1908, for example, S. Douglas Russell of the *Western Age* suggested it was "about time to stop the . . . loafing and marble playing on the principal streets" in Langston.[20] Those involved would have been wise to respond. Russell was also justice of the peace.

Furthermore, almost all editors opposed leisure time spent in idle activities. The work ethic was essential to the economic success of the community, and adults, they believed, should place high priority on the example they set for the younger generation. Men and women who spent time at the local croquet court, at baseball games, on Sunday excursions rather than at church, or whiled away summer hours on street corners encouraged idleness among the young and degraded work in their eyes. Since it was believed that gambling was a direct result of boredom and monotony, the city fathers of each black town passed ordinances prohibiting games of chance. Similar to most small rural communities of the time, however, the town marshal, either by design or neglect, failed to visit the back rooms of some businesses on main street. Years later, a resident of Nicodemus recalled that lodge meetings and public gatherings were always held on the second floor of one particular building, while the "back room of the Talbert Drug Store was used by those seeking less educational entertainment."[21]

The attitude toward drinking intoxicants varied over time and from town to town depending upon its legality, prohibitionist sentiment, the influence of local ministers, and the personal preferences of the current owner or editor of the newspaper. Since the sale of liquor was illegal in Bolivar County, Mississippi, the leaders of Mound Bayou faced no open opposition when they banned it from the town. When

S. Douglas Russell, editor of *Western Age,* Langston. Courtesy Oklahoma Historical Society.

an election was held to legalize liquor sales in the county, Mound Bayou voters rejected the proposition, perhaps responding to the warning of Isaiah T. Montgomery that alcohol attracted undesirable whites into the community. In those towns where the sale of intoxicants was permitted, persons selling wine, beer, and liquor usually paid a high occupations tax in order to operate such a business. In Langston, for example, the town treasurer received $9 per month from its one liquor retailer, an amount exceeding the total monthly fees collected from all other licensed businesses. During its settlement, Nicodemus promoters made clear their opposition to alcohol. At the time people bought lots in Nicodemus, they signed an agreement which forbade them from selling intoxicating beverages on their property for a period of five years from the date of purchase, and the town charter contained a provision prohibiting liquor shops and saloons. Prohibitionist sentiment remained strong in Nicodemus, encouraged by the town newspaper and the formation of a temperance society in December, 1879. Not all Nicodemus residents, however, favored total abstinence. Approximately fifty people signed a petition in early 1887 seeking permission to allow Walt Korb to dispense "prescription whiskey" at his drug store.[22]

Aside from the legal and religious aspects of liquor sales and consumption, black-town editors pointed to the absence of saloons as an indication that blacks were a moral, law-abiding race and that a segregated community offered the best environment in which to raise children. Editors sometimes invited the leaders of neighboring white towns either to follow the black-town example of banning saloons or to restrain their wandering citizens who overindulged. In July, 1886, the editor at Nicodemus warned Webster, Kansas, to "keep her whiskey guzzling young bloods at home, or they might get taught a little morality when they come up this way in the future."[23] Over and above the moral question and the racial and town image, several black leaders opposed the legalization of liquor in their communities for very pragmatic reasons. Liquor sales, they insisted, encouraged drunkenness among those least able to afford it. More important, saloons attracted promiscuous white men searching for black women, and such encounters increased the possibility of racial conflict and physical violence.

Newspaper editors attempted to project the image of the black town as a peaceful rural village free of the crime and violence they claimed characterized biracial communities. If unmolested by whites, they argued, the race was law-abiding and the tranquility found in their community proved the point. According to Arthur Tallman, editor of the *Western Cyclone*, in May, 1886, Nicodemus had "no whiskey shop; no billiard hall or other gambling hole . . . [and] no drunkeness or rowdyism, no cursing or whooping disturbs the peace of the place."[24] And Mound Bayou leaders claimed that because of the absence of problems the constable and deputy sheriff were the only idle men in the town. Editors seemed especially sensitive to suggestions that black-town conflict or crime equaled that found in other communities of a similar size, and they angrily responded to stories in white newspapers implying the contrary. When a fight between two men broke out at the 1887 Nicodemus Emancipation Celebration, most of the weekly newspapers in Graham County reported the incident. In responding, the Nicodemus editor pointed to the apparent double standard of news reporting applied by the newspapers in Stockton, Logan, and Webster who were "howling about the fracas, [but] say little about the same thing in their own towns . . . and because our skin happens to be a little dark we are to be condemned in the severest terms for what two outside strangers did."[25]

Spokesmen complained that what little violence existed in black towns normally occurred late at night or on holidays and weekends when outsiders entered the community. During its early years Boley residents were sometimes aroused from bed to fight late-night clashes with the ex-slaves of the Indians who tried to shoot up the town or by an occasional brawl with railroad workers.[26] Citizens of Nicodemus faced a similar problem. On July 4, 1888, a railroad construction crew bent upon celebrating American independence visited the town around midnight, and, according to the newspaper, the streets were "alive with noisy, good natured fellows intent on having fun. They got it—several got it in the neck."[27] Despite booster disclaimers, not all serious confrontations resulted from encounters with whites or with those living outside the town limits. Benjamin T. Green, a Mound Bayou merchant and one of its founders, was shot and killed in his store in January, 1896, following an argument with a local customer over a five-cent box of rivets. And at the 1909 Clearview Christmas celebration the town constable shot and killed two blacks. Moses J. Jones, city attorney of Boley, told a reporter for the *St. Louis Globe-Democrat* in February, 1913, that "there has never been a serious quarrel here, and there has never been a killing in the town."[28] Jones evidently forgot the shotgun-rifle duel on Boley's main street six years earlier between Mayor J. R. Ringo and James S. Oldham, a local farmer. Oldham shot and killed Ringo over the mayor's enforcement of a town ordinance requiring the confinement of his livestock.[29]

Such incidents seemed to be the exception, however. Most reported crime or violence in the black towns involved the usual fights between men, public drunkenness, failure to confine chickens, petty theft from households or businesses, galloping horses or driving buggies at high speed, discharging firearms inside the town limits, and a host of other misdemeanors common to small rural communities. The first fight inside Nicodemus, for example, was allegedly a harmless scuffle between two ministers following a heated exchange over the interpretation of a passage of scripture. In 1907, Mound Bayou's leaders claimed that during the first twenty years of its chartered existence only three people from the town had been bound over to circuit court for trial, two of whom were charged with theft. And of the 163 criminal cases in the previous ten-year period, sixty-four were for disturbing the peace and twenty-eight involved trivial offenses that never went to trial. Charles Banks, a Mound Bayou developer, boasted in a 1912 advertising brochure that since its founding there had never been a case of rape in the community and only one homicide.[30]

The actual extent of violence and crime probably fell somewhere between the black claims that no serious conflicts occurred in the towns and the reports of some white newspaper editors in surrounding communities who seemed to delight in exaggerating the most minor deviations of blacks from the exact letter of the law. Excluding conflicts stemming from racial antagonisms—that is, when whites or Indians entered the black towns, during the early years of their existence—the towns were probably more peaceful than biracial communities of a similar size. Several forces worked simultaneously to mitigate violence and reduce crime. Many town leaders possessed a good deal of power and were quick to point out that antisocial behavior hindered moral uplift, projected a poor racial image to whites, and jeopardized the future of all. Black criminals who committed even minor offenses were worse than white criminals —they betrayed the race. Many residents owned property, some for the first time, and even those who did not hold title to a farm, house, or town lot enjoyed an economic security unknown in their previous environment. Leaders continued to preach to this group that their continued upward mobility in large part depended upon the success of the town-building venture. Many members of the community were thus intolerant of any conduct which might threaten their new status. People who refused to work or were considered undesirable citizens were either asked to reform or physically forced to leave. Finally, in most cases the black towns lacked a large propertyless lower class that would have been frustrated by the economic exploitation of whites and, therefore, prone toward acts of crime and violence. Although exploitation existed, that suffered by those occupying the lower stratum of black-town society was probably less than the exploitation imposed upon blacks living in a mixed community. Furthermore, it seems obvious that once most residents recognized that the black town would eventually fail, or had reached a growth limit far short of that anticipated, frustration increased, precipitated by the enormous discrepancy between the raised expectations of the settlers and their actual achievement. At that point, violence and crime no doubt became more commonplace.

Town leaders usually blamed blacks for past and current problems and warned that acceptance into American society would come slowly and only after it was earned. Until that time, leaders stressed that the race question could be solved if blacks built a spotless reputation, superior even to that of whites, and acquired property. Although the total environment of a segregated community provided the ideal setting, moral uplift began at home, and the ownership of that home was the first step. Residents and potential settlers were told that all great races had achieved greatness only after they stopped wandering, and that as long as blacks continued to move from place to place seeking better conditions (but never finding them) they would be subservient to less transient races. Property provided its holder and the race with stability and dignity as well as political, economic, and social status. Buying a farm or home and laboring to pay for them set an excellent example for the young, showing them the personal economic rewards to be reaped from hard work.

Like much of rural America at the turn of the century, black-town residents believed that young children were born innately cruel, amoral, lazy, and dishonest.[31] Since the younger generation represented the key to racial uplift over time, they could become worthwhile adults only through strict discipline at home and especially in school. Black-town parents insisted that teachers concentrate on maintaining order in the classroom while instilling pupils with the work ethic and Christian principles. Naturally, black-town churches and schools worked hand-in-hand toward that end. Teachers were usually active in local Sunday school classes. Some ministers earned a livelihood during the week teaching school, and those who did not entered classrooms to give brief talks on such topics as punctuality, thoroughness, vanity, and ambition.

Although black-town residents supported education, some newspaper editors ridiculed "high book learning," arguing that the race must first educate children's hands and avoid useless school subjects of little immediate value in everyday life. Blacks with too liberal an education, it was believed, lacked courage and refused to stand and fight for the race, and the editor at Clearview failed to count the well-educated among those "trying to earn an honest living."[32] Vocational education, on the other hand, would bring economic classes together, prevent the abuse of child labor, and eventually bring racial prosperity. Teach them a trade, argued S. Douglas Russell at Langston in 1909—children must "first learn how to earn bread and butter."[33] Training in manual skills began early in most black-town schools and, consistent with the Washington philosophy, such courses extended into the college years. At Mound Bayou, first-grade children learned sewing and basketry, while three of the four departments at what later became Langston University emphasized training useful in workshops, homes, and on farms. Businessmen in some towns also helped. One Mound Bayou blacksmith shop filled the needs of area farmers and also served as a training school for the instruction of young boys wishing to learn the skill.[34]

To encourage school attendance and to boost circulation, editors sometimes held contests offering to fund for one year the educational expenses of the child who sold the most newspaper subscriptions. Despite such efforts, few black-town schools ran a nine-month term, and those that tried found parents reluctant to send children during the planting and harvesting seasons. "You can always raise another cotton crop," lectured the *Boley Progress* in late September, 1905, "but there is only one time the child can get an education."[35] Attendance at Clearview was compulsory, but employed children were excused as long as they were working. As late as December 21 the editor at Clearview was still urging farm parents to enroll their children in school and keep them there for the remainder of the 1911–

1912 term. In general, the attendance rate for boys, as compared to girls, remained low, with many boys dropping out completely before finishing the seventh grade.

Although isolated from the dominant society, black-town school patrons attempted to compete with whites for county funds, and the resulting discrimination hindered black attempts to provide adequate educational facilities and qualified teachers. In 1904, Clearview parents were forced to form a "subscription school" after they learned that the Okfuskee County Superintendent had failed to submit a list of children living in Clearview, depriving the town of any public funds for education. During the same year, white schools in Bolivar County, Mississippi, in which Mound Bayou was located, received 79 percent and black schools 21 percent of all available funds even though black children outnumbered white.[36] Such a situation forced black-town residents to finance their own schools, many of which operated for only a few months each year, or to seek outside philanthropy.

In laying out Mound Bayou in the late 1880's, Isaiah Montgomery and Benjamin Green set aside a plot of land for the location of the Mound Bayou Institute. The town then entered into an agreement with the American Missionary Society, which constructed several buildings on the site and financed a portion of the instructional costs. The institute offered instruction through the twelfth grade concentrating on courses in domestic science and agriculture. By 1912, the school served approximately 172 students per year, some of whom were black children from nearby communities in the Yazoo Delta. In 1900, the General Baptist Convention helped to establish the Mound Bayou Industrial College, which also specialized in vocational training. The two institutions, plus a public school, coexisted until 1920 when a merger was arranged. Boley also received help in a similar form in 1906 when the Colored Methodist Episcopal Conference authorized creation of a high school for blacks who lived in districts without them. Throughout the school's brief operation, the CME Church funded most of the costs of the Oklahoma Normal and Industrial Institute near Boley. In 1893, two years after Langston's incorporation, a priest and two nuns from Belgium opened a Catholic school there. A gift from the Drexel family of Philadelphia made the school possible and permitted Father Anciaux and two sisters to instruct approximately one hundred students free of charge.[37]

Enterprising teachers or businessmen who sought to establish private schools and colleges in the black towns found it difficult to operate them on a paying basis. Residents witnessed several such attempts, however, and the career of J. C. Leftwich typified a few who exploited the black hunger for education. After traveling in Oklahoma and surrounding states seeking students and funds in 1910, he opened the Creek-Seminole Industrial College at Boley. In recruiting teachers, Leftwich neglected to inform them that upon their arrival in Boley they would be expected to hustle their own salaries as well as food for the students. When confronted with complaints, he is said to have responded, "This school is organized to train minds, not appetites."[38] After the building burned and some teachers instituted legal action against him, Leftwich left Boley. Four years later he was in Clearview where he opened the Creek-Seminole Agricultural College. In order to help finance the new school, James E. Thompson, Clearview's most prominent citizen, appealed to the State Board of Agriculture for funds. Leftwich, meanwhile, had assumed the editorship of Thompson's newspaper, the *Clearview Patriarch*, and in addition to advertising the college through its columns, he embarked on a speaking tour asking for aid from white groups in Shawnee, Oklahoma City, and other towns. The pair evidently met with some success, because in August, 1916, the college advertised the opening of the fall term with seven separate departments. Leftwich's location and activities during the next three years are unknown, but by 1919 he had established the Agricultural School for Negro Boys and Girls at

Bookertee, Oklahoma, another black town in the immediate area. In March of that year the *Guymon Herald* reported the introduction of a resolution in the Oklahoma Senate proposing to buy the Bookertee school building and its adjoining eighty-acre tract of land for $1 with the proviso that the state would continue to fund its operation in the future. Fortunately, not all those who attempted to bring private education to the black towns possessed Leftwich's entrepreneurial spirit. Many, such as G. W. Wood, who incorporated the Boley Agricultural and Business College in 1912 to offer night classes to adults, found the desire for education strong but the money necessary to attend lacking.[39]

When black children were not in school, it was assumed that they would respond to a gentle, yet strong-willed mother who worked to create a home environment conducive to personal and racial uplift. In addition to performing ordinary household tasks, married women were perceived as a strong moral force, lovingly controlling and manipulating their men in order to channel male energies into those areas considered beneficial to family, race, and nation. "You very seldom find a harsh, unpleasant man where you find a loving wife," argued L. W. Warren, the editor at Clearview in 1911. A good woman brings "hubby home early, [and] keeps him from the Club, [which] fills the larder and puts better clothes on the wife's back." Those women who doubted him were advised to "manage your husbands . . . and see results."[40]

Warren, like other black-town editors, believed that historically all great races had advanced because of the strength and purity of their women, and he frequently editorialized on the duties and obligations of wives and mothers praising their virtue and devotion.[41] If, on the other hand, the speed of racial uplift appeared to be slowing, he was quick to point to jealous, self-centered females as the cause. In addition, young men contemplating marriage were cautioned to search for sincere, hard-working partners while avoiding "worthless girls who have the giggling and spending vices reduced to a frazzle."[42] In divorces, Warren blamed the wife 98 percent of the time, husbands 1 percent, attributing the remainder to the absence of love.

It was through such spokesmen that black communities were able to exert considerable social and legal pressure to keep marriages together, separate those living out of wedlock, and point eligible young people toward matrimony. Although for several issues during the spring of 1895 the *Langston City Herald* jokingly followed the nightly romantic exploits of "The Fast Stepper," a mysterious, unidentified local bachelor, single men were usually encouraged to marry at an early age, buy a home, and raise a family. One literary society echoed an attitude common to all segregated communities when its members debated the proposition that "Batchelors Are A Detriment To Langston."[43] Divorces and unmarried couples living together were disapproved of. Town opinion-makers preached against divorce and lent moral and political support to local judges who refused to grant them except on serious grounds such as physical cruelty and desertion. Single and divorced women were denied membership in the Ladies Commercial Club of Boley, a group organized in 1908 to meet biweekly for sewing and social activities. When a local church survey revealed approximately forty unmarried couples living together in Mound Bayou, the offending parties were contacted and offered the choice between a quick wedding ceremony or assistance in leaving the colony. Most opted for matrimony.[44]

Prostitution was seen as an evil which threatened family structure, the very core of racial uplift. During the early years of settlement, officials in some of the towns found it necessary to close the back room of the local billiard parlor and invite its temporary occupant to move on. The money earned from picking cotton or from the sale of crops also prompted local marshals to watch out for enterprising ladies who visited during special celebrations or on fall weekends. Prostitution and extra- or pre-marital relations were considered bad enough, but sexual intimacy between a blacktown woman and a white man was worse. It jeopardized racial purity. Some residents would have agreed with the editor at Langston in January, 1908, when he proposed that the Oklahoma legislature pass a law against miscegenation; male offenders would be hung, females imprisoned.[45] Although whites were usually blamed for initiating such contacts, the community condemned black-town women who sold themselves. In 1910, for example, the *Boley Progress* warned that "this thing of our women meeting white men at the trains, under any pretext, don't go with the people [here]."[46] Black men were very defensive about whites who entered their town searching for female companions. Newspapers such as the *Western Age* at Langston cautioned white men to "keep out of our back yard after sun-down."[47]

The emphasis upon a stable family life and its protection from forces threatening to destroy it stemmed directly from the black towns' patriarchal family structure. During the early years of their development, large family groups, not single transients, settled most of the towns. Thus, the so-called matriarchal family was absent.[48] In a few cases the grandfather stood at the apex of a pyramid composed of many members; and if the extended family owned property, controlled capital, or could advance credit, kinship ties were very important in determining one's social and economic position in the community. In the case of Mound Bayou, membership in the Montgomery, Francis, Green, Banks, or Booze families, all of which were interconnected in some way through blood, marriage, or business investments, assured a certain degree of security and status.

Although newspaper editors and promoters alike preached egalitarianism while boasting of an internal consensus spawned by race pride, each black town possessed a definite class system. During the first few years of settlement, classes were less definable—servant and worker, master and mistress hoed the same fields, ate at the same table, and slept in the same tent or cabin. But as population increased, fortunes grew. Each new day witnessed the arrival of newcomers who had not endured the early years of hardship and hunger, and distinctions in wealth and position became more discernible. Even then, classes tended to blend into one another, and upward mobility remained possible for those with enough ambition or good fortune to acquire property. The black town lacked capital, and it was only a matter of time until those who had it to invest or loan would come to occupy positions of social as well as political and economic prominence.[49]

Local businessmen and those owning large farms in the immediate vicinity of the town occupied the upper stratum of society. This small proprietorial group, along with less prosperous lawyers, physicians, teachers, ministers, and a few white-collar workers, made the relevant decisions affecting the town. Because these two groups needed each other, much more so than in a racially mixed community where the proprietorial class would have enjoyed contacts with influential whites, they usually united on most issues. Occupation, length of residence, family membership, and education also helped in determining class ranking. Family connections were important, but membership in a poor family was of little value. Since the black-town ideology stressed training in practical skills, formal education alone, even at the college level, failed to provide status. Income, economic security, and business aggressiveness, however, overshadowed all other factors.[50]

Laborers, artisans, and those small farmers living close enough to be affected by town development made up the large black-town middle class, but this group usually deferred to members of the proprietorial and professional classes who held leadership positions in the community. Merchants and ministers dominated a few black towns, but in most cases the banker, through the allocation of capital in the form of credit and loans, came to be recognized as the premier citizen. In addition to their investments and financial control, the power of such individuals quickly spread to all aspects of town life. They presided over school boards and town councils, funded local newspapers, influenced churches, and or-

ganized lodges and fraternal societies. In a few instances
bankers even displaced the original town promoter as the actual leader of the community. Although Thomas M. Haynes

The Boley town council, about 1906. Courtesy Oklahoma
Historical Society.

in Boley and Isaiah T. Montgomery of Mound Bayou remained the symbolic father figures for most residents, David
J. Turner, head of the Farmers and Merchants' Bank, and
Charles Banks, cashier of the Bank of Mound Bayou, had
assumed leadership in their respective communities within a
few years after their arrival.

The wives of many black-town leaders exerted considerable influence in their own right and helped their husbands set the tone of the community by teaching in both
public and Sunday schools, directing charities and celebration programs, giving parties, and organizing social clubs.
To the people living in Clearview in 1911 there should have
been little doubt which family occupied the top position in
society. A large picture of James E. Thompson appeared in
each weekly issue of the *Patriarch* along with an article written by him, a discussion of his latest activities, or the transcript of a speech he had recently delivered to a local audi-

ence. Debates, discussions, or lectures at the monthly meeting of the Thompson Literary Society provided Clearview ladies with intellectual stimulation. Those women seeking entertainment might join Mrs. Thompson at one of her frequent parties, attend meetings of the Sisters of Ethiopia, a sorority, or the Alpha Club, a social group, both organized by Thompson's wife, Neva.

Over and above income, investments, and political and social influence, town leaders were readily identifiable by the location and size of their residence and their membership in a particular church. Excluding a few wealthy landowners who resided in the country, most upper-class members lived in one section of the town, and the cost and size of their houses clearly set them apart from the average citizen. The most prominent members of Boley lived in its northeast area, while Mound Bayou's upper class constructed homes near the periphery of the town away from the business district. Charles Banks' $12,000 house and Isaiah T. Montgomery's well-shaded twenty-seven–room brick mansion offered a marked contrast to other Mound Bayou residences. The attendance of Banks and Montgomery at the Sunday services of the African Methodist Episcopal Church—although second in total membership in Mound Bayou—indicated their status within the community. In Boley, the size of the Baptist congregation made it a powerful force in the town, and those who sought political office and social prestige found it advantageous to join.[51]

Lower-class inhabitants of a black town—primarily transients and a few people temporarily attracted there by the novelty of the community—were too few in number to oppose town leaders. And even some members of the middle class who deeply resented the ostentatious display of wealth and power felt economically intimidated and afraid to voice their feelings publicly. One resident of an Oklahoma black town who was brought there as a small child remembered bitterly that the upper class "built large houses like southern plantations, had luxuries, owned lots of land, possessed tenants, drove horses with beautiful buggies, and had or tried to have the same thing as a southern aristocrat. . . . Those old boys really controlled everything; they even owned the church; that is, the bank held the mortgage and almost every member of the church owed the bank, so nobody could ever object to nothing."[52]

The institution of slavery and previous geographic location in part determined class structure and antagonisms in the Clearview-Boley area. The physically violent confrontations between Creek freedmen ("Natives") and the ex-slaves of southern planters ("Watchina" or "State Negroes") who moved into what became Okfuskee County subsided after the two towns were permanently established. Natives and Watchinas continued to maintain social distance, however, the former objecting to what they considered Watchinas' acceptance of white discrimination and their willingness to acquiesce to it. Those Natives who had previously held positions of authority in the Creek Nation, or who were listed on Indian rolls and had received land allotments, identified with their former captors. During their early years Boley and Clearview both contained a Native population of approximately 10 percent. In a short time, however, no freedmen lived inside Clearview's town limits although a few freedmen children attended school there. One freedman recalled that "when I went to Clearview Negro School there was more of them than us [so] I buddied with my own."[53] Even where Watchinas and Natives resided in the same immediate vicinity, they seldom mingled. Natives usually isolated themselves into social "neighborhoods" with activities centered in small rural churches. Such a group was the one composed of fifty freedmen who lived at Grassy Lake near Clearview. Some freedmen seemed proud of any physical characteristics which they thought set them apart from other blacks. "Everyone in Boley knows I'm a Freedman and part Indian," proclaimed one man. "They just look at my beard and know."[54]

Because of their isolation, black-town residents escaped

the daily reinforcement of their subordinate rank in the larger society. In general, their emphasis on physical characteristics in determining social position was the exact opposite of that found among blacks living in a mixed community.[55] Indeed, during the years when optimism concerning the town's future was at its height, black-town citizens rejected light skin color as a status symbol in the community, and individuals with such complexions sometimes suffered. An older man remembered that as a child his color made a difference in Boley: "I happened to be light skinned and, boy, did I have a time. Those 'darkies' in Boley don't like light-skinned Negroes and they show it. I was a victim of their prejudice. . . . All the boys would refer to each other as 'nigger' . . . but I could never use that word." His complexion proved such a disadvantage that when he married he selected a dark-skinned wife so his children "wouldn't have to go through all that mess. . . . It was hell!"[56]

Black-town editors insisted that past association with whites had corrupted the race and that before racial uplift could progress blacks must voluntarily stay away from them and cease what one newspaper called "the inherent worship of a white skin."[57] For example, in a June, 1911, front-page article entitled "COLOR NOT THE CAUSE," a writer for the *Clearview Patriarch* claimed that most Americans favored black over white as evidenced by the public preference for dark shoes, suits, and horses. The race suffered discrimination, he argued, because of certain objectionable customs and manners found in people possessing the color. Continued emphasis upon color made members of the race ashamed and desirous of ridding themselves of it, rather than concentrating on the real cause. With moral uplift, he argued, any prejudice against black would completely vanish.[58]

The black-town press sought to bolster race pride with reports on the accomplishments of past and present national figures. Most of the speeches of Booker T. Washington and the events at Tuskegee Institute were either covered in separate stories or carried in syndicated columns like "Afro-

American Cullings."[59] Holiday and public school programs usually recounted the loyalty and bravery of Crispus Attucks, Peter Salem, and blacks with George Washington at Monmouth or with Andrew Jackson at New Orleans, as well as the deeds and exploits of the 9th and 10th cavalries. In December, 1909, the *Boley Progress* ran a story on the National Negro Doll Company of Nashville, Tennessee, hoping to encourage parents to order black dolls for their small children. The story related the suspicion that white merchants were attempting to bankrupt the firm through a boycott of its products. For a time the fights of Jack Johnson, the world heavyweight champion, received elaborate coverage, with one newspaper even carrying a round-by-round account of his victory over Jim Flynn at Las Vegas, New Mexico, in July, 1912. Praise for Johnson quickly faded, however, because of his marriage to a white woman and his social escapades which many felt disgraced all blacks.[60]

Despite such efforts, leaders could never completely conceal their recognition that color determined class and status in the white world outside the town. Asked by a reporter writing a feature on Mound Bayou in 1909 if he thought other blacks in the South could duplicate the experiment there, Isaiah T. Montgomery, the town's founder, responded, "Why not? We are plain negro men and women, not any better or whiter than other American negroes." In issuing an invitation to Graham County residents to come to Nicodemus to celebrate American independence on July 4, 1888, the editor of the *Cyclone* assured prospective visitors that "you will have a way up time and be treated white."[61]

For some editors, profit superseded pride. They apparently saw no contradiction between their lectures to the race on black pride on the front page and advertisements on page two for skin bleach and hair straightener. Such items usually appeared in the "patent" or "readyprint" sections of the newspaper ordered from a publishing house in a large city. Occasionally, however, readers of the *Boley Progress* and the

Western Age at Langston might find advertisements for Ford's Anti-Kink Pomade, The French System Hair Straightener, or Complexion Wonder Creme interspersed with town news items on those pages run off on local presses.[62] A few black-town visitors were quick to point to what they thought was a dichotomy between race pride and a desire to be white. Hiram Tong, a white reporter who journeyed to Mound Bayou in 1909 to conduct interviews and collect information for a story on the town, commented on cosmetic advertisements in the Mound Bayou *Demonstrator* and a picture which appeared on a promotional calendar given away by the local bank. Tong noted that the well-dressed lady on the calendar was "clearly African, but is light-chocolate brown, has red on her cheeks and straight hair."[63] When questioned, the cashier of the bank there argued that the physical characteristics shown in the picture had no significance since the calendars had been ordered from a black company in Louisville, Kentucky.[64]

Although they tried, leaders could never totally control those who sought to make skin color a criterion for social position. As each community grew larger, and once some citizens recognized that the black town no longer held out the promise of freedom and prosperity, emphasis on black pride subsided. In 1910, three women in Boley formed a club emphasizing better English, good housekeeping, and the social graces, with membership open only to ladies with light skin.[65] Community reaction was immediate. As one early settler remembered the "crazy bastards tried to organize a 'Blue Vein Society' . . . but we run them out of town. I helped run them out 'cause we [could not] divide up on the color question."[66] Boley's leaders must have felt besieged. In early January, 1910, businessmen W. A. Kennedy and O. H. Bradley announced plans to open the White Way, a hotel designed to cater to whites visiting the town. Except for those who worked there, Boley blacks were prohibited from entering the lobby without permission. The White Way was all the more bitter to take because, as editor of the

Progress during 1905 and 1906, Bradley had frequently preached race pride. In two scathing editorials, Ernest D. Lynwood, the Boley editor, found it impossible to understand how "Negroes as black as Kennedy and Bradley" could sponsor such an undertaking; a week later Lynwood concluded that it was just "another story of Jacob and Esau, wherein Jacob sold his birthright for a mess of pottage."[67] As a commercial enterprise, the White Way was shortlived. It was never again mentioned in the newspaper, and within one month Bradley was back in his old office editing the *Boley Progress.*

At first, color distinctions were unimportant in Mound Bayou, "a community in which only a few persons, mostly women, were lighter than medium brown."[68] Also the social mores of the community dictated total isolation from the dominant race in the Yazoo Delta. Even those whose normal business activities brought them in contact with outsiders found little prestige inside the town from their intimacy with middle- and upper-class whites in Mississippi. All this changed. When Eugene P. Booze moved there sometime after 1904 and married Mary Montgomery, Isaiah's daughter, the color line was drawn. Because of his light skin, Booze was immediately suspect. Benjamin A. Green, the mayor of Mound Bayou in the early 1940's, remembered him well but disliked him intensely because, as Green put it, Booze "always pretended he was a white man's nigger."[69] Either Mary or her husband, Eugene, persuaded the elder Montgomery to donate $2,500 and a small tract of land for the construction of an Episcopal mission. The new mission attracted few members, partly because the town already had four churches, but, more importantly, it had definitely been established for residents with lighter-than-average complexions. Only Mary and a few light-skinned blacks from the county attended during its brief existence, but when it closed, color had become a factor in the community.[70]

Hazy and at times contradictory attitudes regarding color only mirrored a larger black-town ambivalency about whites in general. Through successive generations, it was argued, all whites had exploited the race in order to satisfy their own greed and lust, in the process choking the spirit and pride from its members. And, since whites continued to block the path of black advancement, they obviously could not be trusted in the future. Yet, some town leaders clearly distinguished between two classes in white society. "Poor Whites," who the Clearview *Tribune* charged would "wade through hell to steal a dinner pail,"[71] were blamed for most of the violence directed at the race. On the other hand, the "better class of white men" really wanted blacks to advance, opposing only that progress which offered direct economic competition to them. Self-segregated from the larger society, the black town offered protection from the harassment and terrorism of lower-class whites while posing no competitive threat to either group. Townspeople were told that as the community prospered and the race uplifted itself, intelligent whites would soon recognize that current racial theories were invalid and would have to be modified. Racism would cease. Until that day arrived, however, residents were urged to keep their distance from all whites.

Of course, total isolation was impossible, and the black-town proprietorial class recognized the necessity of some external interaction. In their contacts, usually to transact business, such individuals demanded respect. One prominent town leader related that "in Boley, the white people we deal with treat us as equals because we don't deal with them on personal terms unless they *need us* for something. . . . You see, if we needed them, we would have to stand any treatment, like being called 'Boy,' or 'Sam,' or by our first names. . . . A white man will call you 'Mister' all right, if he needs you."[72]

Respect worked both ways. Editors lectured their readers on the necessity of making a favorable impression on whites. Every white person who left the town feeling he or she had been courteously treated represented another convert for the cause, one who might help to dispel fallacious rumors and misconceptions about the race and the community. In April, 1906, O. H. Bradley, editor of the *Progress*, pointed out that every time a white left unmolested it refuted the claims of some people in the nearby town of Paden that they were in danger while inside Boley. Bradley had aimed his short editorial directly at "a certain Negro (if that is not a misname)," who made a practice of insulting white gentlemen. It might be better, he hinted, for the offender to leave town peacefully while it was still possible to do so. Like other editors, Bradley sometimes lost his temper over comments in out-of-town newspapers suggesting that whites were unwelcome, discriminated against, or mistreated. He seemed especially riled in July, 1905, after reading a story about Boley in the *Kansas City Journal* claiming that "if a white man is in it or near it he stays blacked up or under cover."[73] Bradley insisted that many whites lived near Boley, several shopped there, both day and night, and most used it as their post office. Furthermore, on any weekday, white drummers could be found at the hotel or on the streets soliciting orders from local merchants. Regardless of color, he said, all people in Boley were treated with respect.

The black towns varied in regard to segregating the races and providing whites who visited with separate facilities. For the $1 daily rate, J. F. Gooden, proprietor of Hotel Boley, which was located on Main Street near the rail depot, offered equal room accommodations and dining service to all guests, irrespective of color. At times, however, a white traveler in Mound Bayou was isolated from others during his stay. Whites who wished to remain overnight in the town were ushered into hotel rooms reserved for the exclusive use of Caucasians. Rather than joining other boarders at the hotel dining table, or being seated separately, meals were sent to them. Isaiah T. Montgomery's house contained one bedroom which, it was claimed, had never been occupied by a black, and two white men who stayed there around 1910 remembered eating in the regular Montgomery dining room —alone. In Nicodemus, the Emancipation Day Celebration attracted a large number of outsiders to the town once each year. Candidates for public offices and prominent white and black leaders delivered speeches to the assembled crowd of several thousand, and during the early years it was said that the races danced together.[74]

The respectful treatment of white visitors helped to promote a positive racial and community image, but permitting them to live inside the town limits served no useful purpose. "Where do we need their presence as citizens?" asked Ernest D. Lynwood, the editor of the *Boley Progress* in November, 1909. "They are not our fellows and why should we encourage them to live among us . . . if a white man can make a 'lily white' town why can't we make a little black settlement . . . ?"[75] In both Boley and Mound Bayou, whites were discouraged from buying real estate. From time to time a few whites lived inside Nicodemus and white men operated stores there.[76] Most residents, however, objected to absentee ownership and to white laborers who entered the towns looking for work. During September, 1904, Ernest Lynwood, the editor at Clearview, noted the continued presence of a white carpenter who believed "in the ethics of southern social customs," yet continued to loiter on the streets attempting to underbid local contractors. Lynwood suggested that the people of his home town of Weleetka should find steady employment for "this poor outcast of Southern aristocracy."[77]

In the three Oklahoma towns, black leaders displayed mixed feelings concerning treatment of American Indians. Envious of what they perceived as the Indians' relatively higher status, yet sympathetic to a people facing discrimination and dishonesty, newspapers like the *Boley Progress* cautioned Indians to be wary of legal promises, remembering that in the past "the white man had taken the labor of the Negro and the lands of the Indian, under full protection of the law." Displaying great insight, black-town editors predicted that as soon as the federal government had broken tribal autonomy, clearing the path for white land speculators, both groups would occupy a similar position in American society. Furthermore, blacks considered it unfortunate that Indians failed to comprehend the possibilities of a red-black political coalition. In June, 1905, S. Douglas Russell at Langston pleaded with Indian leaders to look to the immediate future and recognize that "negroes and Indians would have the political balance of power in the future state of Oklahoma, provided those votes would form a solid, undivided phalanx at the polls." Such was not to be. And the editor at Clearview lamented, "Uncle Sam has got a half Nelson on the Indian. He'll win in the next round."[78]

Such sympathy was not automatically extended to all other minorities in society, however. While Indians were pictured as honest, yet innocent children, slow to perceive the realities of American life, Jews were seen as perceptive, sinister, and untrustworthy. Convinced that Jews constantly pursued material wealth, blacks thought they controlled the money supply of the United States. Yet, because Jews had no permanent home and especially because of the discrimination and persecution they had suffered, blacks thought they could see in Jewish history many parallels with their own experience. Although disliked, Jews had to be respected, and residents were told that blacks might do well to follow their economic example. Newspaper subscribers at Langston, Boley, and Clearview were scolded for fretting about the plight of their race when they should be observing the Jews who were piling up wealth, building character, and acquiring prestige and position.[79] On the other hand, to put down an opponent, the black-town press sometimes delved into its repertoire of anti-Semitic terms. Following a few derogatory references concerning Jews and the crucifixion, editor Hugh Lightfoot at Nicodemus reported on a heated political race in September, 1886, concluding that "Jew Harwi and Judas Dr. Fuller led the Republican party of Graham county up to the cross at Millbrook yesterday. . . ."[80]

Jews were considered outsiders rather than native Americans, and this partially explained the black-town attitude toward them. Editors and other leaders visualized the horrors of a future America filled with foreign-speaking immigrants willing to work for less than local laborers. If the immigrant tide continued unabated, they warned, blacks would soon lose their only means of livelihood, small as it might be, as well as the one region they could still call home. Speaking at the black Baptist church in Paris, Texas, in May, 1912, Clearview promoter James E. Thompson pointed to the horde of foreign immigrants currently flooding the South, crowding blacks into towns and cities where they must turn to crime or starve.[81] Because of a few isolated, yet well-publicized experiments using Chinese and Japanese workers on large farms in the West and South, Orientals posed the greatest danger. Therefore, discrimination against them was considered justified. In December, 1887, M. C. Inlow, editor of the *Nicodemus Cyclone*, praised a recently passed city ordinance in Wichita, Kansas, deliberately designed to penalize Chinese laundries. Ironically, Inlow advised the Chinese in Kansas to return to their native country "where their appearance is more acceptable." As time passed, the black-town paranoia over immigration increased. "America for American laborers," proclaimed editor Russell at Langston in 1907. And four years later, the *Clearview Patriarch* warned readers that "if the Chinamen and Japs become citizens . . . it would not take a very heavy emigration of them to get a majority of the Pacific states." Such an invasion, the editor argued, was obviously an easier and cheaper means of acquiring territory than a declaration of war.[82]

Although partly a reflection of the national mood, much of the black-town push for immigration restriction stemmed from a sentimental attachment to the South as their ancestral home. Some blacks who moved north into segregated communities saw colonization there as temporary, lasting only a few generations, perhaps less. Believing that they, their children, or grandchildren might someday enter the larger society, they hoped to keep it much the same as when they left, but how could blacks return to a South filled with strangers? Excluding those strangers seemed the obvious answer. But, whether good or bad, black-town residents were interested in the latest news from the South. And editors usually obliged them with items of local interest about the folks back home whether in Banks, Texas; Evergreen, Alabama; or Cotton Plant, Arkansas.

If the South was home, then Africa was not. As long as the black town remained economically and politically viable, with some prospects for future growth, residents there rejected various back-to-Africa schemes. Those who migrated thousands of miles to Africa were admitting that the race problem in America had no solution—the black-town settler had found it. To its citizens, living in a segregated community was neither a substitute for migration to a foreign country nor the acceptance of defeat inside the United States.[83] Although some were fleeing discrimination and violence, most settlers entering the black towns came with great expectations for the future, convinced that the towns held out the promise of eventual entrance into the mainstream of American life complete with economic prosperity and full social and political rights for all. Newspapers at Clearview, Langston, Nicodemus, and Boley chided those contemplating an African exodus for failing to recognize that America was their home and that they would surely perish in transit or soon after they arrived. "Oh ye Africanites . . . who will not listen to reason. I see thy fate," warned A. R. Wheeler of the *Clearview Patriarch* in February, 1914.[84] But as Wheeler wrote, the five black towns were dying. Despite their efforts, promoters found it increasingly difficult to counteract the lure of Africa, a land where plentiful game and rich soil supposedly offered economic security, free from the discrimination of whites.

That the black-town image and ideology contained contradictions merely indicated the extent to which people living there were echoing the ambiguity found in black thought throughout the country. Although promoters and residents espoused absolute allegiance to Booker T. Washington's philosophy, some of their ideas were close to those of W. E. B. Du Bois—much more so than many perhaps realized or would have been willing to admit. The concept of racial uplift, both moral and economic, was not unique to Washington. Indeed, the same year that Langston was named as the site for Oklahoma's black university, Du Bois published an article telling blacks that their first step involved "the correction of the immorality, crime and laziness among Negroes themselves, which still remains as a heritage of slavery."[85] Before his complete break with Washington after 1900, Du Bois supported industrial training, although arguing that such programs should complement a liberal university curriculum. At no point were the black towns closer to Du Bois than with their emphasis on race pride and especially their praise for the virtue and devotion of black mothers. Blacks, Du Bois argued, had a distinct mission as a race; and although he was at times vague concerning the exact contribution of blacks to civilization, the key to the black mission rested with the strength of the black mother figure. Racial and sexual purity were important elements in black destiny. "Unless we conquer our present vices," he said, "they conquer us."[86] Du Bois called for the creation of black colleges, newspapers, and businesses for the uplift of the race, in time permitting its members to make the black spirit felt in America—but not for the purpose of a "servile imitation of Anglo-Saxon culture."[87] The Washington approach, he came to argue, led to complete acceptance of American capitalism and the spirit of avarice inherent in that system; what was needed was a sense of community among blacks, rather than extreme individualism. Like many leaders before him, Du Bois struggled with the dilemma of wanting to see blacks develop their own culture yet being free to participate fully in American society. Finally, in 1908, he asked if "it is going to be possible in the future for the races to remain segregated or to escape contact or domination simply by retiring to themselves?"[88] No! Such a dream he considered impracticable and contrary to the

79

trend of the age. More and more, Du Bois came to focus on black civil rights.[89]

3
Politics
and Discrimination

MOST BLACK-TOWN RESIDENTS were disciples of
Booker T. Washington's philosophy, which at least overtly
emphasized concentration on the economic and moral betterment of blacks at the expense of political and social demands.
From the beginning, however, settlers entered the new towns
intent upon enjoying a full political life. For some, this represented their first opportunity to direct their own destiny
through the ballot box. Although lacking experience, most
citizens refused to be deterred and were soon engrossed in
the raging battles over the merits of various candidates and
issues. Local politics were serious business, and, as election
day approached, the heat of the campaign spread throughout
the town. Just before an election in Boley, mass meetings
were called and candidates took turns publicly tracing and
commenting on each other's life histories, sometimes nearly
coming to blows in the process.[1]

Even though the black towns possessed a formally elected
government, usually a mayor and council, leaders sometimes
called open meetings to provide a forum for debate or to
gauge public sentiment on a specific issue of mutual interest.
Women were prohibited from voting in elections, and in

early Clearview only property owners could cast a ballot. But in specially called town meetings all adult members of the community, regardless of sex or economic standing, could take part in the general discussion. For example, in 1904 the federal government designated Clearview as the name of the post office there and refused several requests to change it to Lincoln. At a mass meeting in August, citizens passed a resolution changing the town name to correspond to the postal designation. And on at least two occasions between 1905 and 1910, Mound Bayou residents met en masse, once to formulate plans to close a "blind tiger" (illegal saloon) operating within the town limits, and again to present a united community front against the repeal of prohibition in Bolivar County.[2]

Newspaper editors boasted of racial solidarity and argued that the consensus found within the black towns clearly set them apart from neighboring white communities, said to be constantly besieged with political squabbles. Despite typical claims like "There is no town where the people work more in harmony than those who inhabit this . . . city," the distrust of public officials and factional fights were commonplace.[3] As in most small communities, politics revolved around cliques which warred over the adequacy of services, taxes and their use, the cost of business licenses, and operation of the public school. Although the editor at Langston attempted to calm tempers on all sides, citizens there were embroiled throughout most of 1895 in conflicts with the school board and town council over attempts to pass bonds for school construction and what some residents felt was an excessive occupations tax. By mid-August, one irate group threatened to circulate a petition to dissolve incorporation of the town unless council members resigned. Some Langston settlers charged that during the community's early years town organizers used the local government and school district as a screen to write fraudulent warrants amounting to $20,000. Once detected, most of those involved in the scheme fled, leaving the people to pay the obligation, a task which took until 1915 to complete.[4]

Unlike blacks living in mixed communities, people in the black towns were shielded from white domination, and, as their political interest and involvement grew, ordinary disagreements were sometimes blown out of proportion. During the spring of 1911, City Clerk E. R. Cavil charged that the Boley council, dominated by promoter Thomas M. Haynes, accepted illegal claims presented to it. At a May council meeting, the Haynes majority voted to remove Cavil as clerk, declaring the office vacant. He refused to accept their decision, resign, or to surrender his records, contending that the council possessed no such authority. When Cavil's books were later forcibly seized, he instituted legal action and sought public support, publishing an extended account of the incident in the local newspaper.[5]

Disputes over this and other issues continued in Boley, and by the time of the 1914 meeting of the National Negro Business League in Muskogee, the conflict in the town had come to Booker T. Washington's attention. Boley businessmen were anxious to have Washington visit there sometime during the league meeting in August and had extended him an invitation. Washington hesitated. Always careful to avoid any public display of racial disunity in his presence, he instructed Emmett Scott, his private secretary, to check into the matter and correct it before he would accept the Boley offer. Scott in turn contacted T. J. Elliott, president of the Oklahoma State Negro Business League and prominent black merchant in Muskogee, asking him to visit Boley to investigate. Elliott, however, was "already aware of a somewhat unpleasant situation over there" between two rival factions. In early January, 1914, Elliott met with what he called "two political clubs, each clamoring for supremacy," and warned both that unless their differences were resolved a Washington visit was out of the question. On January 21, Elliott assured Scott that Washington could now safely include Boley on his itinerary, because "they are all in line . . .

and agree to work under the leadership of the State Business League movement."[6] Scott checked again during the summer before finally committing Washington to the visit, and on June 22, 1914, Elliott assured him that all factionalism in Boley was wiped out and that leaders there were now working together.

Booker T. Washington also took a keen interest in Mound Bayou's development, and from Tuskegee he channeled funds donated by Andrew Carnegie, Julius Rosenwald, and other white philanthropists into various town projects. Washington was well acquainted with Isaiah T. Montgomery, the town father, but it was Charles Banks, the energetic cashier of the Bank of Mound Bayou and promoter of several local enterprises, who became his personal confidant. In addition to his many business investments, Banks was an active Republican, and for several years he kept Washington abreast of political affairs in Mississippi. By 1907, he had risen to the first vice-presidency of the National Negro Business League, second only to Washington himself, and president of the state organization in Mississippi. After Washington's death in 1915, the ill feeling between Banks and Montgomery, smoldering for years, finally surfaced, and the two leaders and their respective following battled for political and economic supremacy in the town. For a time, two separate governments attempted to rule Mound Bayou, each claiming legitimacy. After a mysterious murder there in early 1917, Governor Theodore Bilbo intervened in the struggle, sending in the National Guard and issuing a proclamation recognizing the Montgomery faction as the legal government.[7]

In comparison to the general apathy found in American society, black-town residents were almost totally politicized. During Boley's early years, an average of 80 percent of its eligible voters flocked to the polls. The elimination of registration in advance of municipal elections and the use of secret ballots after 1915 encouraged political participation. Although Boley was strongly Republican, two parties vied for public support inside the town. At the first general election held there in April, 1906, voters could choose between candidates, all of whom had paid a $3 filing fee, running on either the Citizens' or the People's ticket. Nicodemus, too, was Republican, and as an illustration of political interest, 70 percent of the qualified voters in Nicodemus Township cast ballots in a March, 1887, bond election.[8]

In addition to taking an orthodox stand on taxes, law and order, improvements, and schools, black-town politicians appealed to voters on the basis of past service to the community, concern for the common people, and practical business experience. Since many residents lacked formal education, candidates frequently belittled it as a necessary prerequisite for holding public office. In announcing his candidacy for justice of the peace in March, 1908, Thomas R. Ringo informed Boley voters, "I am not a graduate of any college neither have I taught law. I am simply a laboring man . . . [but] I have done more to supress horse stealing at a sacrifice to myself than any other man in the community. . . ."[9] Success in business gave candidates an advantage over less fortunate opponents. From its founding to 1914, Mound Bayou's five mayors were all prominent in business or agriculture, while at least seven of Boley's nine town officials elected in 1906 could claim substantial business investments.

The mayor-council form of government found in Boley and most of the other black towns represented the system most commonly employed in working-class communities in the United States. Boley's town council, composed of five aldermen elected by wards for two-year terms, met twice monthly. At the first meeting following a general election, the council selected one of its number to serve as mayor. He, in turn, appointed councilmen to head standing committees on ordinances, streets and alleys, sanitation, and education. During a regular meeting, Boley citizens could address the council only by invitation. The marshal, justice of the peace, treasurer, assessor, and clerk were elected to office.

In conjunction with the marshal and justice of the peace, council members enforced ordinances ranging from prohibitions against discharging firearms inside the corporate limits and blocking public thoroughfares to keeping lots raked and free of trash and ensuring that private outhouses were maintained in a sanitary condition. New ordinances and fees for business licenses emanated from the council, but questions involving new taxes, bonded indebtedness, or permitting a private company to supply the community with services were usually put to the voters at a special election.[10]

As long as they remained inside the confines of the black town, the people who lived, worked, and played there could conduct campaigns, pass laws, and grumble about the inaction of their elected officials. Beyond the road signs which marked the town limits, however, whites dominated county politics. Perhaps new-found freedom and isolation blinded black-town residents to the realities of American life. They rushed headlong into politics in the county, seemingly oblivious to the certain disaster awaiting them. In the fall of 1886, Hugh Lightfoot, the editor at Nicodemus, reflected the political optimism of the other towns when he predicted that inequalities would soon be a remnant of the past and that men would cease to classify one another by color.[11]

The black town gave its residents a false sense of security. But, had they thought back over their previous experience with whites or had they simply observed daily events in the wider world, few would have welcomed the future. Some settlers had fled to the towns to escape the terror of night riders, and as late as 1910 the *Boley Progress* claimed that southern blacks en route to that town were stopped, harassed, and molested.[12] Even before the incorporation of Langston and Boley, blacks were driven forcibly out of many biracial communities in the twin territories. Such violence accelerated during the 1890's, and by the time of statehood a host of Oklahoma towns prohibited blacks inside their limits except during daylight hours.[13]

A full year before the dispute over the permanent location of the county seat, blacks living in Nicodemus were already beginning to sense the white resentment and hostility toward their involvement in politics in northwestern Kansas. The first issue of the *Western Cyclone* appeared on the streets of Nicodemus in May, 1886, and by early July its editor, Arthur Tallman, found himself engaged in journalistic exchanges with several newspapers in both Rooks and Graham counties. What normally would have passed as harmless bantering between two country editors lingered on, and racial antagonisms quickly surfaced. W. L. Chambers, editor of the *Rooks County Record*, published at Stockton, initiated an argument with Tallman when he announced that "[Edward P.] McCabe will dispense 4th of July 'tiffy' to the Ethiopians of Nicodemus on Independence Day." This slur prompted the *Cyclone* editor to question Chambers' ancestry, referring to him as "an almond eyed shoat." Tallman went on to advise Chambers, "you had better learn to pound sand into a rat hole, Creamy, before you get so 'flip.' "[14]

In late July, 1886, Hugh K. Lightfoot assumed editorship of the *Cyclone*. Lightfoot, who had previously worked on newspapers at Logan, Phillipsburg, and Webster, immediately pushed Nicodemus as the most desirable location for the permanent seat of Graham County. Leaders in Nicodemus hoped that the two leading contenders, Hill City and Millbrook, would reach a stalemate and turn to their town as a compromise, thus avoiding a divisive and costly campaign. Millbrook, located south of the Solomon River, had been designated temporary county seat at a special election five years earlier, but W. R. Hill, founder of Hill City, wanted the prize for his town. James P. Pomeroy, Atchison coal dealer and speculator in western Kansas lands, backed Hill, and promised to construct an elaborate courthouse in Hill City if voters would relocate the seat of government there. From the beginning it was obvious, except perhaps to the citizens of Nicodemus, that neither the boosters of Millbrook nor Hill City would ever tolerate moving the county seat to a black town.

During the spring of 1887, Hill purchased the *Western Cyclone* from Lightfoot and installed George Sanford, a white employee of Hill's newspaper, the *Hill City Reveille*, as the new editor. Sanford maintained his residence in Hill City but traveled back and forth to Nicodemus on weekdays to conduct the business. Coming as no surprise to anyone, the *Cyclone* now openly endorsed Hill City for the county seat. From May on, the political pot continued to boil, and, as Nicodemus residents paused for a holiday on August 1 to hold their Emancipation Day Celebration, racial hatred in the area continued to grow. At that gathering, an altercation between two blacks over a business deal resulted in the shooting of an innocent bystander, and a fist fight broke out between an intoxicated white man and an Indian.[15]

The fracas at Nicodemus generated responses from some of the white newspaper editors in the immediate vicinity. H. N. Boyd at the Logan *Freeman* simply reported the fights without comment, but W. L. Chambers of the *Rooks County Record* implied that such violence was typical of black behavior, telling his readers that Nicodemus visitors "had a monkey and parrot time up there, in which two men nearly lost their lives, and in which a revolver, a razor, and a pair of knuckles figured largely." Chambers was especially irked by "our wooly-headed Ethiopian friend, H. R. Cayton," a Nicodemus resident, who, in the columns of another newspaper, charged that Chambers' news coverage of the event reeked of bias against blacks. In a letter to the Nicodemus newspaper, Cayton pointed out what he considered the "deep seated prejudice of this miserable puke . . . who thought a good nigger was one who worked as a hotel porter, a boot black, or as a monkey for the amusement of the general public." M. H. Hoyt and R. D. Graham, of the *Webster Eagle*, joined in the attack, arguing that "Rinehart's tonic, pistols, shooting, stabbing, etc.," evidently constituted the normal holiday attractions in Nicodemus.[16]

Politics increased racial tension. Representative James Justice called Graham County Republicans to order at their regular party convention held in Millbrook on September 8, 1887. Justice, a close friend of W. R. Hill, and party secretary W. L. Wallace acted as a self-appointed committee on credentials to determine which delegates would be seated. The major plank of the Justice-Hall faction, as the opposition labeled it, was support for Hill City as county seat. Disputes over the seating of contesting delegations split the convention and a group of bolters walked out, nominating a competing slate of candidates. Of course, the Hill-owned *Western Cyclone* at Nicodemus supported the regular party ticket backed by Justice and Hill.[17]

The county seat fight now threatened to divide Nicodemus. For the first and only time in Nicodemus' history, its residents could purchase and read two newspapers published inside the town. On August 12, approximately three weeks before the Republican convention had convened, Hugh Lightfoot launched the *Nicodemus Enterprise*. In its columns, Lightfoot supported the bolting faction of the party and personally attacked the character of W. R. Hill, indirectly boosting the Millbrook cause in the county seat contest. As Hill campaigned for re-election as county coroner, Lightfoot maintained a constant barrage of criticism, at one point suggesting that the "unsavory record of Mr. Hill morally unfits him for the office." Lightfoot chided Hill for running a Democratic newspaper in Hill City and one of the opposite political persuasion in Nicodemus, both for the purpose of securing the county seat. During the extended illness of George Sanford, the succession of part-time editors at the *Cyclone* also received their share of Lightfoot's venom. On September 28, for example, he noted that the "Cyclone changes assistant editors every week. H. R. Cayton is doing Hill's bidding this week."[18]

Never one to avoid a controversy, Lightfoot continued a stream of chatter at what he considered hostile newspapers in the area. Reflecting the black-town attitude toward Orientals, he suggested that one editor in a nearby town "was badly mixed with Chinese blood and wears his 'pig tail' under his coat." In late September he ridiculed the organizers of the Hill City Fair for segregating black and white babies in their annual contest and offering separate prizes for the prettiest child in each race. In early October he commented on the quality of the *Freemont Star*, describing it as "a disgrace to the newspaper fraternity and craft in general . . . make up. The *Star* looks like bird tracks on a very frosty morning and after closely scrutinizing it we are led to believe that [William H.] Cotton uses common shoe pegs for type."[19]

Lightfoot also went after the regular Republican ticket, painting some of its members lily white and accusing them of prejudice and discrimination.[20] In this respect, he possessed strange allies. Since Nicodemus' founding, a few whites in the county had distrusted Hill's original motives, suspecting that he had founded the colony to control politics and eventually to maneuver the county seat to Hill City. As early as September, 1879, the *Graham County Lever* at Gettysburg had claimed that Hill admitted he had brought blacks into Kansas to ensure the success of his town. Two months later, the *Lever* quoted Hill telling a friend that "we will have to make concessions to the niggers and give them a few little offices, but when we get the county seat at Hill City they may go to hell."[21] Hill denied the charge. Despite such attempts to weaken his support in Nicodemus, most of the residents there continued to remain loyal to him.

In the county-seat struggle, Hill City made much of its supposedly superior location north of the Solomon River. As soon as Nicodemus residents were convinced that their town was out of the running, they threw their support to Hill City, primarily because of Hill's part in settling Nicodemus and the dangers involved in attempting to cross the river south to Millbrook during high water. Natural disaster also played a role. In late August, 1887, a severe windstorm, probably a tornado, virtually leveled Millbrook's business district. Lightfoot apparently changed few minds; the regular Republican ticket swept the November elections. He printed the final issue of the *Enterprise* two days before Christmas, but remained in Nicodemus to practice law and sell farm implements. The following spring, Graham County voters chose to relocate their courthouse in Hill City; Nicodemus Township voted 115–1 in favor of the move. Some political observers in the county were convinced Lightfoot had cast the one dissenting vote.[22]

Whites responded quickly to the threat of black political participation in Okfuskee County, but for a few short months Boley citizens lived and voted in a fantasyland of unrestrained privilege. On April 6, 1905, the *Boley Progress* invited southern blacks to join their brethren in a future county of their own, free from want and fear. Blacks living outside the town, however, saw no reason for such rosy predictions. Other signs foretold the future. For example, throughout the twin territories, whites brutally forced blacks from mixed communities, sometimes allowing them only twenty-four hours to depart. On April 7, the *Lexington Leader* heralded the triumph of an all-white ticket in the Guthrie city elections, proudly announcing, "Great Guthrie ungoggles her eyes after sixteen years of darkness. . . ."[23] And delegates to the Muskogee meeting of the Western Negro Press Association in September passed resolutions asking for protection from lynching and assurances that Oklahomans would impose no Jim Crow laws after the territory gained admission to the Union.[24]

With great enthusiasm, Boley blacks turned out in large numbers to elect their first slate of town officials in April, 1906. Undaunted by events outside the town, they looked forward to elections later that year to select delegates to the state constitutional convention. Unfortunately for their future, Boley citizens were unaware they held the balance of political power in the Seventy-Ninth District. Through gerrymandering, Boley had been included with the larger white towns of Okemah, Henryetta, and Weleetka. In the election, the three white communities split almost evenly between the two major parties, but Boley's vote, 265 Republican to 26 Democrat, carried the Republican candidates to the convention by a margin of less than two hundred.[25] The political joy ride would soon end.

The dynamiting of two homes in Okemah in January, 1907, marked the beginning of open violence against blacks living in the county. In mid-August, Okemah hosted the meeting of the Republican county convention, and on the opening day several white delegates refused to sit with the blacks in attendance. After the convention elected a white president and O. H. Bradley, former editor of the *Boley Progress*, as secretary, several whites walked out, later meeting separately to nominate an alternate slate of candidates. The remaining delegates, fifty-eight black and twenty-four white, presented a ticket with James E. Thompson, Clearview town promoter, and another black as candidates for county commissioner.[26]

Immediately after the convention, the Democratic *Okemah Ledger* and *Weleetka American* both launched a systematic campaign of racial hatred. On the front page of the August 29 issue, readers of the *Ledger* found photographs depicting Reverend A. J. Walker of Boley leading the Republican convention in prayer, a caucus of black and white convention officers, and racial mingling before the opening of a session. The following day the *American* pulled out all the stops, asking the Republican "candidate for sheriff on the nigger ticket . . . whether or not, in your canvass, you met a Clearview nigger . . . and promised to give a deputyship to a Boley nigger . . . ?"[27] By the middle of September, the *American* had become totally paranoid, desperately warning whites:

STOP! LOOK! LISTEN!
TO A RAILROAD DANGER SIGNAL! THE COUNTY IS IN DANGER OF NEGRO DOMINA- TION—WHITE VOTERS, CRUSH THE INSO- LENCE OF THE NEGRO! PROTECT YOUR HOMES WITH YOUR BALLOT![28]

In commenting on the political activities of W. B. Toney,

candidate for county judge on the regular Republican ticket, the *American* on September 13 finally sunk to its lowest level. Toney had visited Boley and, like many whites before him, had stayed overnight in the hotel there. The headline to the brief story reporting the incident read, "SLEEPS WITH NIGGERS."[29]

On the grounds that the ticket was incomplete, the Democratic-controlled Okfuskee County Election Board refused to certify the slate of regular Republican candidates nominated at the Okemah convention in August. Although the regular Republicans finally appeared on the ballot, the election board threw out the returns from predominantly black precincts and the Democrats took political control of the county.[30] The *Weleetka American* endorsed the decision to reject black ballots because at the polls "the niggers chased out the white judges . . . and allowed every nigger big, little, young, and old to vote as often as they desired."[31]

Despite the Democratic victory, the white fear of black participation in politics continued unabated. The selection of the permanent location of the county seat still lay in the future, and the animosity between the races intensified during the fall of 1907. In October, Clearview narrowly avoided a small riot. As a large number of Clearview residents waited on the depot platform to board a passenger train, Charles Allen, a white man, charged through the crowd, hitting people with a suitcase and umbrella and demanding that blacks step aside and let him go first. Blacks outnumbered whites by at least five to one, and violence was avoided only by locking Allen in the train and persuading the conductor to move it farther down the track away from the station. Two months later, the first lynching of a black in the new state of Oklahoma occurred at Henryetta, twenty miles east of Okemah.[32]

Pending the outcome of a later election, the State Constitutional Convention had designated Okemah temporary county seat. Although Boleyites dreamed of a two-story stone courthouse standing in the center of their town, most whites living along the Fort Smith and Western Railroad from Weleetka to Paden shuddered at such a thought. Violence erupted again. In two successive weeks in April, 1908, dynamite blasts ripped through a hotel and black-owned restaurant in Okemah.[33] With an eye cast toward the coming county-seat election, the editor of the *Okemah Ledger* abandoned any semblance of objective journalism and moved to discredit Boley, picturing it as a lawless community unworthy of the seat of government. A brief story in the May 14 issue, for example, reported a burglary at the United States post office at Castle. Officials investigating the crime had found what they believed to be the robbers' footprints in the mud just outside the post office window. Although the police had only indicated that the footprints led west of the building, the *Ledger* headlined, "Post Office Robbed at Castle . . . Trail Leads Toward Boley." During the next two weeks the black town was featured by headlines reading, "A Wanted Negro Found at Boley," and "Woman Publicly Whipped in Boley."[34] Although Boley citizens voted by a narrow margin to award the county seat to Weleetka, Okemah retained permanent possession in a very close election in August, 1908.[35]

Politically, Boley died. To be sure, citizens there continued to vote in municipal elections, but out in the county approximately 90 percent of Boley's adult population was disenfranchised. Even before Oklahomans enacted a grandfather clause in 1910, Okfuskee County whites utilized their hold on registration and the threat of violence to ostracize blacks politically. Moreover, to neutralize Republican strength, Democrats gerrymandered Boley and simultaneously relocated the registration and polling site in Paden. Those few blacks who traveled the six miles to Paden to register and vote met open hostility and intimidation. Agreeing to allow only a limited number of blacks to participate in each election, white registrars required "legible" handwriting and a clear indication that voters could "understand" the state constitution. Blacks who still attempted to vote found precinct lines redrawn again and again in order to confuse them. One newspaper suggested that black voters needed a search warrant to locate the poll.[36] The hatred sown by the Okemah and Weleetka newspapers finally matured. Its ultimate harvest came in 1911. In May of that year, Paden residents Mrs. Laura Nelson and her teenage son, charged with murder, were forcibly taken from the Okemah jail and lynched. Mrs. Nelson was raped several times, and then she and her son were hanged from a bridge over the Canadian River.[37] For a time, terror gripped blacks in eastern Oklahoma, and some who lived in Boley must surely have remembered their past experiences in the South.

Most of the people of Mound Bayou never enjoyed the opportunity to take part in politics outside the community. Long before the town was incorporated, Mississippians had moved to disenfranchise blacks living in the state. Ironically, Isaiah T. Montgomery, Mound Bayou's promoter, led the drive to disarm his race politically. A Republican and loyal party worker, Montgomery served as a delegate to both the Warren County and Congressional District Conventions during the late 1880's, later sat on the Bolivar County Republican Committee, and held a patronage position in the federal land office at Jackson. On at least one occasion he joined a state delegation traveling to Washington, D. C., to testify before a Senate committee studying flood problems on the Mississippi River. In a July, 1890, election, he and George Melchoir, a white man, were chosen to represent Bolivar County at the State Constitutional Convention.[38]

During the post-Reconstruction period, Montgomery had taken part in the fusion politics endemic to Bolivar and a few other counties in the state possessing heavy concentrations of black laborers. Under the arrangement, black Republicans joined forces with Democrats, agreeing in advance of an election to the exact number of offices each race would receive. Under normal circumstances, blacks could expect low-paying jobs with little authority, a few spots on the County Board of Supervisors, and perhaps a seat in the state legislature. As the two delegates to the State Constitutional Convention, Melchoir and Montgomery represented the candidates of the fusion ticket in Bolivar County.[39]

When Montgomery entered the convention hall in Jackson on August 12, 1890, he encountered a body composed of 130 Democrats, one National Republican, one Conservative, and one Greenbacker. He was black, Republican, and alone. Public demands for prohibition and cleaning up state government were offered as reasons for the convention call, but the quest for a legal method to eliminate black voters in Mississippi constituted the major purpose for convening the body. Some blacks—John R. Lynch, a Mississippi congressman, for example—believed that Montgomery had already committed himself to support a group with announced intentions of barring blacks from the polls. And on the opening day, Montgomery helped to vote this faction into the chair, giving it control over the organization of the convention.[40]

Montgomery was appointed to the Committee on Franchise, Apportionment, and Elections, which returned a report to the convention calling for a state literacy test. At the discretion of an election judge, voters could be required to offer a "reasonable interpretation" of the constitution when read to them. If adopted, the plan would eliminate at least 124,000 blacks from politics, leaving the state with a white majority of more than 48,000. On September 15, Montgomery gained the floor to join in the debate. "My mission here," he told the white delegates, "is to bridge a chasm that has been widening and deepening for a generation." In an hour-long speech, Montgomery went on to evoke visions of an ante-bellum South where master and slave worked hand-in-hand, sharing mutual admiration and respect. But war had destroyed that beautiful world ruled by "the proudest aristocracy that ever graced the Western hemisphere," and outsiders had gained the confidence of his people, upsetting the harmony between the two races. Now, "every form of demoralization, blood-shed, bribery, [and] ballot stuffing" plagued the politics of a once-proud state. In his opinion, most blacks had failed to attain the "high plane of moral, intellectual, and political excellence" reached by whites, and blacks were currently stalled at an "inferior development in the line of civilization." To those soon to be disenfranchised, Montgomery justified his support of the proposal on the grounds that "we have not taken away your high privilege, but only lifted it to a higher plane." The restriction, he argued, would encourage blacks to improve, allowing them to re-enter the electorate once they had earned the right.[41]

The convention loved him. What better endorsement for disenfranchisement than a supportive speech from the lone black delegate whom many considered a leading spokesman for his race? Any opposition to the committee report quickly faded, and by a lop-sided margin the literacy test was incorporated into the draft of the new state constitution. White newspapers in Mississippi were elated. The *Raymond Gazette*, for example, praised Montgomery for his perception of the race problem. Some black leaders were less pleased, however. In the neighboring state of Alabama, Booker T. Washington remained silent on the issue, but T. Thomas Fortune, editor of the New York *Age*, blasted Montgomery for the serious wound inflicted on his people. Montgomery returned home to Mound Bayou, and later became one of the half-dozen residents there eligible to vote in elections held outside the limits of the town. Fourteen years later, in a letter to Booker T. Washington in 1904, Montgomery privately confessed that his stand at Jackson had been a serious blunder.[42]

Disenfranchisement plagued the other black communities as well. By the time Oklahomans enacted a grandfather clause to eliminate black voters in 1910, the residents of Clearview, Langston, and Boley were accustomed to discrimination. Many had moved there to escape the open hostility of whites in the South. Geography changed nothing. In Indian Territory, separation of school children was left to county option until 1904; thereafter, children of African descent were legally isolated. And white missionaries dispatched to the area after the Civil War had already established separate Indian churches. In December, 1907, the legislature of the new state of Oklahoma passed a statute requiring Jim Crow cars on all railroads operating within its borders. In May of the following year, Governor C. N. Haskell signed a bill officially outlawing interracial marriage. More terrifying, however, were the number of "sundown" communities prohibiting blacks inside the town after dark and the acts of violence inflicted upon blacks.

During the early territorial and statehood years, racial hatred in Oklahoma exceeded that found in either Kansas or Mississippi. Despite the emotionalism of a few Democratic newspaper editors in northwestern Kansas, blacks living in or near Nicodemus never seriously threatened the white control of Graham County politics. Most of the early white settlers of Graham County, moreover, had come from the North and lacked the intensive racial animosity found among many southern whites. Thanks in part to Isaiah Montgomery, blacks were already disenfranchised in Bolivar County, Mississippi, before Mound Bayou incorporated. Oklahoma was unique. With its various land runs and lotteries, what became the state of Oklahoma represented an open frontier in which both races, each antagonistic toward the other, vied for the economic exploitation of the area's resources. While they never accounted for more than 10 percent of the total population, blacks competing for those resources intensified white antagonism toward them. In addition, Oklahoma's late statehood, in 1907, allowed the large number of southern whites who migrated there the opportunity to draw upon the segregation laws already adopted in other states. Once blacks were economically and politically neutralized and socially segregated, racial hatred in Oklahoma subsided to levels found elsewhere. As late as 1915, however, white Oklahomans still felt insecure. In that year, the legislature authorized the State Corporation Commission to establish separate telephone booths for black and white callers.[43]

By their very existence the black towns encouraged segregation. Reflecting much of the current attitude toward the ghetto of a major city, prejudiced whites could point to the towns as an indication that blacks wished to live apart from the rest of society. Black-town leaders worked to ensure the location of segregated institutions in their communities and state legislators willingly obliged. Although whites continued to control their operation, facilities for the deaf, dumb, blind, and orphans, a girls' reformatory, the hospital for the insane, the state training school for boys, and a university were all located in the various blacks towns of Oklahoma.[44] In Okfuskee and Logan, the county superintendent of schools usually designated Boley and Langston, respectively, as the site for the summer "normal" or "institute" held for the training of black teachers. As discrimination increased, the towns also became a haven for blacks wishing to hold public and private meetings, and fraternal organizations gravitated to them. In 1911, for example, the black Masonic Lodge of Oklahoma authorized construction of a $20,000 temple at Boley.

To the people living in or near Clearview and Boley, the treatment of blacks by some Indians was perhaps more galling than white discrimination. Of the Five Civilized Tribes, the Choctaws and Chickasaws perhaps held the strongest views toward other races. In 1866, the federal government withheld $300,000 owed to the two tribes until they adopted their former slaves. Both refused. The Indian freedmen problem, which continued for some time, was compounded by an illegal invasion of blacks from Texas and Louisiana who slipped across the Red River into Indian territory. Chickasaw light-horse police and vigilante committees met little success in attempting to turn back the immigrants or to remove those already located. Such action, in fact, prompted a flood of black petitions to Congress pleading for army protection from Indian cruelty. In 1883, the Choctaws reluctantly accepted $10,000 to include their freedmen in the tribe (the Chickasaws never capitulated), but racial animosity continued.[45] Blacks were socially segregated and excluded from Indian schools, and as late as 1891, the *Lexington Leader* reported that the "Choctaws are driving the negroes out of the Nation. Anyone employing a colored servant is subjected to [a] $50.00 fine."[46]

Okfuskee County blacks expected little sympathy, or even kindness, from the Choctaws or Chickasaws, but the Creek attitude toward them was difficult to accept. Clearview and Boley were located in the Creek Nation, and blacks had married into the tribe. Creek freedmen generally enjoyed amiable relations with their former masters. One freedman born during slavery later remembered that right after the Civil War "we live right in amongst them, sometimes a nigger in one side of the house and an Indian in the other . . . no Jim Crow then."[47] The rapid influx of white southerners into the area quickly changed such red-black intimacy. Creek freedmen identified with the Indians, assuming a higher status position than newly arrived blacks from the South. Whites refused to recognize these fine class distinctions. Such comments as, "The Creek niggers are niggers just like the rest of them . . . ," and, "In any mixture nigger blood will dominate and show out," represented attitudes common among most whites.[48] In fact, many whites pointed to miscegenation as the major reason for what they considered Creek backwardness relative to other tribes. By the turn of the century, most full-blood Creeks had accepted the white southern racial ideology and were moving toward total segregation.

Black-town editors like Ernest Lynwood in Clearview and S. Douglas Russell at Langston felt empathy for Indians. When Indians discriminated against them, however, or when whites placed Indians in a superior position, black tempers flared. Generally, Lynwood supported Indian rights, but when the Creeks established segregated schools in 1904 he slipped into a bitter denunciation of the school board of the Creek nation, calling it an educational fake. Lynwood pondered about the plight of the Creek freedmen and those blacks listed on tribal rolls. Would "they be permitted," he wondered, "to 'butt in' to the sacred confines of a government civilizing machine?"[49] In Langston three years later, Russell commented on the new Oklahoma constitution, sarcastically lamenting that at least for the time being "every blanket, raw meat eating Indian is recognized by the constitution as white persons to associate, marry and give in marriage with white persons." This would no doubt continue, he argued, until the land sharks had eaten their fill of the Indian domain. He questioned "whether [then] they will be able to march to the music of the white man's civilization?" Eventually, both black and red would face the same problem, and once Indians felt the full force of white discrimination they might come to recognize the absurdity of their haughty attitude.[50]

Because black-town residents were totally isolated from them, most whites who expressed an opinion on the subject generally supported the idea of a separate community at least during the early years of its existence. In referring to Boley in 1905, the editor of the *Weleetka American* felt that having "the colored people all to themselves beats the Guthrie system," where the races attended school together and where a white customer was "forced to refresh himself at a bar where the colored man's money was good."[51] Contact between white and black towns was sometimes cordial. Such was the case in December, 1879, when a Nicodemus minister delivered a speech on prohibition to a large audience in the nearby town of Gettysburg; in turn, two Gettysburg residents visited Nicodemus to organize a temperance society.[52]

A viable black town, however, made the white argument for disenfranchisement and segregation seem all the more contradictory. If blacks were excluded from the electorate on the grounds of their inability to make an intelligent decision at the polls, how could one explain their success at self-government in their own community? And if their economic and social behavior inside their own corporate limits contradicted the white stereotype of the race, by what standard could one justify segregation? As soon as the black towns made it clear that they expected to share equally in public funds available for schools, road maintenance, and bridges, or threatened to disturb the balance of power in county politics, such questions were easily brushed aside. To the extent that they ever recognized or faced the dichotomy between their racial prejudices and the realities of black success, whites solved the dilemma in several ways.

In the minds of some whites, the people who dwelled in the black town were atypical of the race. Those holding strong racial views had sometimes pointed to the possibility of mixed blood in an effort to account for the abilities of Booker T. Washington, Frederick Douglass, and other black leaders. The dark complexion of many black-town residents, however, quickly nullified that argument. Yet, if blacks were supposedly inferior, an explanation for their success must surely exist, and eventually an answer was found. In the January, 1910, issue of *Century Magazine*, Hiram Tong, a white reporter who had visited Mound Bayou to write a feature story on the town, admitted that the "maximum amount of white blood in the colony is so slight that Mound Bayou's ultimate success cannot be attributed to Caucasian race qualities." Rather, Tong argued, "the negroes of Mound Bayou are black; five sixths of them are descendants on both sides of African slaves." Tong suggested that only a cursory comparison of the photographs of Mound Bayou's leaders with that of Booker T. Washington would "reveal the racial purity of the Mound Bayou type."[53] In June of the same year, Thomas Arnold, a writer for the New Orleans *State*, elaborated upon the same theme, contending that the people of Mound Bayou were the pure offspring "of the real old-time African race into whose veins has crept no germ of that shiftlessness, worthlessness, criminal tendencies, or self-importance that characterizes so many of the race who have grown to be such a fester upon the average city. . . . That kind of blood has never found permanent lodgement in the citizenship of Mound Bayou, nor of the farming element of the 'colony.' "[54]

Rather than issuing such testimonials praising the accomplishments of the "African race" or groping for other rationalizations to explain black achievement, some whites in nearby communities refused to acknowledge explicitly the existence of a black town in the immediate vicinity. The newspaper at Coyle, located approximately ten miles from Langston, seldom mentioned the black town either in news items or among business advertisements. But the people of Coyle were well aware of the presence of blacks in the area. Mears Drug Store there discriminated against them and the owner of Shellhammer's Barber Shop assured customers that "only white workmen [were] employed." Although Langston residents frequently shopped there, the proprietors of the New York Cash Store rejected appeals to advertise in the *Western Age* at Langston or in other black newspapers.[55]

In most cases, black-town leaders refrained from publicly commenting on acts of discrimination aimed directly at the community or its citizens. In fact, they sometimes pretended as if brotherly love characterized all contacts between their town and those in the larger society. "The Negroes of Langston and the white people of our twin town Coyle are living within a stone's throw of each other, on terms of perfect American friendship," boasted S. Douglas Russell in June, 1905.[56] And, in concluding a brochure on Mound Bayou, Charles Banks felt it would be "unjust to close this brief write-up . . . without making mention of the kindly disposition of the white people near here in laying no barriers in the way of the effort to build up a substantial and creditable Negro town and colony."[57] Such statements were designed for white consumption, but they frequently produced adverse results. By ingratiating themselves, praising whites for what little freedoms they enjoyed, and accommodating to segregation, leaders reinforced the white belief in black inferiority, thereby encouraging further injustices. Not to fight back was one thing and, given the times, was quite understandable, but to glorify white prejudice and inhumanity was quite another. When queried in 1910 about the possibility of an armed attack on Mound Bayou, Isaiah Montgomery seemed confident that a race riot would never come to northern Mississippi. "Up here," he said, "our own people are being guided by the wisdom of the best negroes in the United States. And the whites understand this. They are trusting us more and more to control our own criminals."[58] Montgomery would live to see a white deputy sheriff from Merigold beat some of his townspeople with a whip. The accommodating attitude of Montgomery, Banks, and others was evident to whites who visited the town. In the summer of 1910, a white newspaper reporter just recently returned from Mound Bayou was struck by the "entire frankness and complacency with which they regard the fact . . . that they are in reality an inferior race."[59]

The black-town reaction to segregation reflected some of the trends in black thought in the United States. Certainly, Isaiah Montgomery's support for Mississippi's literacy test in 1890 paralleled the shift from protest to accommodation throughout the South.[60] But because of their location in a frontier environment, which briefly permitted the exercise of freedoms denied most blacks in older states, those residing in Langston, Clearview, and Boley were slow to respond to the realities of open discrimination. Even as they rode in Jim Crow railroad coaches, watched their children come and go to separate schools, and listened to legislators debate disenfranchisement, leaders in Oklahoma's black towns remained optimistic. As late as October, 1907, readers of S. Douglas Russell's *Western Age* at Langston were advised to ignore talk of segregation, keeping in mind "that this is not a real southern state, remember that the majority of Oklahoma people are for fair play and full enjoyment of personal liberty."[61]

Russell knew, of course, that such rhetoric might temporarily raise the spirits of a few people, but it would never curb the white drive for total segregation. Earlier, in April of the same year, he had chaired a convention of three hundred blacks meeting in Oklahoma City to protest the new state's proposed constitution. Out of that gathering came the Negro Protective League, a statewide organization set up to coordinate opposition to the document before it came up for ratification by the voters in August. Russell was elected chairman of the league's executive committee, and the *Western Age* became its official organ. Since the Democrats were screaming "race" in Oklahoma politics, Russell gradually conceded ground on the issue of total black equality. In his April 26 issue, he advised blacks to blot "out the word social equality but by the eternals write in burning letters POLITICAL EQUALITY," and one month later Russell captioned an article on state politics with, "SOCIAL EQUALITY COUNTS 0."[62]

When the Republican party convened its state convention at Tulsa in September, 1907, blacks were persuaded to withdraw all demands for representation on the ticket, as Russell put it, "to save our party from the ignorant democratic prejudice and harang of Negro domination, and social equality."[63] Neither did blacks sit on the Republican Central Committee. Party leaders, however, agreed to allow blacks to select two representatives from each congressional district to act as an advisory body. As secretary and manager of the Black Advisory Committee, Russell secured a suite of rooms in the Melrose Hotel in Oklahoma City, installed office equipment, employed a staff, and opened a state headquarters. When criticized about the separate office, Russell responded that the race was segregated in all other areas and the arrangement would immediately disarm any Democrat charging black equality inside the Republican party. Russell combined his duties for the party with those of the Negro Protective League, collecting signatures on a petition to the federal government seeking rejection of the constitution and mailing out thousands of letters to black Republicans.[64] All efforts failed. With constitution intact, Oklahoma entered the Union on November 16, 1907. Democrats controlled the first legislature; and on February 15, 1908, the state's Jim Crow law went into effect.

On the same day, Edward P. McCabe, former Nicodemus resident and promoter of Langston, filed suit in United States Circuit Court at Guthrie. McCabe's legal protest, the first of a succession of failures, sought a temporary injunction against the establishment of separate railroad coaches until their constitutionality could be determined in court. In early February, McCabe appealed to blacks across the state for funds to carry on the legal battle, and at Boley the editor of the *Beacon* urged readers to send money to him, "as we have a good show at winning; and if we do it will make the difference in the world to Boley."[65] On February 25, William Henry Harrison Hart, professor of law at Howard University in Washington, D. C., who had previously won a 1905 case in Maryland against segregation in interstate travel, joined McCabe.[66] Despite their combined efforts, however, legal challenges to Oklahoma's Jim Crow law eventually ended in failure.

As soon as it became apparent that newspaper editorials, political organization, and court action would fail to hold back the Jim Crow onslaught, black-town leaders abandoned such efforts. Most demands for social equality ceased, but instead blacks insisted that all laws must be enforced to their letter. At Langston, S. Douglas Russell argued that if Oklahoma must have a Jim Crow statute, the state had to ensure "equal accommodations for black and white—not the way it is done in the rabid southern states." In December, 1908, Russell filed a complaint with the State Corporation Commission charging that blacks were being denied equal accommodations on four railroads operating inside Oklahoma.[67] In Mound Bayou, promoter Charles Banks frowned on such methods, however. In a July, 1914, letter to Booker T. Washington, Banks claimed that the separate day coaches offered black travelers between Memphis and Vicksburg equaled those provided for whites. Banks told Washington that the few blacks who instituted lawsuits against the railroads in that state hindered his efforts to persuade officials of the Yazoo and Mississippi to upgrade the facilities for all blacks. Some way had to be found, he told Washington, to discourage such legal action in the future.[68]

In time, black-town leaders accepted segregation as a *fait accompli*, but they demanded that it be total. Specifically, they called for absolute black control over their own institutions, facilities equal to those offered whites, and equal pay for equal work. Whites conceded little. At Langston, two blacks sat on the Board of Regents of the Colored Agricultural and Normal University, but remained in the minority. In May, 1907, the *Western Age* pointed out that the faculty at CA and N received less pay than comparable white teachers throughout the state.[69] Although CA and N President Inman E. Page had openly endorsed the Booker T. Washington approach of concentration on industrial education, the school's regents voted to remove him in 1916. According to *Harlow's Weekly*, Page, who had previously been president of Lincoln Institute in Missouri, was fired because he had embraced the philosophy of W. E. B. Du Bois and "could not be convinced of the inapplicability of the idea in Oklahoma."[70] Most state institutions for blacks were located in black towns, but whites continued to dictate policy and control operations.

For years, black-town promoters had preached that isolation from whites constituted the first step toward a solution to the race problem in the United States. But their actions, especially attempts to gain the county seat and to participate in politics, belied their public statements. When segregation and disenfranchisement came, however, most leaders abandoned any semblance of opposition, in time even praising them as blessings in disguise. Separation would spur black-town population growth and bring racial solidarity, something impossible, they said, before the advent of Jim Crow and the grandfather clause. Indeed, segregation was good. It provided blacks the opportunity to learn self-government, built character, and offered employment for teachers.[71] For

Inman E. Page, president, Colored Agricultural and Normal
University, Langston. Courtesy Western History Collections,
University of Oklahoma Library.

those blacks who could still vote in Oklahoma in 1912, the
Clearview Patriarch advised them to seek out a candidate
who stood for the separation of the races and "vote for that
man, and let the politics take care of themselves."[72]

Politics, however, had always been an important part of
black-town life, both in and outside the community, and
some leaders were reluctant to advise residents to forsake all
demands for political equality. Yet, whites might permit
black participation in county and state elections if they could

be shown that such activity offered no real threat. The answer seemed obvious—make peace with the Democrats. The idea of splitting black votes equally between the two major parties had been suggested by several prominent blacks as early as the 1880's, but S. Douglas Russell, editor of the *Western Age* at Langston, set out to bring the proposal to fruition in Oklahoma. Shortly after Oklahoma entered the Union in 1907, a Democrat sat in the governor's mansion and the party controlled the legislature.

Beginning in November of that year, Russell embarked on a campaign aimed at convincing blacks to abandon their solid support for the Republicans. Russell praised Governor C. N. Haskell as a brave and fearless leader, thanked the Democrats for their continued financial support for the university at Langston, and asked his race to study the cardinal principles of the Democratic party; most would come to recognize that justice and fair play constituted its chief cornerstone. In early January, 1909, Russell sent a circular letter to all members of the Oklahoma legislature and high state officials, asking Democrats to refrain from making derogatory remarks about the race and to pass no legislation endangering the civil rights of blacks. In return, Russell assured them that through the columns of the *Western Age* he could convince his people of the futility of voting solidly Republican at the polls.[73]

The response to Russell's proposition came in the form of a letter from Oklahoma Attorney General Charles West. West told Russell that open antagonism toward the "ruling class whites" had done much to damage race relations in the state and that vote splitting might help to alleviate the problem. Furthermore, West thought it extremely foolish of blacks to seek office in the Oklahoma Senate or House of Representatives, "or to put themselves in any position where they attract the fire of economic and political hostility." He also hinted that Russell had overlooked an important yet simple alternative—blacks could refrain from voting.[74]

Russell's overtures to the Democrats represented one

last attempt to forestall passage of Oklahoma's grandfather clause. Russell's subsequent career also suggests that other motives may have prompted his behavior. As early as the fall of 1908, Russell had pushed for establishment of a state-supported institution for black orphans and deaf and blind children. Governor Haskell and the legislature responded in the following year, agreeing to locate it in Taft, a black town ten miles west of Muskogee. From the beginning it was obvious that Russell wanted to head the new institution, and in March, 1909, he scolded those who voiced concern over who might be appointed superintendent. Blacks should be thankful, he told his readers; and although the new institution was his idea, "who manages it is not of importance." By the time he spoke to the annual meeting of the Western Negro Press Association in Topeka, Kansas, in late November, 1911, Russell was editor of the *Tribune* at Taft and superintendent of the school for the blind there.[75]

For a time, the idea of vote splitting between the two major parties was more rhetorical than real. Most black-town settlers had migrated from the South, and few could forget the wounds of the past. Inside the towns, the terms "Democrat" and "race prejudice" were synonymous. Years later, one of Boley's early residents recalled, "We hated them democrats down south and we kept them out. One man was shot when he tried to make a speech. In them days, if you was a democrat you had to keep it to yourself."[76] Farther north, in Nicodemus, Democrats collected only fifteen of the 652 total votes cast in the nine presidential elections from 1880 to 1912.[77]

Later, as Democrats gained control over registration and elections in the county, black-town citizens seemed more disposed to switch parties. Practicality entered the picture. Those who refused to give up their Republican affiliation were denied the right to vote. Lawyers in Boley, for example, found it advantageous in their law practice in the county court to ally with the dominant party. At least in name, the black towns became progressively more Democratic.[78] One old settler objected to the trend, however, lamenting that "Boley was a good little town 'til we started dealing with them damn democrats."[79] In the formative years of Nicodemus, only avowed Republicans could expect to win election to local office, but in September, 1887, eight Democrats met at Hays' Drug Store to form the party's first town caucus.[80]

The shift of some black-town residents to the Democratic party in no way represented an ideological commitment to its principles. But recognition of the practicalities of county politics along with what some considered the Republican betrayal of the race made the switch more palatable. At least the Democrats had always been honest; they had never attempted to conceal their racial feelings. Republicans, on the other hand, had paraded as the champions of black rights. In a strange way, the hatred of some blacks for the Republicans overshadowed their traditional aversion to the Democrats. Although Democratically controlled legislatures disenfranchised and segregated black-town citizens, Republicans received the bulk of their criticism. Editors and other leaders frequently singled out Republicans who voted for Jim Crow laws, refused to stand and protect the race, or failed to appoint blacks to office.[81]

In general, the black towns remained loyal to the Republican party on the national level, but between the first election of Theodore Roosevelt and that of Woodrow Wilson their devotion was sorely tested. The black-town oscillation of first praise and then rejection for both Theodore Roosevelt and William H. Taft reflected the frustration of all blacks throughout the country. Roosevelt seemed to move back and forth between appeasing blacks, reflected by his invitation to Booker T. Washington to visit the White House, and accommodating the demands of the lily-white elements of his party. The nationwide uproar over Roosevelt's dishonorable discharge of three companies of black soldiers accused of rioting in Brownsville, Texas, in 1906 seeped into the black-town press.[82] Yet, although they grumbled and threatened to withdraw their support, few blacks followed that course. Experience had shown that no other home awaited them in the American party system.

By the same token, socialism found few converts inside segregated communities. Most citizens there failed to perceive that, at least in the abstract, the proponents of socialism and those favoring economic self-help shared many common assumptions and goals. Furthermore, the idea of a class conflict, irrespective of color, completely eluded them. Editors, however, sometimes attempted to pressure white Republicans, suggesting that blacks might abandon the party and embrace socialist candidates on the local level. In January, 1906, the *Western Age* at Langston warned Republicans seeking office that if Logan County blacks joined in a political alliance with Socialists they could elect an entire Socialist ticket. "Will the corrupt and arrogant white men who have been running Republican politics stop, think and act this year?" asked the *Age*. Such statements represented nothing but shallow threats. Black-town leaders quickly learned that hostile whites could point to socialism as an alien philosophy and use it against the race. During the fall and winter of 1911, for example, the editor of the *Okemah Ledger* equated socialism with black demands for justice. In its December 14 issue, the *Ledger* ran an article entitled "SOCIALISM URGES NEGRO EQUALITY."[83]

To some people in the black towns, the Populist solution also seemed too radical; to others, Populist candidates represented nothing more than temporarily displaced Democrats. Mary Elizabeth Lease, the well-known Populist orator from Kansas who once counseled farmers to raise more hell and less corn, spoke to a large audience in Langston in October, 1895. In part reflecting his attitude toward the Populist party and in part echoing the black-town reaction toward a woman in politics, R. Emmett Stewart, editor of the *Langston City Herald*, argued that Mrs. Lease's address proved that "ladies must stay at home and take care of the babies while the men run this great government."[84] In Nicodemus, on the other hand, the Populist platform evidently appealed to several residents. The Populist candidate for president garnered 35 and 39 percent of the total votes cast in Nicodemus Township in 1892 and 1896.[85]

Although some blacks had never forgiven Theodore Roosevelt for the Brownsville Affair, or for his failure to act decisively in their behalf, by 1912 he seemed the least of several evils. To most black-town spokesmen, the election of Woodrow Wilson, Eugene Debs, or William H. Taft spelled certain disaster. In August of that year, Clearview town promoter James E. Thompson felt that, given the realities of American politics, Roosevelt's views on the race question seemed the most tenable. And when Roosevelt appeared as the presidential candidate of the Progressive party, Thompson reluctantly supported him. In general, however, Thompson, along with blacks living inside the towns and throughout the nation, saw little in the entire progressive reform movement of any great benefit to the race. Progressives, they argued, should concentrate on purifying the ballot and permitting each individual the opportunity to express their will at the polls. The reform of city government, recall of judges, or referendum meant nothing to a black person who could not vote.[86]

The black-town excursion into politics had proved disastrous. Coming in quest of economic security and arriving with little experience in political matters, yet eager to exercise their legal rights as citizens, residents met discrimination and disenfranchisement. With the opportunity to enjoy political and social equality now gone, only one other area remained. As early as October, 1907, S. Douglas Russell at Langston had argued that the recent Democratic sweep of state offices in Oklahoma meant nothing for the race or the town. Look from the ballot box to the soil, Russell advised. "Your farm land will produce just as good a bale of cotton now as before."[87]

4

Economy and Society

AS THE COTTON BELT spread north and west into Oklahoma and Texas, blacks generally refused to follow. But the early settlers of Langston, Clearview, and Boley who had migrated from the South brought some knowledge of cotton culture with them to the area. According to *Herald* editor R. Emmett Stewart, Langston, in September, 1895, was already recognized as the "cotton belt center of Oklahoma."[1] Despite some bad years, the interest in cotton remained high in and around Oklahoma's black towns. In early 1913, the U. S. Department of Agriculture dispatched agents to Clearview and other communities to demonstrate the techniques of planting, plowing, harvesting, and marketing the crop. In February, officials of the Fort Smith and Western Railroad joined in the effort, sponsoring a "cotton train" to transport the USDA agents and their equipment. The arrival of the group in Clearview prompted a day-long celebration, and school children in the upper grades enjoyed a holiday from regular classes in order to attend the "cotton lecture."[2]

Concentration on cotton meant a serious lack of diversification. Some farmers continued to grow a variety of agricultural produce ranging from corn and beans to melons and potatoes, but as early as 1895 the editor at Langston warned local farmers that total dependence on cotton might eventually prove disastrous. After crop failures in 1910 and 1911, Clearview farmers were urged to turn to truck gardening. To encourage the move away from cotton, Clearview town promoter James E. Thompson proposed establishment of a cooperative canning factory in the community to provide a market for those who switched to truck farming. Thompson's factory never materialized, and, when some disgruntled farmers complained that there was no place to sell their produce, the *Clearview Patriarch* advised them that at least the 1912 crop could be eaten.[3]

Specialization in cotton, coupled with a lack of capital, made sharecropping inevitable. At first, black-town promoters heralded each community as a haven from the horrors of the crop lien system. "That none may be mistaken," announced the editor at Langston in 1895, "this is no share business with the negro on the cotton bound for town," and in 1905, the *Progress* invited southern farmers to come "to Boley where every man is a man, and when you raise a crop the whole of it is yours to dispose of as you see fit."[4] Such pronouncements applied only to those possessing sufficient funds to finance their own farming operations. Few black-town settlers fell into that category, however. By 1911, those advertising Clearview had abandoned all pretexts of economic independence, advising prospective newcomers that general "farming is run on the credit or supply system, just as it is in the southern states," and that farmers could rent land on a third and fourth basis, getting supplies while working their crop.[5] Those unable to find credit inside Clearview might receive an advance from A. H. Tyson, a furnishing merchant who operated a loan company in Wewoka, a small town twenty miles to the south.[6]

Among the first to join Isaiah T. Montgomery and Benjamin T. Green in the founding of Mound Bayou, Simon Gaither, a former slave, typified many black-town farmers.

Although he purchased a forty-acre farm inside the colony, Gaither found money scarce and deprivation a way of life. After making the initial payment on his land, purchased from the Louisville, New Orleans, and Texas Railroad, and buying a few necessities, Gaither possessed only $10 in cash. In 1888 he cleared a plot of land for a garden, constructed a crude log house for his family, and planted one-fourth acre of corn, cane for molasses, and a small quantity of rice. He next searched for opportunities to make money. While his wife and children traveled as far as thirteen miles to pick and chop cotton, Gaither contracted to clear land for others in Mound Bayou at $4 per acre and to cut timber for stave boards at $6 per cord. In 1890, he found it necessary to turn to sharecropping, agreeing to cultivate four acres of cotton for J. C. Lauderdale, a white man, on the share system. Under the arrangement, as Gaither later recalled, Lauderdale "was to furnish the land, the team, team feed, tools, and seed, while I was to supply the labor and to tend and harvest the crop which was to be divided equally between us."[7] By the turn of the century, Gaither had added an additional forty acres to his farm, attributing much of his success to his wife's willingness to endure hardship.

The desire to own land in part sustained the Gaither family and others in the black town during hard times. Holding title to a farm or town lot represented much more than the ownership of property. To some black-town residents, land constituted the first step in a long march toward economic independence, and community leaders frequently capitalized on such feelings. "Real estate is the basis of all wealth," proclaimed promoter Edward P. McCabe in the *Langston City Herald* in 1892. Property, according to the boosters, provided its owner with individual dignity, free from the economic and political control of others. As S. Douglas Russell at Langston phrased it in June, 1908, when "a farmer owns the land and raises his meat and bread, he is a prince, a king or a monarch within himself, and don't have to bow to the whims of oily politicians and sharks."[8]

During the formative years land was cheap in most towns and credit was available, and many settlers took advantage of the opportunity. In early Mound Bayou, undeveloped farm land cost from $7 to $8 per acre, with $1 down and the balance in yearly installments. As a consequence, by 1907 approximately 50 percent of the farmers near Mound Bayou owned the land they cultivated, most holding forty-acre tracts. In Nicodemus Township in 1881, most land was held by individual owners, each of whom possessed 160 acres. Within a few years, however, property appears to have been less well distributed. By 1887, James P. Pomeroy, one of several speculators, had acquired approximately 15 percent of all the land in the township.[9]

If blacks could buy land, they could also lose it. Leaders urged black-town farmers to work hard, diversify crops, and save for future emergencies. Newspapers like the *Tribune* at Clearview and the *Progress* at Boley ran long articles on the need for blacks to learn to economize and to understand the value and dignity of hard work.[10] Some went beyond lecturing. The wife of a black-town banker in Oklahoma recalled that her husband had "run the good-for-nothing Negroes out of town." She remembered that in the early days the streets were nearly empty from Monday morning until Friday night because when her husband saw a black farmer on weekdays "in town having a good time, he would tell him to get back out on that farm where he belonged. He was good to all of them . . . but he saw to it all people worked."[11] Charles Banks, cashier of the Bank of Mound Bayou, exerted a similar pressure in his town. In a speech before the Washington, D. C., Commercial Council in 1910, Banks made it clear that "there is not a loafer or idler in the community—men who won't work cannot stay there."[12]

Despite his dictatorial attitude, in large part a reflection of his economic power as cashier and major stockholder in the Bank of Mound Bayou, Charles Banks worked to encourage and help local farmers during good and bad times. With the aid of Booker T. Washington, he convinced the

U.S. Department of Agriculture to send a permanent extension agent to the town. J. A. Booker, the agent, established a Farmers' Institute to teach better methods and improve crop yields. In addition, Booker demonstrated the use and maintenance of the latest farm implements, touring Bolivar County farms in a Jessup Agricultural Wagon. To promote competition among area farmers, in 1909 Banks proposed creation of an annual Mound Bayou Fair to display agricultural produce and award prizes each fall. And, in late April, 1910, he attempted to gain a county agricultural school for the community.[13]

Banks periodically mailed letters to black farmers in the county giving advice on crops and predictions on future prices. In such letters, he frequently lectured them on what he considered their extravagance and lack of industry as well as the need to keep abreast of new trends in agricultural production and marketing. During the fall of 1909, for example, Banks scolded farmers for hiring cotton pickers while family members remained idle, warning that merchants and bankers would no doubt demand full payment on all accounts before advancing credit for the coming year, since crop failures seemed imminent. Thus, money foolishly spent would be needed later. In January, 1910, he told farmers to straighten "your fences, white wash farm houses, paint the house, build new out-houses and otherwise improve your premises and make farm life attractive and pleasant." Each family should subscribe to at least one farm newspaper or magazine, having the children of the house read it aloud to the adults. To those who thought they knew everything about farming, Banks responded that most had been working since emancipation yet had little to show for their efforts, living on credit from a local store. When the boll weevil infected nearly all the Yazoo-Mississippi Delta in 1911, Banks pleaded with farmers to remain in the area rather than abandoning their land. The arrival of the weevil, he argued, represented a blessing in disguise because many merchants had refused to extend credit, thereby leaving more total profit for blacks than in previous years.[14]

In regard to the land, black-town settlers generally shared the contradictions of the larger society. Well-grounded in the tradition of a homestead, they believed that a farm was something to be purchased, improved, added to, and passed on to future generations of the family. Close to nature and well removed from the decadence of a large city, a farm was an excellent environment in which to raise children and agriculture a superior means of livelihood. Black-town parents were urged to sacrifice now so that their offspring might hold land in the future because contact with the earth instilled virtue in the farmer and his family. Invoking the pastoral ideal, more common to the nineteenth than the twentieth century, the *Clearview Patriarch* in 1912 assured residents that out "of the pastoral life springs the moral brawn and sinew, the physical endurance, that wins in the race of life."[15] Farmers were respected. The picture on a calendar given away by the Bank of Mound Bayou in 1910 showed a man with his arm around a small boy. The man was pointing to a bale of cotton and the caption under the picture read: "As long as there are mouths to feed, backs to clothe, and lands to be tilled, the place of the farmer in the hearts of the American people will be supreme."[16] To its boosters, each community was securely nestled in nature. In 1895, Langston was destined to become "one of the garden spots of Oklahoma." Not to be outdone, Boley achieved the remarkable feat of becoming the "garden spot of the Southwest" in the same year it was incorporated.[17]

In reality, however, and more consistent with other Americans, black-town promoters treated land as a commodity, something to be bought, sold, and speculated with in much the same way one made a profit from trading horses or grain. Boosters assured potential settlers that land speculation held out the promise of quick wealth. The *Western Cyclone* in May, 1887, proudly proclaimed that "50 to 200 percent has been realized on money invested in Nicodemus lands." Those considering Clearview as a permanent location in 1912 were advised that the first year's cutting of alfalfa would pay for the farm. The less industrious need not be discouraged, however. They could rest at night content with the assurance of developers that "CLEARVIEW land EARNS MONEY while you sleep."[18]

The image of large cities produced contradictions similar in many respects to the dichotomy of the farmer as both land speculator and noble yeoman. Much of the rhetoric concerning black-town life dealt with residence in a rural paradise. Like Booker T. Washington, leaders projected the image of urban areas as wicked, tempting young members of the race into gambling, prostitution, drinking, and extravagance.[19] "What chance has the negro boy or girl who lives in the 'nigger quarters' of the cities?" asked J. W. Covington, editor of the Mound Bayou *Demonstrator* in 1910. "They soon learn to think they can never amount to anything and to despise their race no matter how hard they work or moral they be."[20] The editor at Clearview preached the same theme two years later, arguing that the so-called good life in the cities drove the race into crime. "There can be plenty of pleasure in the country," he said, "to satisfy any conservative mind."[21]

The skin color of a town promoter, however, had little impact on his basic objective—rapid population growth. Like every other booster in the American West and South, black-town promoters equated bigger with better. In writing to a possible investor in 1908, Charles Banks clearly indicated what he had in mind for the future. Rather than the idyllic community envisioned by its founder, Banks planned to make Mound Bayou "a larger and more pretentious town." Instead of buying thirty thousand acres in the immediate vicinity, Banks meant to "own and control all the land that can be brought under our influence."[22] Cities might be condemned on moral grounds, but images of a small agricultural service center quickly faded, yielding to visions of a giant city complete with all the paraphernalia associated with urban life. In a paper read before the November, 1911, meeting of the Patriarchs of America, a fraternal order, a local schoolteacher visualized what was in store for the residents of "CLEARVIEW Ten Years Hence":

> Main Street will have changed its appearance from the few present stores to five or six blocks of large business stores interspersed with one or two "Skyscrapers." . . . The place where the Printing Office stands will be occupied by a large Garage Shop. Autos, Taxicabs, and motors will be of common use. There will be at least two aeroplanes. . . . There will probably be three railway lines . . . and at least two good depots of stone or brick. . . . The size and population of the town will necessitate electric railways. . . . There will be three, two-story School-houses, Primary, Grammar, and High School, one University, and a Conservatory of music and a Business College.[23]

Indeed, Clearview was destined to become an industrial center. In early December, 1911, the editor there assured those who might scoff at such a prediction that the immediate locality contained "plenty of stone and sand to build a second New York."[24]

Of course, growth and development required population and capital. Whether it was called the Businessmen's League, Chamber of Commerce, Board of Trade, or Commercial Club, every infant community, regardless of the color of the inhabitants, spawned one. The purpose of such booster groups, usually dominated by business and professional men, was to "boom" the town, hoping to attract permanent residents and increase sales. Typical of the other black towns, A. R. Wheeler, editor of the *Patriarch*, presided over the Clearview Commercial Club in 1913 aided by James E. Thompson, the town's most prominent merchant and land speculator. Such organizations arranged trade excursions, sponsored celebrations, and maintained a constant chatter of optimistic pronouncements concerning local prosperity (always good) and opportunities for quick wealth. Accuracy was no virtue. Few seemed concerned that promotional literature or newspaper editorials exaggerated the beauties of the local climate or grossly over-estimated the number of new arrivals during the past week.

New settlers were important, but most welcome were those people who brought money with them into the community. During their formative years most of the towns were inundated by a flood of poverty-stricken sharecroppers from the South, many of whom possessed only a few personal belongings. The success of the town building venture in large part depended upon capital for business ventures, the establishment of schools (since blacks seldom received their fair share of county tax revenues), and for the extension of credit through local stores. Speculators and developers also needed money to finance the sale of land both inside the town limits and in the surrounding countryside. Much of the black-town promotional effort was thus focused on those who had the capital to fund their own operations or to extend credit to others. In June, 1908, S. Douglas Russell at Langston stated the priorities as he saw them, arguing that "the dollar is next to the Almighty."[25]

Although a few came, black-town boosters found in difficult to attract enough people with capital to meet the increasing demand of each community. The absence of money forced the early residents of Nicodemus to resort to simple barter inside the town. The $18,000 annual payroll of the Colored Agricultural and Normal University probably saved Langston citizens from a similar fate.[26] Promoters quickly recognized that bank formation offered the only way to generate a sufficient supply of money necessary to carry on normal business operations. In 1905, the same year the town sought incorporation, Boley druggist and land speculator David J. Turner convinced the Business Men's League there to seek a state charter for the organization of a bank. Turner, who later became cashier and one of the bank's largest stockholders, purchased one-third of the first subscription taken by the public. Within three years, Turner's Farmers and

Merchants' Bank was joined by the Boley Bank and Trust Company, also with a capital stock of $10,000. Unfortunately, the latter institution lost much of its money through embezzlement in 1910. Some investors in black-town banks lived in surrounding communities. W. H. Dill, a stockholder and president of the Farmers and Merchants' Bank in 1908, resided in Okemah, and J. W. Walker, a Muskogee grocer, succeeded Dill in that office. When Clearview promoter James E. Thompson called a meeting in October, 1912, to discuss the organization of a bank in that town, he received promises of stock subscriptions from local citizens and from black businessmen in Atoka, Boley, and Wewoka.[27]

Banks provided the community with a circulating medium of exchange, advanced crop loans to area farmers, and financed the merchants' extension of credit through local stores. But a few residents resented bankers and felt they abused their power. Several settlers had come to the black towns hoping to escape economic exploitation by whites. To some, exploitation had merely changed colors. Exhibiting a great deal of bitterness, one early resident of an Oklahoma black town argued that the bank "prospered on short loans with high interest. . . . Even the grocery stores were run *like* the commissary plan of the plantation—seasonal loans, to the grocer by the banker, who made creditors sign notes which were in turn sold to the bank."[28] One Boley resident claimed that living there offered the opportunity for the exploitation of others and to "get rich in this town, for it's full of 'dummies.' "[29]

The meteoric rise of Charles Banks of Mound Bayou from grinding poverty to financial success exemplified the opportunities open to those people with money to invest in black-town enterprises and the entrepreneurial talent to do it wisely. Banks' career also illustrates how it was possible for a few individuals to acquire power, prestige, and wealth while most black-town citizens struggled just to survive. Born in 1873 in a shack later used for a chicken house, Banks grew up under the influence of a prominent white family for whom his mother labored as a cook. Financed by white friends, he attended Rusk University at Holly Springs and at the age of sixteen entered into a mercantile partnership with his brother in Clarksdale. In 1903, he moved to Mound Bayou and, within one year, organized a bank there with a capital stock of $10,000.

Before the establishment of the Bank of Mound Bayou, area residents faced heavy mortgage payments. Moreover, most farm families found themselves perpetually owing from $600 to $1200 per year, paying interest charges of 25 to 30 percent for supplies advanced by white furnishing merchants in the nearby Delta towns of Shelby and Merigold. To compound their problems, when the Louisville, New Orleans, and Texas Railroad sold its interests to the Yazoo and Mississippi line, the fear of total failure spread throughout the black farmers of the colony. The new owners threatened to foreclose on all outstanding loans. Charles Banks, however, renegotiated contracts and organized the Mound Bayou Loan and Investment Company to aid those who failed to meet mortgage payments and to fund improvements in the town. Banks assumed the secretary-treasurer post in the investment company, capitalized at $50,000, and served as cashier of the bank. Both firms occupied the same two-story brick building.[30]

Indicative of the demand for its services, the Bank of Mound Bayou earned 17 percent during the first eight months of operation and declared annual dividends of at least 7 percent for the next six years. Armed with an increasing supply of capital and a growing reputation for his contribution to the community, Banks sought additional investment opportunities. In 1907, he formed a partnership with John W. Francis, a local undertaker. Banks and Francis operated a mercantile firm, dealt in lumber and building supplies, and speculated in town lots. Later that same year, the pair opened a real estate development called the Banks and Francis Addition to Mound Bayou. For the next five years Banks increased his holdings. Everything he touched seemed

Board of directors, Bank of Mound Bayou, with Charles Banks seated second from left. From *Alexander's Magazine*, July, 1907.

to succeed. He organized a sawmill, directing its financial operations, and became the general manager of the Mound Bayou Oil Mill and Manufacturing Company, one of the largest black manufacturing enterprises in the South. By 1910, he lived in a $10,000 house, "commodious enough to house a small-sized army," owned one thousand acres of land in Bolivar County, held title to 250 town lots valued at approximately $7,000, was a stockholder in most of the eleven banks controlled by blacks in Mississippi, held an interest in several smaller businesses in the town, and employed a full-time manager to handle his cotton speculations, paying him $5 per day, including Sundays. As his wealth increased, his prestige spread throughout the state. He was a director of two insurance companies and sat on the board of trustees of two colleges.[31] In *My Larger Education*, published in 1911, Booker T. Washington called Banks "the most influential, Negro business man in the United States."[32]

The close relationship between Charles Banks and Booker T. Washington began in 1900 at the first meeting of the National Negro Business League. Banks, at that time a merchant in Clarksdale, Mississippi, traveled to the Boston convention in the company of Isaiah T. Montgomery, the founder of Mound Bayou, who talked to the group on "The Building of a Negro Town." In 1905, Banks organized and assumed the presidency of the Mississippi State Negro Business League; and the delegates to the 1907 national organization meeting in Topeka, Kansas, elected him first vice-president, second in rank to Washington. For the next eight years, until Washington's death in November, 1915, the Tuskegee Institute and Mound Bayou, Mississippi, worked hand-in-hand.

In articles, speeches, and books, Washington used Mound Bayou to support his philosophy of self-help and racial uplift. Isolated from whites, he argued, the black town acted as a laboratory, proving that under the correct circumstances the race was hard working, law abiding, and capable of self-government. In "Law and Order and the Negro," published in *The Outlook* in 1909, Washington cited statistics from Mound Bayou to illustrate the absence of serious crimes there. Blacks also benefited from their residence in the community. "As I look at it," he wrote in 1911, "Mound Bayou is not merely a town; it is at the same time and in a very real sense of that word, a school."[33] Inside the community, he claimed, blacks gained inspiration through observing the achievements of other racial members while learning the duties and obligations of social and civic life.[34]

Washington derived several benefits from his close association with Banks and others in Mound Bayou. In September, 1908, for example, Banks contacted C. P. Mooney, editor of the *Commercial Appeal* in Memphis, and a number of other southern newspaper editors, asking them to provide extensive press coverage of Washington's proposed tour through the South later that year.[35] During the summer of 1910, Washington invited Banks to New York to speak to several groups composed of influential whites. In his presentations, Banks was urged to discuss the success of the town and wherever possible "to equate the growth of Mound Bayou with the work being done at Tuskegee."[36] In a letter to the *New York Sun* in December of that year, Banks came to the public defense of Washington and his philosophy, attacking his critics and labeling them "calamity howlers" and a "whining impotent contingency."[37] Apparently unknown to Washington, Banks tried to boost the Tuskegeean's books. In March, 1910, he expressed concern to Emmett Scott, Washington's private secretary, that the sales of *The Story of the Negro* appeared to be lagging. Perhaps, he said, "it may be well for us to get some things in motion among our own people that might increase the demand. . . . Just at this time, we want no stumps whatever."[38]

Publicly, Washington disavowed direct participation in politics, advising blacks to concentrate on economic and moral betterment. Behind the scenes, however, he worked closely with Banks, an avid Republican, to keep informed on political appointments and discrimination against blacks in Mississippi. Banks' involvement in state politics began in 1890 with an appointment as federal census enumerator for his district. With the support of whites, he became supervisor of the Twelfth Census for the Third District of Mississippi in 1900. In 1904 and 1908, he served as a delegate to the Republican National Convention, supporting William Howard Taft at the latter meeting. According to one account, black delegates there selected Banks to second Taft's nomination, but "for the sake of political expediency this honor was not conferred upon him."[39] Banks turned Progressive in 1912 and served as a delegate-at-large from Mississippi to the Bull Moose Convention which nominated Theodore Roosevelt.[40]

From the neighboring state of Alabama, Washington sometimes asked Banks for information on political developments in Mississippi, usually cautioning him "not to use my name." In February, 1910, for example, he wanted Banks to investigate the circumstances surrounding the removal of the postmaster at Ocean Springs, Mississippi. Federal officials had apparently informed Thomas I. Keys, the black post-master there, that a white man would replace him in office. Banks was instructed to check on Keys' character, the number of years he had held the post, and the "extent he is backed up by white people."[41] Banks also sought to apply pressure in the case, asking Fred R. Moore, editor of the New York *Age,* to run an article in his newspaper exposing discrimination at Ocean Springs. In return, Washington tried to help Banks with federal patronage positions inside the state. Such was the case in early 1910 when Banks wrote to Tuskegee seeking assistance in naming a white woman to a postal position in the nearby town of Rosedale.[42]

In the Rosedale matter, as in a number of other cases, Banks was trying to maintain some influence in Republican politics in the Yazoo Delta. That struggle remained. In a letter to Washington in October, 1915, one month before the Tuskegeean died, Banks expressed his disillusionment with the party structure in the South. Now was the time, he told Washington, for northern Republicans to think about strengthening their position in the southern states, but they might find it difficult to work through the southern wing of the party. It was Banks' opinion that entrenching themselves for the disposal of patronage constituted the major aim of most Republican officeholders. In Mississippi, as elsewhere in the South, Republicans failed to "command the following of the other Whites and the independent, self-sustaining Negroes who can be relied upon for real party growth." Reflecting his own experiences, he predicted that political disaster would ultimately result from "ostracizing and curbing the Negro."[43]

Like the other black towns, Mound Bayou periodically suffered from a shortage of skilled and semiskilled artisans and laborers. To alleviate the problem, community leaders looked to Booker T. Washington for help. Beginning as early as 1908 and continuing for several years, a procession of Tuskegee graduates, trained in such areas as carpentry, teaching, bricklaying, and business management, moved from the institute to Mound Bayou. As examples, during January, 1910, Banks wrote to Washington asking him to send a qualified blacksmith and later, in April, a woman trained to operate a laundry. In both cases, Banks offered to arrange to finance the new ventures. Emmett Scott channeled letters from black farmers who wrote to Tuskegee asking for crop loans to the Bank of Mound Bayou. People writing to Washington seeking investment opportunities were advised to contact Charles Banks.[44]

As the economic and political ties between Mound Bayou and Tuskegee grew stronger, Charles Banks and Emmett Scott became close personal friends. By 1910, both were stockholders and directors of the Mississippi Beneficial Insurance Company, and Scott supported Banks when he won the post of secretary-treasurer of that organization. Scott held stock in the Bank of Mound Bayou and sat on its board of directors. The pair also arranged for mutual donations between the school and the town. Banks, a member of the AME Church and one of its prominent lay leaders in the South, yearly contributed $25 toward the "Banks Prize" at Tuskegee awarded to the outstanding student of the Phelps Hall Bible Training School there. When Mound Bayou dedicated its new library, Scott purchased two chairs for the building.[45]

Other than an honest admiration for Scott and a strong commitment to the Washington philosophy, Banks nurtured the Mound Bayou–Tuskegee relationship for a very practical reason. Association with Washington, the most influential black leader of his time, offered the tiny community a direct connection to white philanthropy. In a letter to Scott in late November, 1908, Banks initiated the suggestion of funneling some white capital through Tuskegee to the town. "I am writing to have you start a campaign," he said, "to have Mr. Rockefeller or Mr. Carnegie, or some other philanthropist, built a Y.M.C.A. building, a library building or a school building for the Negroes of Mound Bayou."[46] One week later after discussing it with his mentor, Scott responded, instructing Banks to write directly to John D. Rockefeller and Andrew Carnegie, mentioning Washington's name.[47] As he thought on the possibilities, Banks' vision of Mound Bayou apparently grew much larger. Through Scott, he asked Washington to approach Carnegie in February, 1910, about the possibility of funding the purchase of large tracts of land around the town to be held in trust for future settlers. "You have an idea," he confided in his friend, "what it would mean for us to ultimately control this corner of the county as we now control Mound Bayou. Talk this over with the Dr. and let us see what can be done."[48] Over the next few years, Banks proposed a similar scheme to several white business-men, including W. L. Park, vice-president and general man-ager of the Illinois Central Railroad.[49]

Most of those contacted, including Rockefeller, politely declined to invest in the town or to contribute to its develop-ment through a direct gift. Although Banks failed in his efforts to convince philanthropists to buy up the unoccupied lands surrounding the community, he enjoyed some success in other areas. In late 1908, as he had done in so many other places in the United States, Carnegie agreed to donate $4,000 to finance construction of a public library for Mound Bayou. In turn, the town council offered to raise 10 percent of that amount for the maintenance of the building and grounds. The Rosenwald Fund provided $1,000 for a school in the community in 1909, and Banks gained the aid of the Jeans Fund of New Orleans for rural schoolteachers in Bolivar County. Banks' most striking success, however, made pos-sible through Washington's endorsement, was convincing Julius Rosenwald of Sears, Roebuck and Company to invest in a proposed $100,000 cottonseed oil mill which opened for business in November, 1912.[50]

At its 1907 meeting, held in Meridian, the executive committee of the Mississippi State Negro Business League, chaired by E. P. Montgomery of Mound Bayou, voted to establish the oil mill. In order to gain wide support from blacks all over the state, representatives from fourteen communities sat on the Ways and Means Committee of the new corporation. Banks soon discovered that disposal of $40,000 in bonds and the $100,000 worth of stock posed a formidable problem. He approached Washington. In a series of meetings at Tuskegee, the pair formulated a plan to fund the enterprise. Isaiah T. Montgomery was sent to New York and other northern cities to seek out white philanthropists, Banks launched a stock-selling campaign in Mississippi, and Washington agreed to use his influence with Julius Rosenwald as a possible investor. After an exchange of correspondence and a final meeting with Banks in Alabama in February, 1913, Rosenwald offered to take $25,000 of the $40,000 in bonds bearing 6 percent interest. Rosenwald was to hold a first mortgage on the plant and equipment, and the bonds were to be retired at the rate of $2,500 per year. Banks insured the building and its contents for $45,000.[51]

Washington risked using his name and throwing his support behind the mill. He realized that its failure might harm his reputation as well as jeopardize future support from prominent whites. In a September, 1912, letter marked "Private and confidential," he lectured Banks on his responsibilities in the matter, warning him to be certain "that every promise which you have made to Mr. Rosenwald be strictly and fully carried out. If Mr. Rosenwald be disappointed in this investment he will lose faith in our entire race."[52] Washington also wrote to businessmen in Ohio, California, and Massachusetts, seeking their assistance in buying the remaining $15,000 worth of bonds. B. B. Harvey, a white owner of an oil mill in Memphis, finally purchased the remainder of the issue and agreed to lease the mill.[53]

To promote stock sales, Banks, Montgomery, and other officers utilized an appeal to race pride, arguing that the mill would stand as a monument symbolizing black business acumen to future generations. Each investor received a letter advising him to frame and hang the stock certificate in his home to indicate his contribution to racial solidarity and to encourage "neighbors and . . . friends to join in this uplifting of the rising banner of race progress."[54] Banks asked for Washington's help in this area as well. With much advance publicity and great fanfare, Washington arrived in Mound Bayou on November 25, 1912, to open the mill officially. In his dedication speech, the Tuskegeean stressed two major points. Whites in Mississippi should also be proud of the undertaking because it helped blacks while benefiting the entire state. And those in the audience with money to invest should buy stock in the corporation. Since Banks still needed to dispose of from $10,000 to $15,000 worth of stock and because he always tried to accommodate whites, Banks had written Washington on November 2 asking him to emphasize these two areas in the address.[55] Some of the stock issue, costing $1 per share, was taken by the Odd Fellows, Pythians, Masons, and other black fraternal organizations in Mississippi.

Other than Mound Bayou, to which he seemed totally committed, Washington exhibited some interest in other

Booker T. Washington dedicating the Mound Bayou Oil Mill and Manufacturing Company, 1912. Courtesy Library of Congress.

133

black towns. He was familiar with Boley, Oklahoma, visiting there in 1905 at about the same time its promoters sought incorporation. Three years later, he published an article in *The Outlook*, entitled "Boley, A Negro Town in the West," in which he called the community "another chapter in the long struggle of the Negro for moral, industrial and political freedom."[56] Yet, the Tuskegeean remained ambivalent about most segregated communities. In general he opposed northern migration, believing that blacks must work out their destiny in the rural South. Towns like Boley, therefore, were temporary experiments, a resting place along the path of racial uplift where blacks could improve themselves, gain self-confidence, and show their capacity for self-government.[57] In the report of the 1914 meeting of the National Negro Business League, which Washington edited for publication, William Arey of the Hampton Institute argued that Boley was undoubtedly a success and reflected credit upon the race. If, however, "the Boley idea were carried to its logical conclusion, the Negro would suffer and so would his white friends" from the lack of mutual contact.[58]

Because the philosophy of Booker T. Washington coincided with that of most black-town promoters, they supported him and his ideas long before the Tuskegeean reached the pinnacle of his power and attracted the attention of white philanthropists. As early as 1896, newspapers like the *Herald* at Langston ran weekly news items on the activities at Tuskegee Institute. By 1905, the editor of the *Boley Progress* was running reprints of Washington's speeches, praising him as the greatest living member of the race. When Washington spoke at the Opera House in Guthrie, Oklahoma, in November of that year, Inman E. Page, president of the Colored Agricultural and Normal University at Langston, headed a delegation of 236 people from the community who traveled the twelve miles to hear the address.[59] Like Charles Banks in Mound Bayou, leaders in other black towns recognized the importance of direct contact with Tuskegee. Typical of similar requests, Boley banker David

J. Turner wrote to Emmett Scott in the fall of 1914 hoping that Scott and Washington would "say a good word for us wherever you think best, and to send us some good people with money to help build our town."[60]

Black-town leaders rushed to join the National Negro Business League after its formation in 1900, and Washington used them to increase membership in the organization. Usually through a personal letter, Washington urged the towns to affiliate with the league. In December, 1914, he wrote to J. Harold Coleman, promoter of Blackdom, New Mexico, seeking more information on that community and encouraging formation of a local chapter there. Such prompting frequently produced results, and from the league's first meeting in Boston until Washington's death fifteen years later, representatives from segregated communities attended national conventions and appeared on the programs. At the 1914 meeting, held in Muskogee, Oklahoma, businessmen from the black towns of Mound Bayou, Mississippi; Allensworth, California; and from Taft, Foreman, Rentiesville, Tullahassee, Wybark, Clearview, and Boley in Oklahoma either spoke to the convention or sat in the audience. Black-town leaders were active in the state organization as well. In Oklahoma, three of the ten state officers and 20 percent of the executive committee resided in a black community in 1914.[61]

To guarantee a large turnout at the Muskogee meeting, Washington accepted an invitation from Boley businessmen to visit the town by special train. Ralph W. Tyler, ex-auditor of the United States Navy and hired by Washington as a traveling organizer for the league, felt the site chosen for the convention was a mistake. Since Chicago, Boston, and other major cities had usually hosted previous meetings, Tyler felt it unlikely that members would be willing to travel to a small and somewhat isolated town in the Southwest. The unique character of Boley might entice delegates, however. Approximately one month before the convention, Washington wrote to Emmett Scott from Castine, Maine, hoping that

Tyler could be proved wrong and suggesting that "the idea of going to Boley will attract a great many people if it is kept constantly to the front."[62] Accompanied by a delegation of league members, Washington spoke at the Boley city park on Saturday, August 22. At that time, some blacks in eastern Oklahoma were joining a back-to-Africa movement headed by Alfred Sam, an Akim chief from the Gold Coast. Reflecting his attitude toward African migration, the Tuskegeean advised Boley residents not to follow "Chief Sam or Chief anybody else." Much to the consternation of Boley leaders, Clearview promoter James E. Thompson also convinced Washington to visit his town as well. At the railroad depot, Washington was met by Clearview school children and later entertained by the "Rough Riders," a group of local horsemen.[63]

A Washington visit raised spirits for a few days and perhaps even sparked a minor "boom," but, soon after his departure, residents returned to the everyday problems of life. As in all communities, large and small, taxes had to be paid. In Boley, property owners were assessed an ad valorem tax of 2 percent, 1.5 percent of which went for schools with the remainder allocated to the town's general fund. Boley schools also received all the revenue collected from the $1 poll tax. Since money was scarce, some communities accepted or required payment in labor rather than cash. Mound Bayou pioneers constructed the roads in the settlement by serving ten days per year. Later, each male citizen of Mound Bayou was "taxed" three days' work on the roads of the colony. Boley's town council in 1909 directed property owners living on certain streets to lay their own oak-plank sidewalks and, by the mid-1920's, males of voting age were required to work on town streets four days, eight hours a day, or face a fine of $10. Communal volunteers also helped. Town residents and nearby farmers subscribed money for bridge construction, donated time, and supplied teams and the crude apparatus necessary for street and road maintenance. Heavy rains in March, 1888, for example, made Nicodemus streets nearly impassable, prompting the editor of the newspaper there to call for volunteers to repair them.[64]

In addition to the usual property and poll taxes, businessmen paid license fees to their respective town treasuries. Costs varied. In Boley in 1905, businesses of a less permanent nature—fortunetellers, auctioneers, and peddlers—were charged $1 to $2 per day, while circuses paid $10 for every twenty-four hours of operation. More established firms received yearly rates, from a high of $25 for banks and $6 per table for billiard parlors to a low of $4 each for drug stores and drays of two horses. Half of all tax revenue collected from businesses was earmarked for the Boley school fund.[65]

Like their white counterparts, black-town businessmen were of course interested in increasing sales. Based on the frequency of use, most felt that an appeal to race pride constituted an effective device to attract customers and to ensure that local consumers shopped at home. The black-town trade area extended well into the surrounding countryside, and merchants were eager to entice farmers away from neighboring white communities. "Buying Black" inside the town kept capital in black hands. "Where does most of your money go?" Boley attorney Moses J. Jones asked a local group in March, 1905. "To the white merchant. Why not circulate that money among ourselves and allow our boys and girls to become business men and women?"[66] Moreover, some leaders argued that those who purchased from whites financially supported prejudice and discrimination. In June, 1905, S. Douglas Russell at Langston insisted that self-respecting blacks should boycott all businessmen who refused to respect the race.[67] Typical of most supporters of the National Negro Business League, Jones and Russell apparently failed to recognize the internal contradiction of their own argument. If economic laws were color blind, why encourage blacks to buy only from other blacks? As Jones put it, "A man in business is not recognized by the color of his skin nor his curly hair, but by the amount of business he does."[68]

Although Arthur Tallman, editor of the *Western Cy-*

clone, assured residents in June, 1886, that "you can buy anything from a wheelbarrow to a twine binder right here in Nicodemus, and it is your duty to patronize home industries,"[69] black-town businessmen faced competition from other communities. People living in Clearview, Boley, and Mound Bayou could board the train at the local depot and be shopping in a nearby town in a few minutes, in part attracted there by advertisements run in the columns of the black-town press. In November, 1904, for example, firms in Boynton, Weleetka, and Okmulgee sought customers through advertisements in the Clearview newspaper. And in December of the following year, advertisements in the *Western Age* invited Langston citizens to trade with merchants in the neighboring towns of Coyle and Guthrie. When out of town on business, however, black-town editors urged their readers to trade with businesses operated by members of the race.[70]

If the black-town merchant, or the banker who backed him, failed to extend credit, many customers were compelled to shop elsewhere. Local residents were upset during the fall of 1887 when a severe drought and lack of funds forced Henrie and Brothers, a Nicodemus dry goods and grocery store, to announce a "cash only" policy in August of that year.[71] To be sure, hard times affected white storekeepers as well, but the overall scarcity of capital in the black community, even during prosperous years, imposed severe limitations on the black merchant.

The greatest threat, however, came from another source. By the turn of the century, all country storekeepers, regardless of location, felt the competition from mail-order houses such as Sears, Roebuck and Montgomery Ward.[72] In time, merchant concern turned to fear and then to panic. In a November, 1905, article entitled, "LOCAL MERCHANT VS Mail Order Houses," Boley editor O. H. Bradley described the firms as a growing evil threatening to destroy the prosperity of the small towns and cities in the West. In Bradley's eyes, females were in large part responsible for their continued success. Women purchased from mail-order houses for many of the same reasons one attended a séance, patronized an oriental honky-tonk, or read a dime novel—because of the mystery and romance and the thrill of getting a package from some "monster corporation." Bradley placed those who bought from mail-order houses on a par with persons who married through correspondence. Unlike the local merchant, mail-order houses never extended credit, and they "never tell you to send them any farm products that you may have, all they want is your cash, and when you send them a dollar you may as well kiss it good-bye forever."[73] And besides, Boley blacks were already sending too much money east for insurance payments. Bradley pleaded with residents to support local firms as a matter of race and town pride, even if mail-order goods were cheaper.

The scarcity of money in Boley, to which Bradley indirectly alluded by mentioning the outward flow of cash, was manifested in several ways.[74] Four of the five black towns possessed at least one, and sometimes two, joint-stock trading companies organized to deal in a general merchandise business. At the 1914 meeting of the National Negro Business League, Eugene P. Booze of Mound Bayou, a brother-in-law of Charles Banks, discussed the reasons underlying the formation of the Farmers' Cooperative Company in his town. Because of the lack of capital to stock goods and to extend badly needed credit to customers, Mound Bayou merchants could handle only 25 percent of the business available there. The remainder of the population shopped in the neighboring towns of the Yazoo Delta, paying high interest charges on accounts held by white storekeepers. Although they perhaps could never totally solve the problem, Booze felt that several such ventures might make Mound Bayou a more attractive trading center.[75]

The Abe Lincoln Trading Company of Clearview, incorporated in June, 1904, typified the methods employed by the promoters of such firms in the other black communities. With a capital stock of $2,500, company directors offered shares to the public at $25 each. To reach smaller investors, residents could pay 25 percent of the price of each share in cash, with 10 percent of the remaining balance due each month. By mid-September, $280 worth of stock had been paid in, and the company held assets, including cash, fixtures, hardware, and groceries, valued at $338. Sales from June 1 through August 30 amounted to approximately $300. Dividends for those few with money to invest were handsome, on one occasion reaching 21 percent, but the overwhelming majority of Clearview citizens lacked the capital to benefit from the enterprise.[76] In November, 1909, Clearview boosters suggested a similar approach in an attempt to organize a joint-stock canning factory in the town.

The multiple ownership of businesses by a very few individuals also indicated the absence of a large pool of investment capital, but more importantly it also illustrated the unequal distribution of income in most black towns. Perhaps to an even greater extent than that found in corresponding white communities, the control of the black-town economy rested in the hands of a small group. The list of the officers and directors of the Farmers and Merchants' Bank at the time of its formation in March, 1905, read like a directory of Boley's most prominent businessmen. Included were the owners of the cotton gin, hotel, drug store, and three general merchandise firms, plus a lawyer, the railroad station agent, and the town promoter, most of whom speculated in real estate. David J. Turner, the bank's leading stockholder and its cashier, held investments in town lots and farms, a drug store, ice plant, brickyard, newspaper, and lumberyard, and was an agent for the Equitable Life Insurance Company. Economic and political power went hand-in-hand. The mayor of Boley and four of the five town aldermen were either officers or directors in the Farmers and Merchants' Bank.[77]

Partnerships proved ephemeral, as small entrepreneurs, committed only to the opportunity for a good return and a rapid turnover of money, searched for possible investments.

The movements and activities of Jay C. Trimble, one-time resident of Boley, illustrated both the geographic mobility and peripatetic nature of many black-town businessmen. Born into Alabama slavery during the Civil War, Trimble lived with his parents on a farm until the age of twenty. He taught "subscription school" at Marion, Alabama, for one year, receiving fifty cents per pupil, and then worked as a laborer for two different railroads in Tennessee. Hearing stories about Indian Territory from acquaintances, he decided to relocate there, arriving in Claremore in September, 1900. From his savings as a railroad worker, he purchased a barber shop and leased 160 acres of Indian land for a coal mining operation. Losing his mining lease in a court dispute with an oil company, Trimble sold the Claremore barbershop and signed on as a traveling barber with the Sills and Dumas Circus, where he received $100 per month and expenses. In 1904, he moved to Boley, opened a barbershop there, started a contracting company, and entered into a partnership with two other individuals to manufacture bricks. With Issariel Johnson, he purchased forty acres of land and plotted it into town lots. Trimble donated $50 to John C. Leftwich toward the founding of the Creek-Seminole college in Boley, and he taught manual training there for two years. In later life, Trimble suffered from cataracts and eventually lost the sight of one eye. In 1937, at the age of seventy-six, Trimble was living in Oklahoma City on a social security pension, but he continued to work, making and selling brooms, leather suspenders and belts, and rubber doormats, which he fabricated from discarded automobile inner tubes.[78]

Black-town businessmen like Trimble advertised in the columns of the local newspaper, and their promotional schemes and advertisements paralleled those used by small firms throughout the South and West. Like most country merchants, town shopkeepers ran the same announcement for several months heralding the arrival and a "new" stock of goods. Advertisements often revealed the multiple nature

141

of some businesses, such as the February, 1912, claim of J. A. Roundtree in the *Clearview Patriarch* that he could "make your clothes, cut your hair, clean your clothes and shave you too—Walk in."[79] At T. C. Jordan's in Mound Bayou, customers could buy a meal, purchase meat, and shoot a game of pool. Promotional gimmicks were also commonplace. Hoping to increase sales through a show of community spirit, Abraham Hall, a Nicodemus merchant, offered in March, 1888, to donate $2 of every one hundred in sales toward a library for the town. In Boley, Hosmer's Store gave a new suit of clothes to the man who brought in a wagon with the most women in it; John Eaton, a local resident, crowded fourteen females into his wagon and won. And, during the 1912 season, the Clearview Cotton Gin gave each farmer patronizing that firm a ticket for a drawing on a new wagon.[80]

Money was scarce and unevenly distributed, and, with few exceptions, the black-town class structure was drawn along economic lines. Unlike people living in the black section of most mixed communities, however, those who provided direct personal services—doctors, lawyers, barbers, and undertakers—failed to achieve upper-class positions in black-town society.[81] Rather, the land promoter, merchant, and banker, since each held capital and could extend credit, dominated the economic life of the town. Alliances or feuds between or among economically important families could influence municipal politics and affect town prosperity. In Mound Bayou, Isaiah T. Montgomery and his cousin Benjamin T. Green founded the community and started several of the first businesses there. Montgomery's daughter, Mary, married Eugene P. Booze, a wealthy merchant, who migrated to Mound Bayou from Clarksdale, Mississippi. Booze was related by marriage to Charles Banks, in time the town's most prominent entrepreneur. In turn, Banks formed multiple partnerships with John W. Francis, who had married Benjamin T. Green's widow. Kinship and economic ties among the Montgomery, Green, Francis, Booze, and Banks families could have given them virtual control of Mound Bayou.

Factional fights soon developed, however, and long after the elder Montgomery's death and Banks' departure from the community, the Green and Booze families vied for power.[82]

Consistent with their commitment to the philosophy of Booker T. Washington and their support for the Republican party, the black-town leaders generally favored political programs on the national level which aided the American business community. Editors and other leaders opposed government regulation of the private sector of the economy and antitrust legislation while supporting a high protective tariff aimed at keeping out competitive foreign goods. The tariff supposedly provided jobs and luxuries for American workers and kept the price of farm products high.[83] Following the 1912 election, Clearview town promoter James E. Thompson feared the "tariff tinkering" of Woodrow Wilson and the Democrats. To protect the country from the "radical element" of his party, which Thompson believed had produced financial disasters in the past, Wilson would have to follow the example of Grover Cleveland and use the veto power of the presidency extensively.[84] To the black-town press, ideas threatening to alter the economic status quo endangered American stability and freedom. For example, according to the editor at Nicodemus in October, 1887, Henry George's "absurd and ridiculous" proposal for a single tax on land values was being agitated among "organizations of anarchical inclinations."[85]

Organized labor also came in for its share of criticism. Totally isolated from the daily problems of industrial life in a large city, some black-town leaders felt that labor unions violated the freedom of the individual and disrupted the normal relationship between workers and capitalists, and that union leaders seemed more interested in their own status than in the welfare of their members. Commenting on the Knights of Labor in October, 1887, George A. Sanford, the editor at Nicodemus, argued that serious problems had developed inside that organization when men "who were well satisfied with their employers were forced to surrender their jobs and go out on strike to favor a few figure heads who called themselves bosses."[86] Although the presence of blacks in a labor-management dispute only increased racial antagonisms, occasionally editors rejoiced at a walkout. In November, 1892, the *Langston City Herald* reprinted an exchange from another newspaper commenting on the Homestead Strike at a Carnegie-owned steel works in Pittsburgh. "Where no Negroes were formerly employed," reported the *Herald*, "four hundred of them . . . now have an equal show to earn a living."[87]

For those owning no farm or business or possessing few skills, earning a living in the black town meant part-time work on the railroad or on adjacent farms. During the summer of 1905, Boley provided approximately twenty-five hands for the Fort Smith and Western Railroad, and each fall area farmers entered the community seeking cotton pickers. Such jobs were only seasonal, however, and rural parents frequently sent young children to the cotton field rather than the classroom, thereby eliminating the need to pay for additional help during harvesting. The cotton gins in each black town employed some men, but like all firms oriented toward agricultural service, they operated only a few months each year. To assist the idle in finding work, Boley formed an employment bureau during the summer of 1911. The local newspaper printed notices of jobs available in the community and in neighboring towns along with a listing of people looking for work.[88]

To be sure, black-town leaders recognized the lack of employment opportunities. As a result they concentrated much of their promotional effort on enticing manufacturing firms or inducing the local populace to contribute toward their construction. Residents in nearly every town witnessed attempts at local manufacturing. From February through April, 1908, the L.L.C. Medicine and Toilet Factory in Langston produced Blood Remedies, Magic Linament, Gofer Powders, Cough Catarrh Asthma Balsam, and Bloom and Life Tonic and Hair Preparation among its full line of medicines and perfumes. Four years later, the Boley Carbonating Works, successor to the Boley Bottling Company, was turning out soda water and vinegar for local customers.[89] Aside from Mound Bayou's $100,000 cottonseed oil mill, Clearview boosters embarked on the most energetic campaign of industrial promotion. In addition to a standing offer of "land and water free gratis to any Mfg. Co. who will establish a plant here,"[90] business leaders organized the Clearview Development Association with offices in the Harris Building in Muskogee. In two advertisements in March, 1912, the association announced plans to build six factories in the town within eighteen months, ultimately increasing Clearview's population from three hundred to ten thousand. The boom was on. Residents were urged to write to friends and relatives in other states advising them of the natural advantages of the area and to provide association members with the names of fifty people to be contacted. According to the promoters, the output from the overall, canning, glove, and other concerns would be sold to blacks throughout the United States who would give "preference by buying those articles made in factories owned, operated and controlled by their own race."[91] Within a few months the scheme collapsed.

Promoters of every tiny community in the West and South thought they saw the coming of the railroad as the key to future greatness. Black-town leaders were no exception. Clearview, Boley, and Mound Bayou were plotted along established rail lines. Isolated in a sparsely settled area of northwestern Kansas, Nicodemus was less fortunate. After resigning themselves to the loss of the county seat, Nicodemus citizens turned their attention to attracting one or more railroads to the town. In January, 1887, Hugh K. Lightfoot, editor of the *Cyclone,* and a representative group of businessmen, conferred with W. W. Fagan, superintendent of the Missouri Pacific Railroad, about extending that line west from Stockton. Later, the Nicodemus group met in a local church to sign a petition calling for a special election to approve $16,000 worth of bonds. And, on March 22, by a vote of 82 to 3, Nicodemus Township approved the proposition. In general, Lightfoot opposed "paying tribute," but advised *Cyclone* readers that getting the railroad would provide a home market and boom the town. Meanwhile, the township was asked to consider voting bonds for the Union Pacific also laying track toward the community from the southeast. According to one resident, James P. Pomeroy, a business and political associate of W. R. Hill and a heavy investor in Graham County lands, supposedly sent word advising Nicodemus to forestall any vote on additional bonds. Pomeroy held a financial interest in the Missouri Pacific and virtually guaranteed its construction to the town. Thus, Nicodemus waited.[92]

For some, black-town life proved monotonous. Consequently, any diversion from the everyday routine of hard work represented a welcome diversion. Residents looked forward with anticipation to one or more celebrations usually held each summer or fall. In Mound Bayou, local citizens and out-of-town guests gathered to hold Founders' Day, honoring the original settlers of the colony and those who had contributed its subsequent development. Both Clearview and Boley staged annual festivities commemorating the issuance of the Emancipation Proclamation, while several thousand people converged on Nicodemus every August 1 to celebrate the freeing of the West Indian slaves in 1833. A carnival atmosphere usually prevailed with bands, parades, rides, games of chance, and sporting events, plus the standard rural picnics held under shade trees. Typical was the June, 1911, Clearview Emancipation Day Celebration, which featured prayers, songs and hymns such as "Marching Through Georgia" and "Blessed Assurance," as well as speeches on education, the black press, and town building.[93] Promoters, sensing the possibilities for profit, took advantage of the excellent opportunity to sell town lots while politicians delivered speeches or mingled with the crowd hoping to garner votes for an upcoming election.

Baseball games, excursions, band concerts, and special

programs provided other attractions during the summer months. Like the other Oklahoma towns, Boley maintained a highly commercialized baseball team which traveled to other communities in Oklahoma and occasionally played teams from Texas. Black-town citizens took intense pride in their team, and the enthusiasm of fans plus the large attendance at games sometimes prompted editors and other leaders to lecture residents on what they considered an excessive preoccupation with the sport. In reporting Langston's loss to El Reno in July, 1907, the editor of the *Western Age* noted that baseball was the current rage in his town, and it "may be all right for the unemployed, but there is too great a demand for farm hands now in this section."[94] Editors also criticized groups of people who took "Sunday Excursions" on the train to visit other communities. D. F. Whitaker at Clearview welcomed the warm April days in 1911 but feared that with baseball and excursions good Christians would "never see the inside of a church until cold weather."[95] The cornet band, common to nearly every black town and from which some prominent jazz musicians emanated, also traveled to other communities. Nicodemus organized a ten-member cornet band in April, 1887, and the following spring the group performed at Hill City during the celebration of that town's victory over Millbrook in the county seat race.[96] "Entertainments," as they were called, encompassed a wide range of activities, including specially organized programs staged at a church or school, lectures, speeches, concerts, and recitals. Promoters of such events, usually a church or civic group, used the money collected from the nominal admission charge or donation to fund a specific project.

The literary society, organized to hold public debates, attracted large audiences. In explaining to Clearview citizens why the town needed a literary society in 1911, Georgia Talifaerro, a schoolteacher there, argued that such groups helped participants overcome timidity, trained the mind, and educated blacks by teaching them to speak in public. Resolutions debated seldom dealt with issues of importance to the town or race, such as prejudice, discrimination, poverty, or injustice, but usually concerned trivial topics of limited social, economic, or political consequence. During 1895, for example, members of the Langston Literary Society debated resolutions that "Morality Increases with Civilization" and that "Laziness Is More Common among Males than among Females." And in 1912, Clearview debaters argued whether fire had more power than water and whether a girl had more right to an education than a boy. No doubt reflecting the abilities of the speakers rather than the possible implications of the decision, the negative won a 1905 debate at the Union Literary Society in Boley over the question of whether blacks should celebrate George Washington's birthday.[97]

The black towns contained the usual lodges and fraternities common to the race whether living in a mixed or segregated community. In some cases, membership was large, indicating that individuals belonged to several different organizations. At one time Mound Bayou supported no less than twelve lodges: Sons and Daughters of Jacob, Knights of Phythias, Masons, Odd Fellows, Knights and Daughters of Tabor, Eastern Star, Order of Calanthe, Independent Order of Eagles, Royal House of King David, Benevolent Industrial Association, Woodmen of Union, and the Household of Ruth. In addition to five of those mentioned, some Boley blacks held membership in the Elks, American Woodmen, Brotherhood of Friends, and Sisters Mysterious 10. The Patriarchs of America, and its women's auxiliary, the Sisters of Ethiopia, were unique to Clearview. James E. Thompson formed the fraternal order in January, 1911, to promote a colonization scheme. As the title indicated, the *Clearview Patriarch* served as the official organ of the group as well as the town newspaper. After his proposal failed to receive serious consideration, Thompson and the Patriarchs concentrated on economic self-help, moral uplift, racial solidarity, and boosting the community.

Black-town lodges were more social than benevolent.

Certainly, the United Brotherhood of Friends and Sisters Mysterious 10, who constructed a home for orphans and the elderly in Boley, the Daughters of Zion and the Benevolent Association in Nicodemus, who worked for community welfare, and the Knights and Daughters of Tabor, who later brought a hospital to Mound Bayou, all worked on improving the quality of life and aiding the less fortunate. But impromptu groups of volunteers and clubs less formally structured than the fraternal orders generally handled the civic improvements and charity on a small scale. In Langston, the women of the community made and sold fancy needlework and gave socials to buy fifteen gas lamps for the main street, while a Clearview minister solicited money on his own in order to light the streets of the town. Individuals and small groups also initiated direct assistance to the needy. The Women's Club of Boley met in February, 1908, and took up a collection of provisions and clothing for a poverty-stricken woman. In 1911, the townspeople of Clearview donated money to a family in which the father was disabled and the following year to another whose house had been totally destroyed by fire. In both Nicodemus and Clearview, citizens depended upon private donations or volunteer labor in order to attempt the digging of a town well.[98]

Like people living in other farm communities around the turn of the century, black-town residents seemed obsessed with their health. Editors reported attacks of consumption, grippe, diphtheria, typhoid, and a number of other diseases. By carefully scrutinizing local news items, readers could determine who was confined to bed, near death, or was up and about following a brief or extended illness. Contrary to previous claims that the area was "unexcelled for a healthy climate" and assurances that the water "contains many medical properties," the town fathers of Boley announced in August, 1905, a thirty-day postponement of the annual celebration because of what the *Progress* editor diagnosed as "yellow fever." Through advertisements in the readyprint section of the newspaper, residents became familiar with the latest patent medicines of the day such as Anti-Grippine, Castoria, Piso's Cure for Consumption, St. Jacobs Oil, Carter's Little Liver Pills, Lydia E. Pinkham's Vegetable Compound, and Hostetter's Celebrated Stomach Bitters. Evidently, the practice of medicine was a lucrative profession, and for that reason some black towns possessed an overabundance of physicians, in time making it difficult for any one of them to earn an adequate livelihood. In the mid-1920's, for example, seven doctors tended to the medical needs of 3,500 people in Boley. Despite the presence of physicians, even during the early years of settlement, the use of midwives was common during childbirth.[99]

In addition to doctors, most black towns contained a large number of practicing ministers as well. Some editors, such as Lee J. Meriweather at Langston, saw the "preaching plague" as one of the major stumbling blocks impeding racial progress, believing that "many turn to it to avoid hard work." Meriweather advised young men contemplating a career to consider business rather than "school teaching and preaching, for the world is getting full of them." At Boley, Ernest D. Lynwood, editor of the *Beacon* in 1908, thought his town could still use "a few lawyers, dentists, and doctors, but for the present we are overstocked with preachers."[100] Too many churches dispersed the limited funds available, leading to underpaid ministers who were compelled to work at other jobs, and a lifeless religious environment. In 1904, the settlement at Mound Bayou listed ten churches, and, twenty years later, the people of Boley attempted to support thirteen different ministers. Most towns claimed the usual denominations—several Baptist, a Christian, African Methodist Episcopal (AME), Colored Methodist Episcopal (CME), Methodist Episcopal (ME), African Methodist Episcopal Zion (AME Zion), Church of God, and, in a few cases, Catholic and Seventh-Day Adventist. Intracongregational feuds, such as the one at Clearview in 1912, frequently led to different branches of the same church inside a community.[101]

During the initial years of settlement the absence of

permanent buildings made intense denominationalism less common. In 1888, the pioneers of Mound Bayou held religious services under a brush arbor regardless of church affiliation. And in early Boley, the Methodists met in the morning and the Baptists in the afternoon, both utilizing the same one-room schoolhouse. Church-going members of the community usually attended both gatherings. Although the AME and Baptist churches in Clearview conducted separate Sunday Schools in 1911, ministers from the two denominations delivered sermons on alternate weeks.[102] In most instances, ministers concentrated on racial solidarity and boosting the community rather than purely spiritual topics. Few extant sermons or articles contained the admonition of the Reverend L. B. Bryant of Clearview to "forget difficulties, hardships, and disappointments, and with our eyes upon the goal, overlook obstructions and continue to press forward to the mark of the high calling which is in Christ Jesus."[103] On the contrary, pastors normally advised congregations to concentrate on this life, uniting to advance the race and town. In a December, 1911, article for the *Clearview Patriarch*, the Reverend B. L. Lockhart praised black progress and his community "with its businessmen, its stores, a Printing Office to herald the news to our millions of people; its schools, its churches. Bless God!"[104] Characteristic of the secular nature of many religious services, Boley's ME Church celebrated Heroes Day on the second Sunday in March, 1906, to honor Abraham Lincoln, Frederic Douglass, and Ulysses Grant.[105]

Barring inclement weather, spare time after church provided the opportunity to socialize with friends. During Boley's early years, townspeople gathered outside the church to visit with farm families who were in town for services, or joined those sitting on logs and stumps placed along mainstreet near the town well. Occasional out-of-town guests brought news from other localities. The arrival of a relative from another community or state usually provided the host or hostess with an excuse to hold a "social" to introduce the stranger, and in order to ensure thorough coverage of the event in the next issue of the newspaper, the editor usually received an invitation to such gatherings. Editors also expected visitors from nearby towns to drop by the printing office to pay their proper respects, and those who failed to do so were sometimes indirectly scolded for their poor manners or lack of appreciation concerning community protocol.

Although isolated from the dominant white society, residents kept abreast of changes in the outside world. Ready-print sections in the newspaper carried information on Booker T. Washington and other prominent black leaders on the national level, local editors ran special columns on activities in other black towns or provided news about blacks living in biracial communities, and, through their attendance at state and national meetings, town leaders encountered the views of blacks living in other localities. A meeting of black post-masters in Oklahoma City in September, 1915, for example, brought Caesar F. Simmons of Boley in contact with representatives from thirteen black towns and seven racially mixed communities in the state.[106] Perhaps because they shared common values and problems, the residents of Oklahoma's black towns visited each other frequently. Other than people in Boley who were only a few miles away, families in Clearview hosted friends and relatives from the black towns of Lima, Lewisville, Taft, Langston, Porter, Red Bird, Bookertee, and Rentiesville during the summer and fall of 1911.

Except for a special celebration, or an occasional drummer seen scurrying from store to store to display samples and take orders for merchandise, those entering or departing the town were usually black.[107] During the summer and fall, the place bustled with activity. Cotton or grain wagons slowly rumbled through the streets headed for the local gin or grist mill where fleece would be cleaned and baled or grain ground into cornmeal and flour. On Saturday nights farm families filled the same wagons, coming to trade eggs, butter, and cream for groceries and later joining the knots of people visiting along mainstreet. After a hard day in the fields or spent clearing brush and trees, older farm children within a radius of several miles sought out the town for entertainment, walking there or catching a ride with rural families bound for mid-week church services. At the height of the town's prosperity, blacks from the outside always seemed to be present, attending this or that meeting of the Masons, the Business League, a Sunday School convention, the Teacher's Normal, or one of the many lodges with mysterious sounding names.

Although the details and layout might differ slightly, a visitor walking the unpaved but well-graded streets of Mound Bayou in 1910 could gain an impression of the typical black town in the United States. The forty-plus shops and stores lining the mainstreet, running from the rail depot through the town, were designed to serve the daily needs of a community of one thousand and the four thousand farmers who considered Mound Bayou their town. Small yet well-kept houses lined most streets, and farther out stood the larger, more pretentious homes of the town's most prominent citizens. Several unsteepled churches, showing little appre-

A Mound Bayou drug store. From *Alexander's Magazine*, July, 1907.

153

ciation for the niceties of architectural excellence, dotted
the village along with three small schoolhouses. A hand-
some, two-story brick building housed the Bank of Mound
Bayou located in the business district, a structure commen-
surate with the importance of capital to the community.
Four cotton gins handled most of the five thousand bales
exported annually, and a sawmill and lumberyard processed
and stored some of the railroad ties and barrel staves mar-
keted there. Local merchants considered the forty square
miles surrounding the town as their trade area, and most
of the farmers who lived within it owned the forty-acre plots
they worked; approximately 80 percent raised the corn and
hay needed for their livestock.

This was Mound Bayou in 1910. Asked by a newspaper
reporter in June of that year about the future of his community, Charles Banks responded:

> As the years go by and our schools, colleges, and
> churches improve in power and capacity, as our streets
> are drained and paved, our oil lamps replaced by elec-
> tric lights, the old antiquated characteristic Delta pump
> is displaced by bountiful streams of pure artesian water,
> negroes will begin to make this their residence home
> . . . there will be an atmosphere in which to raise their
> children and a social status for their wives and daugh-
> ters very much to their liking.[108]

Ironically, within five years Banks would see his beautiful
dream of contentment and success turn to a hideous night-
mare of frustration and failure.

5

Frustration and Failure

EXPECTING LITTLE MORE THAN a mysterious country with fascinating sights and mysterious customs, black
novelist Richard Wright stepped from the ship at Takoradi
in 1953 to view West Africa for the first time. Shocked, he
stared at the people in disbelief—the workmen, traffic officers, policemen—all of them black. "The whole of life
that met the eyes was black," he later wrote.[1] Black towns
were also black. "You should be here on Saturday night,"
a Boley resident responded to an inquiry concerning the
community's social life in 1913. "This town is black; yes,
literally black with people."[2] And one of Mound Bayou's
prominent leaders remembered that as a child everything
there was black, "from the symbols of law and authority and
the man who ran the bank down to the fellow who drove the
road scraper."[3] A settler departing the train at Mound Bayou
or Boley for the first time no doubt felt a similar experience
—suddenly to be among the majority in a world where everyone around him was black. Just as Wright had seen an occasional white face in Takoradi, a black-town visitor might
have encountered a white person there on business. But

whites looked strangely out of place in a community dedicated to isolation from them.

To attract settlers, promoters had pitched their appeal to black pride and economic self-help. Moreover, advertisements and editorials equated race progress with the success of the town-building venture. Capital and credit, however, generally determined business success, and the black town possessed little of either. Editors made much of the bank accounts of a handful of people in each community, such as the twenty-three men in Boley with at least $1,000 each in 1906, but leaders soon discovered that such meager sums were inadequate to serve a populace needing loans and jobs.[4] As a consequence, Charles Banks, as did businessmen in other communities, pleaded with area residents to invest their capital. "What are you going to do with your surplus money?" Banks asked in a form letter mailed to Mound Bayou farmers in 1912. "Are you going to hide it about the house where fire or robber may consume it? Or, are you going to deposit it in a safe bank?"[5] Although it was certainly a commendable effort to encourage savings among members of his race, Banks found that black farmers possessed little "surplus money." Most, along with some of those living inside the town limits, survived part of each year on credit extended by white merchants in other communities.

During hard times, whites sometimes shut off credit. Farmers in and around Langston found it difficult to get loans in order to carry them through the spring and summer of 1895. Many suffered. In the fall, the cotton looked good and the yields from other crops exceeded previous expectations. By late September, A. J. Alston, editor of the *Herald*, claimed that Langston farmers were free of debt and would ask no one for help in the future. "How do you merchants around Guthrie who refused to let farmers have a dollars worth during the summer like this kind of noise?" Alston asked. Such claims of financial independence were usually short-lived. After enumerating a number of woes besetting his community in April, 1915, Charles Banks confided to

Booker T. Washington that in Mound Bayou "we are having the hardest time of our existence to get advances to make the crops, but," always the optimist, he added "this will be best in the end, as they will not owe it all when harvest time comes, as in the past."[6]

Both the high percentage of business failures and the rapid turnover in ownership attested to the scarcity of black-town capital and the unequal distribution of income. Residents in each community witnessed a succession of new firms, most of which lasted only a few months or years, along with what must have seemed like a constant procession of changing partnerships. From the very beginning, merchants felt the pressure to advance credit. But often overextended at the bank themselves and carrying too many customers on account, they faced quick annihilation should a crop failure strike area farmers. Few enjoyed the success of J. H. McRiley, who operated a lumberyard in Boley from 1907 until the early 1920's. Most businessmen, like the five individuals who one after another attempted to establish a laundry in Boley, failed within five years. Even cotton ginning, which should have prospered because of the concentration of local farmers on the crop, sometimes faced serious problems. In 1905, the promoters of the Langston gin soon found the cost of obtaining water too serious an obstacle to overcome and ceased operations. As the town population stabilized or declined and the "boomer" spirit waned, the number of commercial firms remained constant or increased, thus pushing down the general economic prosperity of all. As late as 1925, long after the potential for growth had ceased, over twenty general mercantile stores competed for 3,500 customers inside Boley.[7]

Even the town newspaper, the very embodiment of booster optimism, found the lack of capital an insurmountable handicap. Like the more than sixty black weeklies published west of the Mississippi River by 1900, most black-town newspapers died in their infancy. Usually established by promoters to boom the community, most newspapers required periodic subsidies from local businessmen to continue printing. And during hard times, when financial support lagged and advertising fell off, presses sometimes remained idle for several months.[8] Typical of most editors, A. J. Alston at Langston only worked on the *Herald* part time, depending instead upon his medical practice or other business investments for a steady income. To counteract the scarcity of money in that town, Arthur Tallman, the Nicodemus editor in July, 1886, agreed to take "all kinds of vegetables, young chickens or anything else that a christian printer can eat, on subscription at this office."[9] As the crops matured during the fall of the same year, Hugh Lightfoot, the new editor of the *Western Cyclone*, extended Tallman's offer, agreeing to trade a one-year subscription for four bushels of corn.[10] Despite such efforts, the turnover of editors equaled or exceeded that of other small businesses. And at least nine different editors directed the *Boley Progress* during the eleven years from its first issue to 1916.

The disintegration of the Mound Bayou economy in the fall of 1914 illustrated the precarious nature of most black-town business ventures and, given the scarcity of capital, their susceptibility to the fluctuations of the market. With Charles Banks as cashier, his business partner John W. Francis, president, and Isaiah T. Montgomery on the board of directors, the officers of the Bank of Mound Bayou hoped to guide the economic destiny of black farmers in Bolivar County, thereby freeing them from the control of white furnishing merchants. Beginning in 1904 with the formation of the bank and continuing for the next six years, Banks and his cohorts loaned money to Mound Bayou storekeepers and advanced crop loans to local farmers, most of whom concentrated on the production of cotton. On crop loans with town lots, land, or other property as collateral, the Bank of Mound Bayou normally charged 8 percent interest, a rate comparable to that of other banks in nearby communities.[11] The demand for funds usually exceeded its supply. In July, 1910, Banks appealed to Booker T. Washington for help in arranging "a loan of five thousand dollars on 90 days for us there. I find some matters very tight in our Southern Centers and Mound Bayou just now must not receive any serious set back."[12] Such loans were only temporary stopgaps. More capital was needed. Again the following year the Bank of Mound Bayou was overextended.

As the bank operated from year to year, sometimes teetering on the brink of disaster, Banks continued to promote the $100,000 Mound Bayou Oil Mill and Manufacturing Company. Built by a black contractor using local laborers, the mill was designed to process the byproducts of the cotton grown by Yazoo Delta farmers. To construct the plant, purchase machinery, and buy raw material, Julius Rosenwald of Sears, Roebuck and Company agreed to take $25,000 of the $40,000 worth of mill bonds. B. B. Harvey, a white man who was also president of the Memphis Cotton Oil Company, took the remaining $15,000 in bonds. In turn, Harvey leased the mill for five years.

Thanks to Rosenwald and Harvey, the mill project was launched; but the sale of stock in the enterprise proved more difficult. Although some black fraternal organizations in Mississippi purchased shares, Charles Banks soon found it necessary to use the Bank of Mound Bayou to finance sales. He loaned money through the bank to buyers and then accepted their stock in the oil mill as security. The relationship was set. The Bank of Mound Bayou and the Mound Bayou Oil Mill and Manufacturing Company were tied together, and pressure on one meant the possible failure of both. In time, the bank held one-half of the $80,000 worth of capital stock sold. Desperately searching for a way to unload it or to convert the stock into the cash needed for crop loans during the coming season, Banks wrote to Washington in February, 1914, asking him to help arrange a loan of $15,000 to $20,000 with the oil mill stock as collateral. Banks also sent George Mays, the mill's financial agent, Isaiah Montgomery, and W. P. Kyle, a mill official, to Chicago where they visited black churches there in an attempt to sell some of the mill stock held by the bank. On at least one occasion, Charles Graves, secretary to Julius Rosenwald, joined the trio in their sales campaign.[13] Kyle, Montgomery, and Mays met some success; but in April, 1914, Kyle wrote to Emmett Scott in Alabama reporting that "frankly, the Bank is in a Hell of a fix."[14]

Disaster struck. In May, 1914, Banks wrote to Washington at Tuskegee pleading for help in salvaging the bank, and the following month the pair met with Rosenwald in Chicago who advanced an emergency loan of $5,000. By that time, Banks had succeeded in reducing the bank's holdings of oil mill stock to $25,000. The crisis appeared to be over just as the bottom dropped out of the cotton market. The Bank of Mound Bayou had advanced loans to farmers on the prediction that cotton would be selling for from twelve to fifteen cents per pound and had accepted mortgages against houses, lots, and farms as security for the loans. As cotton prices fell, real estate values also declined, leaving the bank with no way to convert its holdings into cash. While Washington was in Boley, Oklahoma, to deliver an address there on August 22, he received a telegram from Banks advising him that the state examiners had just voted to close the Bank of Mound Bayou.[15]

As the investigation of the bank's affairs continued, rumors circulated up and down the Yazoo Delta of possible criminal charges against its officials. T. M. Henry, the state insurance commissioner, called for an audit of the Masonic Benefit Association of which Banks was treasurer. Some policyholders had charged Banks with mismanagement of funds; and, on September 10, 1914, the *Enterprise* at Cleveland, Mississippi, carried front-page headlines informing readers that "CHARLEY BANKS FLEES THE STATE, Wanted by Authorities for Alleged Fleecing of Colored Masonic Fraternity." Earlier, the *Vicksburg Herald* had claimed that Banks had used Booker T. Washington to obtain a loan of $10,000 in Chicago to save the Bank of Mound Bayou, using only a small portion of the money for that purpose, and that the Masonic Benefit Association faced unpaid death claims amounting to over $75,000. Banks responded, labeling the charges false. He was still in the state he said, and welcomed a full and impartial investigation of his actions. To help alleviate the plight of those who had invested in the Bank of Mound Bayou, many on his personal recommendation, Banks offered to exchange his own stock in the Mound Bayou Oil Mill and Manufacturing Company on a par basis for stock in the now defunct bank.[16]

The mill, however, was also in trouble. By the fall of 1914, Banks had begun to distrust Harvey and in early December of that year was attempting to force him out as lessee. In leasing the mill, Harvey had supposedly agreed to use the money from the $15,000 in bonds he had purchased to pay the debts outstanding against the plant and equipment. Harvey was to hold the Rosenwald bonds in trust. At the close of the first year of operation, Harvey evidently refused to submit to an audit or to present a financial statement; and Banks, Montgomery, and others were forced to pay the interest on the debt, taxes, and the insurance in order to protect the Rosenwald investment. During the second year, the mill ran only part time, and by January, 1915, it sat idle. On February 4, Banks wrote to Charles Graves, Rosenwald's secretary, accusing Harvey of embezzlement. Banks claimed that Harvey had illegally gained access to the Rosenwald bonds and had negotiated some of them. Banks assured Graves, however, that he now controlled the mill and that matters could be worked out.[17]

According to Banks, Harvey stayed out of Mississippi to avoid a summons, and his attorney later got a change of venue into federal court at Clarksdale. Thus, Harvey succeeded in extending the case well into the fall of 1915. Meanwhile, Banks received an offer from the Buckeye Cotton Oil Company, owned by Procter and Gamble and located in Greenwood, Mississippi, to lease the mill. Accepting the Buckeye proposal would have helped Banks financially, but he declined, telling Washington that signing the lease meant the complete loss of the mill's racial identity. On September 30, Banks sent Washington more bad news. George Mays, a Tuskegee graduate and the mill's financial officer, had sold stock in the enterprise under false pretenses and apparently had pocketed some of the money. Banks had been hiding Mays' actions from the public for several months, hoping to solve the problem quietly. Now he asked Washington's advice on the matter. What should he do? The Tuskegean hoped that when confronted Mays would make restitution, but in the event that failed Banks should hold him accountable for his actions through the courts.[18]

As Banks attempted to force out Harvey during the spring and summer of 1915 and to get the oil mill running under his control, he struggled with Mississippi banking officials over the opening of another bank in the town. Prejudice hindered his efforts. With no competition from Mound Bayou, bankers in nearby communities increased interest charges on crop loans, dictated rental fees for land, and demanded that cotton be brought to their towns for ginning. Based on the losses suffered by creditors, the state bank examiners recommended that criminal charges be brought against Banks and the other directors. But the grand jury hearing the evidence found no basis for such action and voted to quash the indictment. Banks claimed that "designing White men" were trying to gain control of the oil mill as well as block the creation of a new bank in Mound Bayou. The first bank should never have been closed, he told Washington in March, 1915. The method of depreciation of values used by the state examiners would have forced any institution into insolvency. Since he knew how to handle the securities, Banks claimed that if left alone he would have weathered the storm and avoided failure. They would not listen. At first, the state demanded the total liquidation of the defunct bank before the issuance of a new charter, as Banks told Fred Moore, editor of the New York *Age*, "opposition they would not dare show against members of their race." In order to take advantage of the movement of cotton,

Banks pushed to open the new bank by June. State officials, however, insisted upon a fully paid capital stock and a "surplus" of $2,000 before permitting the Mound Bayou State Bank to open its doors on October 21, 1915.[19]

Although Charles Banks was neither a stockholder in the new institution nor one of its officers—apparently a concession to state banking authorities—he put up $11,000 of the $12,000 necessary to underwrite its opening. To aid those who had lost farms through mortgage foreclosures and sharecroppers who had failed to obtain credit, Banks developed two large plantations for their use while personally assuming $30,000 worth of liabilities inside Mound Bayou. If it became necessary in order to save the town's economy, he vowed to Washington that he would sacrifice the remainder of his fortune. In late December, 1914, Banks mailed letters to Mound Bayou farmers trying to raise their spirits, encouraging them to remain on the land, and calling for a public meeting in the library building to discuss the general depression in agriculture and the low price of cotton.[20]

On January 10, 1915, the day of the meeting, the oil mill sat idle, in time to be used as a community recreation hall and ballroom. The Bank of Mound Bayou had been closed since August, its directors faced possible criminal indictments, and the prospects for a new bank seemed dim. The psychological impact of the collapse of the bank and the oil mill permeated the town. Unable to pay their debts, collect outstanding accounts, or to extend more credit, a number of storekeepers had followed suit and closed their doors. Ironically, the very location of the meeting symbolized the failure of the Mound Bayou experiment. Since the town fathers had neglected to provide the necessary funds, the library donated by Andrew Carnegie stood in need of maintenance and contained no reading material. Rather than books, the building housed the Masonic Lodge. Perhaps to convince himself as much as Washington, Banks wrote the Tuskegean in March, 1915, assuring him that there was "nothing fundamentally the matter with Mound

Bayou and our efforts here except that in our efforts in making progress we counted too strongly upon the loyalty and support of our constituency and resources at our command and did not properly discount the chances for reverses and general depression."[21] Certainly the relationship between the oil mill and bank contributed to the catastrophe at Mound Bayou, but the decline of cotton prices which precipitated the collapse clearly indicated the basic weakness of the town's economy.

Although the settlers of Nicodemus battled the hot winds, insects, and inadequate rainfall endemic to the High Plains, most avoided one-crop agriculture. The other black towns were less fortunate. Langston, Clearview, and Boley, like Mound Bayou, were located in "cotton counties" in which most farmers depended upon the staple for a livelihood. The cotton depression of 1913 and 1914 marked the beginning of the end for Boley and Clearview as viable towns, and only the payroll of the Colored Agricultural and Normal University saved Langston. When cotton prices tumbled, businesses failed or merchants operated on a low margin or at a loss while carrying customers on credit during hard times. Some Okfuskee County farmers discussed the possibility of withholding the crop from market until prices improved, but lack of money prevented blacks living in the Clearview-Boley area from considering such an approach.[22]

Even in the absence of falling prices and white discrimination, the black towns' concentration on cotton ensured their eventual failure. Unlike the cereals or livestock, cotton lacked the alternative uses leading to the formation and growth of subsidiary industries and the backward and forward linkages associated with internal development. As evidenced by the American South during much of the nineteenth and early twentieth centuries, cotton culture meant dependence upon outside capital, a shallow internal market, and the absence of diversification. As long as prices remained high, black-town bankers, storekeepers, and the farmers they served basked in prosperity, but a prosperity living on borrowed time. Once locked into the vicious cycle of one-crop agriculture based on credit, the future held only the promise of eventual failure or perpetual stagnation. In 1904, cotton accounted for 75 percent of all the crops harvested by Mound Bayou farmers. In an anniversary booklet published thirty-three years later, a Mound Bayou leader admitted that the town would continue to "rise and fall with the favor of 'King Cotton.' "[23] Farther north, in Boley, a resident reported in 1924 that nearly all the farmers within a five or six mile radius still depended upon cotton for survival.[24]

Furthermore, the hope of building a small agricultural service center with prospects for continued growth ran counter to the entire range of economic and social forces sweeping the country after 1865. The constant encroachment of a nationalizing market challenged the security and ingenuity of the businessmen in the stores along mainstreet in thousands of small communities. Commercial clubs and chambers of commerce struggled to counteract the increased mobility of consumers, the appeal of brand names, and the low prices and variety found in the pages of mail-order catalogs. As railroads corrected track-gauge differentials, transfer charges on goods shipped from urban to rural areas and from east to west declined. Town councils pleaded with local residents to support booster projects with money and votes to entice settlers, retain population, aid merchants, and attract manufacturers and railroads. At the same time, the lure of the big city beckoned to the young and the discontent, draining the vitality from the small town and shriveling the tax base necessary to fund new projects. Given such circumstances, any hope of survival or of delaying the inevitable depended upon fortuitous circumstances, keen perception, and the availability of capital. For every Dallas, Chicago, Minneapolis, or Tulsa that won out in the race for urban status, a multitude of small towns succumbed to the devastating onslaught of modernization. In such circumstances, the probability of success for any new community, black, white, or multiracial, seemed slight.

Yet as late as 1912, Clearview town promoter James E. Thompson advised blacks to stop patronizing and investing in giant corporations and instead to put their money in small local firms which hired blacks.[25] Except in a few isolated areas, as Thompson wrote, small factories of the residentiary type—woolen mills, wagon works, rope walks, canning and clothing plants, and a host of others—had already found it impossible to compete in price or quality with large companies enjoying economies of scale and serving the regional or national economy. Even if the capital had been available for their construction, tiny local firms could not compete in the larger market, and the black-town population lacked the necessary purchasing power to support them. Like the horse and buggy, they belonged to a previous age.

Since those living outside the community controlled the allocation of the revenue collected from taxes, white discrimination also weakened the black-town economy. Through a number of ruses—deliberately underestimating the number of pupils, failing to submit reports on time, reducing the length of the school term as an "economy measure"—or openly withholding funds, white officials forced residents to finance partially their own elementary schools or to form private ones to which parents paid to send their children. In the expenditure of money for road maintenance and bridge construction, county officials in both Bolivar and Okfuskee discriminated against Mound Bayou and Boley. In a July, 1914, speech delivered on Founders' Day, Isaiah T. Montgomery complained that although Mound Bayou citizens had paid $5,000 toward the principal and interest on a recently passed bond issue of $175,000, none of the money had gone for roads inside the colony. According to Montgomery, only three of the twenty-seven miles of roads in the settlement had been serviced by a grader. In Boley, people hoped for a bridge over the Canadian River, and, in April, 1909, the *Progress* urged its readers to support the bond issue for construction.[26] Okfuskee County commissioners voted during July to spend the money elsewhere, however, and

Ernest D. Lynwood, the editor, warned them that the town would "remember this unkind cut in the future and govern her vote accordingly."[27]

Other types of discrimination were more overt than the subtle manipulation of public money for a bridge or school. During the spring of 1909, C. R. Springer, Mound Bayou farm implement dealer, wrote to the Oliver Chilled Plow Works of South Bend, Indiana, seeking advertising brochures to distribute to local farmers. H. R. Beale, an Oliver official, wrote back informing Springer that the material "we send is very expensive and we do not think would be appreciated by the negro population in the Southern States, if, in fact, the larger portion of them could read the booklets at all."[28] Furious, Charles Banks responded to Beale, praising the progressiveness of Mound Bayou farmers. On a carbon copy of the letter forwarded to Booker T. Washington, Banks scribbled, "These people do not know as much about us [as James K.] Vardaman."[29]

More serious, people living in Clearview and Boley found it difficult to find work or to rent land outside the immediate vicinity of each town. During 1911, when the white fear of black domination was at its height, some Okfuskee County whites attempted to block further immigration and to force blacks already living there into segregated communities where they would be unable to support themselves and would eventually leave.[30] Organizing commercial clubs in eight school districts in and near Paden, several white farmers signed an oath pledging to "never rent, lease or sell any land in Okfuskee County to any person or persons of negro blood, or agent of theirs; unless the land be located more than one mile from a white or Indian resident . . . [and] to avoid the hiring of negro labor."[31] Leaders hoped to expand the movement over the entire eastern one-half of Oklahoma.

Black-town politicians who ventured out into the county or state seeking public office also found discrimination awaiting them. Edward P. McCabe, former Nicodemus settler,

167

two-term auditor of Kansas, and promoter of Langston, saw his political career vanish with Oklahoma statehood in 1907. With Democratic control of the first Oklahoma state legislature, McCabe lost his position and in time his influence with prominent Republicans deteriorated. Although considered for several federal appointments, none of these materialized. Personal tragedy struck twice in succession. In 1907, his twenty-two–year-old daughter, Edwina, died, and the following year, Dimples, his younger daughter, lay dying in a Chicago hospital. In September, 1908, the *Western Age* at Langston carried a lengthy interview with McCabe just prior to his final departure from Oklahoma. In general, Oklahoma had been good to blacks, he said, but the new state had grown too fast and the race must become more independent in politics. Referring to his own career, McCabe was bitter over what he considered Republican betrayal, not expecting "when I really needed assistance that the men whom I have assisted to office of preferment for nineteen years would throw me down."[32] After a stop in Chicago to join his wife at the bedside of their daughter, McCabe was bound for Victoria, British Columbia, to start anew.[33]

To be sure, McCabe was neither the first nor the last Oklahoma black to consider a Canadian exodus. To some blacks, western Canada held out the promise of fertile soil and freedom from the prejudice found in the United States. Viewed by local inhabitants as romantic curiosities, the few black pioneers scattered across the plains of the Canadian West prior to the turn of the century generally lived unmolested by whites. Canadian immigration officials, however, worried that increased racial strife in the United States might encourage a northward migration of blacks hoping to take advantage of Canada's liberal homestead law. As early as 1899, the Immigration Branch of the Canadian Department of the Interior cautioned its agent stationed in Kansas City to avoid any promotion of black settlers into western Canada. Two hundred Oklahoma blacks arrived in Saskatchewan in the fall of 1909, triggering rumors of an impending invasion from the south. While some leaders in the Canadian government searched for legal means to stop the "menace" at the border, the Immigration Branch dispatched William J. White, inspector of United States Agencies, to Oklahoma to study the situation. White remained in Oklahoma five days, visiting several black towns in the eastern half of the state. In his report, a blend of prejudice and misinformation, White found Oklahoma blacks immoral, lazy, and poverty-stricken, the result, he argued, of intermarriage between the Creeks and their former slaves. Blacks wished to remain in Oklahoma, he said, but white landowners supported by the railroads were encouraging them to leave. White advised the goverment at home to take steps to block their entrance into Canada. Ottawa hired G. W. Miller, a black minister, to stump eastern Oklahoma preaching against Canadian migration while the government officially used existing medical and character inspections at the border to reject potential black settlers.[34]

Families from Clearview made up the advance guard of the first group of Oklahoma blacks who entered Canada in early 1910. Hoping to escape Jim Crow laws, violence, and the impending grandfather clause, and to take up homesteads, a number of residents departed Clearview in late January.[35] During the remainder of the year and throughout most of 1911, the Clearview editor and other town leaders desperately tried to halt the exodus before the population dwindled even further. In a March, 1911, issue, D. F. Whitaker of the *Patriarch* pleaded with readers to "cease to ramble here and yonder, and be content and," with a direct reference to a line from a famous Booker T. Washington speech, " 'let down the buckets where we are.' " After reprinting an article from an Edmonton newspaper discussing prejudice against the race in Canada in April, 1911, Whitaker chided those still considering migration. Whether in the North, South, East, or West, he argued, blacks had to face up to discrimination and "if we must move, move to Negro towns, Negro colonies and concentrate our forces." L. W.

Warren, the new editor at Clearview, took up the same theme in September. "We hear the cry of Negroes 'I am going to Canada. I am going to Mexico. I am going to Africa. I am going, I am going, I don't know where.' All of this nonsense," Warren argued, created dissatisfaction. As late as October, the *Patriarch* still cautioned residents that "most colored people have NOT considered what it will cost them to break up and leave the United States. . . . You can not beat Oklahoma."[36]

Clearview and Boley were doomed, however. Just as the Canadian mania appeared to subside, Alfred Charles Sam, an Akim chief from the Gold Coast, arrived in Okfuskee County in August, 1913, singing the praises of Africa as a home for American blacks.[37] Long before Oklahoma statehood, a number of colonization schemes had swept through the territory. During the 1890's, for example, James McNeal Turner, a bishop in the AME Church and an active participant in Georgia Reconstruction politics, visited Indian Territory on several occasions urging residents there to migrate to Africa.[38] And later, in 1908, George Washington, an aged black living in Okmulgee, called for a convention of blacks to organize an exodus to Liberia. Except for a few isolated groups, most had failed to follow such advice. To black-town citizens America was home and their earlier move from the South to Boley, Clearview, Langston, or the other towns was in no way a substitute for an African migration.[39] Therefore, as long as the towns remained viable communities with some prospects for future growth, promoters found it relatively easy to discredit those preaching migration. By 1914, however, with the black towns dying economically and with social ostracism and political disenfranchisement, Sam found audiences eager to listen. The extent to which they followed him indicates the degree of their frustration and their recognition that the black-town experiment had failed.

Sam, a short man whose soft voice and distinct accent elicited a feeling of sincerity, concentrated his efforts almost exclusively in rural areas and in small towns. Usually dressed in American clothing, he captivated audiences in Clearview, Boley, and other communities with visions of a land that was "one long, sweet dream for negroes."[40] People living on the Gold Coast, Sam told them, could find diamonds washed up by a heavy rain, grow sugar cane as large as stovepipes, and enjoy the harvest from trees that bore bread. For the sum of $25, blacks could purchase one share of stock in the Akim Trading Company, Ltd., entitling its holder to passage to the African paradise. Even Sam must have marveled at the response. Oklahoma blacks were ready to leave. Despite Sam's advice to the contrary, many people sold their farms, houses, town lots, and furniture and moved into two make-shift camps near Weleetka. By February, 1914, the six hundred residents of "North and South Gold Coast Camps" shivered through a severe Oklahoma winter, many in dilapidated tents without adequate food, clothing, or medicine. A Clearview doctor who went there to offer assistance in February found people in rags, children with no shoes, and outbreaks of typhoid and dysentery. Later, a smallpox epidemic broke out.

As the faithful in Weleetka endured the cold winds of an Oklahoma winter, Sam encountered a host of economic and legal problems. From the sale of Akim stock, he purchased a twenty-seven–year-old, iron-hulled passenger ship in New York planning to move it to Galveston, Texas, for its final departure from the United States. Needed repairs, Sam's insistence upon an all-black crew, the purchase of supplies, including coal to power the vessel, and difficulty in obtaining papers delayed the initial move to Galveston for several months. As Sam and his lieutenants vacillated, most of those in the two camps at Weleetka began moving south to Galveston by train. In April, 1914, five hundred people had taken up residence in a tent city in MacGuire's Park there.[41]

After docking in Galveston harbor, Sam stalled while he and his agents sold more stock in order to buy supplies. Since the *Liberia*, as Sam had rechristened the ship, could

171

hold only a small percentage of the company's stockholders, a representative delegation of only sixty made the first voyage on August 21. This group was to inspect the Gold Coast and return to report to those waiting in Galveston. It took three full months for the *Liberia* to reach Africa, only to be delayed even longer by British inspectors. Finally, on February 13, 1915, over eighteen months after Sam had first entered Okfuskee County, he and a few of his followers reached their final destination. Those who had made the journey found land available, but it was a country of strange customs and primitive agriculture, quite unlike farming near Clearview and Boley. As his debts continued to mount, Sam transferred the *Liberia* to a Canadian company, thereby ending any possibility that other investors would follow the original sixty. A handful of the pioneers followed Sam to Liberia where he later became a cocoa buyer. Most returned to the United States, destitute. Penniless and without hope, several of the campers in MacGuire's Park trekked back to Oklahoma.

Black-town leaders reacted quickly to try and counteract Sam's appeal to residents. In Clearview, he was none too subtly advised to leave the county as soon as possible; that failing, he was arrested in Boley for allegedly obtaining money under false pretenses. Officials found it impossible, however, to persuade any stockholders in the Akim Trading Company, Ltd., to testify against him. Personally thinking Sam a fraud and besieged with inquiries concerning the legitimacy of his operations and the extent to which the state government endorsed the movement, Oklahoma Governor Lee Cruce attempted to discover if the chief was in violation of any state law. After interviews with several black leaders and correspondence with various individuals, Cruce decided to drop the issue and suggested that the U.S. Post Office handle the matter. Some postal officials expressed doubts regarding the validity of some of his claims, but lacked sufficient evidence to charge Sam with using the mails to defraud the public. Although harassed, Sam continued to attract followers and collect money.

Within a few weeks after Sam's arrival in Okfuskee County, black-town leaders began their attack. Clearview town promoter James E. Thompson told a reporter for the Okemah *Independent* in August, 1913, that Sam was claiming that in West Africa "the old folks just sit around and drink whiskey and gin and have a good time."[42] In late September, Clearview editor A. R. Wheeler cautioned possible investors in the movement that Sam had given no security for "the ship that will never sail."[43] Wheeler wondered how people could be deluded into believing in a land where they could "just go along any old place and kick up candy yams" with their feet?[44] Such sarcasm fell on deaf ears. Boley attorney W. S. Peters admitted that "the country negroes around Boley are as wildly excited over Chief Sam's 'back to Africa' scheme as they are around Clearview."[45] And at the *Patriarch*, Wheeler lamented that "our people won't listen," preferring instead to follow the "great African Yam Eater."[46]

Undaunted, Sam fought back. In October, 1913, he funded publication of the *African Pioneer*, published at Boley and edited by M. A. Sorrell, the justice of the peace there. According to its first issue, the newspaper would aid in informing those who wished to join Sam on his journey to Africa and would give the chief more time to devote to colonization. Sam stepped up operations in the fall, holding rallies in various rural communities, and on November 18 he staged a mass meeting at Clearview which netted over $12,000.[47] The week before the Clearview rally, citizens of Boley who opposed Sam indirectly struck out at the movement by calling a public gathering to demand the resignation of Sorrell as justice of the peace. Charged with neglecting the duties of his office in order to work for Sam, Sorrell resigned but continued to edit the *Pioneer*. Fearing the outbreak of an epidemic, officials in Weleetka forced the closing of the two African camps near that town for health reasons.

Such actions, however, only seemed to increase the determination of Sam's supporters.

For months, bitterness toward Sam and those who had followed him lingered on in the black towns. The newspapers at Clearview and Boley seemed to delight in publishing each new report of a delay in the *Liberia*'s departure schedule or the hardships encountered by the emigrants. "Strange, strange it is, that the Negro will go headlong into every scheme that comes along," chided the *Clearview Patriarch* in May, 1914, "we advance the old story that 'a fool and his money soon parts.' "[48] When word reached Boley in July, 1915, that some members of Sam's party were starving and appealing for aid in the United States, George W. Perry, former editor of the *Progress*, advised readers there to "let them stand the pressure of their folly." Turning slightly poetic, Perry wondered what Sam's people would "want with money in that land of milk and honey?"[49] The self-satisfaction of having predicted that Sam would fail offered blacktown leaders little compensation for their loss. Boley and Clearview were dying.

Nicodemus' boom also ended abruptly. In March, 1887, the voters of Nicodemus Township approved the issuance of $16,000 worth of bonds to attract the Missouri Pacific Railroad to the community. Operating on assurances that the Missouri Pacific would build westward from Stockton through their town, Nicodemus leaders delayed action on making a similar proposal to the Union Pacific laying track into Graham County from the southeast. From spring through early fall, Nicodemus buzzed with excitement over the "prospect of two or more railroads in the next twelve months."[50] As a Kansas autumn settled over Nicodemus, optimism turned to doubt—by spring to despair. "Nicodemus township stands ready and willing to vote $16,000 to the first railroad that will come through our town," proclaimed the editor of the *Cyclone* on April 1, 1888.[51] None came.

The Missouri Pacific remained stalled at Stockton. Nicodemus' dream of a rail center connecting "the manufactories of Leavenworth and the coal fields of Colorado"[52] vanished as its citizens saw the Union Pacific track crews stay south of the river, missing their town by six miles. Bogue, once a railroad construction camp, soon blossomed into a full-fledged town, and many Nicodemus residents and businesses moved the six miles to the new community on the Union Pacific. Some leaders looked on in disbelief as a number of frame buildings were torn down in sections, loaded on wagons, and hauled to Bogue for reassembly. Even stone structures were moved, a block at a time.[53] In December, 1888, one resident reported that a young doctor from the East planned to open a drug store in Nicodemus on January 1 "as soon as he can get a building, which is a hard matter as we have loaned all our vacant buildings to Bogue until the CBRR from Stockton is built to this place, which will be in the early spring."[54]

As *Cyclone* editor J. E. Porter watched the town die, he talked to those who remained of the rebirth of Nicodemus and an even greater prosperity yet to come. There was no cause for alarm, Porter told them, and for every businessman presently deserting the town "we will get ten wide awake men next spring. Don't get frightened, hold on to your property and be ready to enjoy the real boom that will surely come."[55] With that prediction, on September 7, 1888, the *Nicodemus Cyclone* ceased publication. Two months later, J. E. Porter opened a drug store in Bogue. The citizens of "Demus" slowly drifted away. In October, 1887, and again in February of the following year, the *Cyclone* editor had ridiculed those who might be considering an exodus to a foreign country. A few families did join one or another back-to-Africa movement, but most left Nicodemus to relocate in Hill City, Bogue, Stockton, or some other hamlet in Kansas. A few moved on to larger sities such as Denver or Chicago. In 1913, Sam Garland, an early Nicodemus pioneer and one of the town's wealthiest businessmen, led six other families to Colorado where they founded the Manzanola Colony near Rocky Ford.[56]

The unity among black-town classes, based almost entirely upon the success of the community, evaporated with the loss of leaders like S. Douglas Russell in Langston, Charles Banks in Mound Bayou, and Moses J. Jones in Boley.[57] Years after the town had started to decline, a bank clerk in Boley saw "too much bickering between the merchants, farmers, and teachers. Some of the merchants try to act like they're better than the farmers, and the teachers try to stand off by themselves. This make the farmers and the teachers take their trade to Okemah, because they distrust and dislike the merchants."[58] A Mound Bayou pioneer argued that "since [Isaiah] Montgomery and [Benjamin] Green died, there ain't been nobody here to help the common man. All of these here now will cut your throat for a dime."[59] An early settler of Langston recalled that "in the good old days we really stuck together . . . [but] things sho has changed here now though. People ain't like they used to be. Everybody tryin' to be a politician and any old no good white trash can come in here and make a speech."[60]

Indeed, "things" had changed. From a population of approximately six hundred in 1877, Nicodemus, Kansas, dwindled to less than two hundred by 1910.[61] Poverty then settled over the town. A visitor there in 1918 found only two businesses in existence, one a restaurant with a "two-by-four counter, a box turned upside down for a table, and the rest of the fixtures of the same type."[62] At the time, most of Nicodemus' sixty residents lived in dilapidated houses, few of which showed a sign of paint in recent years. The old men of the town ritually gathered at the post office around three o'clock every afternoon to talk over the happenings of the day while waiting for the mail to arrive. In 1939, a researcher for the Federal Writers' Project saw children playing "in the dusty streets before wooden or stone huts that contain only the bare necessities—often wooden chairs and a table, a stove and an iron bed."[63] One tavern was all that remained of Nicodemus' once-proud business community, only the churches possessed electricity, and those wish-

An old stone building in Nicodemus, in 1973. Built in 1880, the building had a general store on the lower floor and a lodge hall above. Courtesy Kansas State Historical Society.

ing to make a telephone call had to travel the six miles to Bogue. No stores remained in 1950, and three years later the government withdrew its post office there. The black haven on the Solomon had become almost a ghost town.[64]

As Nicodemus lay dying, Mound Bayou, Mississippi, fought to survive. Town leaders hoped that the opening of the Mound Bayou State Bank in October, 1915, would aid in a quick recovery from the depression hanging over the community following the collapse of the oil mill and the failure of the first bank. Advancing cotton prices during the World War I years heightened their optimism. Many Bolivar County blacks borrowed heavily in order to plant additional acreage. Unfortunately, agricultural prosperity failed to last, and by 1920, with cotton prices depressed well below an amount sufficient to cover the costs of production, many Mound Bayou residents lost homes, livestock, and farms. Several joined the exodus of southern blacks who moved to Chicago and other large cities in the North. Those who remained faced the prospect that whites might gain title to much of the land in the surrounding area. From 1920 to

World War II, Mound Bayou's population stabilized at approximately eight hundred. A fire in 1926 consumed several stores, and another in 1941 destroyed nearly all the original business district.[65] In the latter year, black author J. Saunders Redding visited Mound Bayou and described it as a town more dead than alive. One resident told Redding that it was "mostly a town of old folks an' folks getting old."[66]

Promoted by Edward P. McCabe as a gathering point for settlers from which to launch a much larger colonization scheme, Langston, Oklahoma, reached a peak population of approximately two thousand in 1891. Once McCabe's plan for an all-black state collapsed, he abandoned the town, moved to Guthrie, and became active in Republican politics in the territory. Laid out twelve miles from the nearest railroad and primarily populated by poor sharecroppers from the South who had come in search of cheap land, Langston had little hope of building an economic base of sufficient size and depth to sustain growth and development. Although families moved in and out, usually to reduce the expenses of educating their children at the Colored Agricultural and Normal University, Langston's population stayed at approximately three hundred people from 1900 through the Great Depression. The small amount of money brought in by five hundred students and the state appropriation to the university (proportionately less than that received by corresponding white institutions), kept the community alive. A few stores, catering to the needs of students, faculty, and people on nearby farms, constituted the town's business community. When Ralph Tyler, organizer for Booker T. Washington's National Negro Business League, visited Oklahoma in 1913 he by-passed Langston. Tyler had previously scheduled meetings with merchants there but canceled the engagement, writing to Washington that no harm had been done because there was "nothing at Langston but the school."[67] Ironically, Langston, perceived as the capital of a black state, lived on to serve a public institution created by whites to segregate the race.

Clearview, Oklahoma, remained what it had always been —a tiny agricultural service center lacking the capital and internal market necessary to diversify and grow. Grudgingly, Clearview always stood in the shadow of Boley, a much larger and more publicized community. Like most of the blacks living in Okfuskee County, the town's residents and nearby farmers remained tied to the credit cycle of one-crop agriculture. For a time it appeared that the arrival of James E. Thompson, a wealthy Anadarko coal mine operator, might breathe new life into the community, but Thompson quickly used Clearview and its newspaper to advertise his own real estate speculations. The Patriarchs of America, a fraternal organization founded by Thompson to induce the federal government to set aside land in the West for blacks, lasted only a few years. By early 1914, citizens had witnessed an earlier loss of population to Canada, farmers faced an unstable cotton market, and leaders looked on as Chief Alfred Sam tried to entice the remaining residents to Africa. By that time, Thompson had apparently abandoned all hope of developing the town further. In January of that year, he

The Clearview post office, 1974. Courtesy De Crockett.

179

advertised in the *Patriarch* that his Clearview Land Agency also held large tracts in Mexico and would help potential settlers relocate there. Older people, who made up much of Clearview's population of four hundred during the 1930's, could look to a future filled with more hard times and the continued decay of their town.[68]

The history of Boley, Oklahoma, since World War I offers an excellent case study of a dying community. Cotton failed completely as a cash crop after the mid-twenties, and although some farmers sought their salvation in the production of peanuts, most found the income inadequate to support a family. Boley merchants, totally dependent upon local farmers for their trade, struggled to remain in business. Residents complained of the high prices in Boley stores, the lack of credit, and the poor quality of merchandise offered for sale. Many traveled to neighboring towns to shop. As the agricultural depression of the early twenties intensified, another large segment of the population moved farther west. Many of those who stayed behind lost their farms and houses. As people left or were forced to sell their property, the com-

A street scene in Boley, 1974. Courtesy De Crockett.

munity tax base shriveled, putting additional pressure on the local government.[69] The declining tax base only added to an already difficult problem. Since Boley's population was scattered over a wide geographic area, it made municipal services cost approximately twice as much as normally would have been the case. The Great Depression added more misery. In 1933, the county treasurer estimated that only a handful of people in Boley could afford to pay their taxes, and six years later the town declared bankruptcy. Much of the property in the community went on the auction block, and the locally owned telephone company was sold to whites. The Farmers and Merchants' managed to survive the 1920's only to be closed by the state banking commission in December, 1932. As if to complete the destruction, the Fort Smith and Western Railroad, so important in Boley's establishment and later growth, went into receivership in 1938 and its tracks through Okfuskee County were ripped up. Unable to find work, the young people of the town moved on to large cities. In a survey of sixty farm families living within an eight-mile radius of Boley in 1946, one investigator found that 81 percent were tenants. From a population of approximately five thousand in 1914, the town had declined to 574 in 1960. "Boley is the salvation of the Negro race," went one

The Fort Smith and Western depot, Boley, 1939. Courtesy Western History Collections, University of Oklahoma Library.

line of a song composed by an early settler. Unfortunately, that would never be.[70]

As with most communities, large and small, past or present, a few people had derived the bulk of the benefits from the black towns' existence. Individuals like David Turner and Thomas Haynes in Boley, James E. Thompson in Clearview, Edward P. McCabe and S. Douglas Russell in Langston, and Charles Banks and Isaiah Montgomery in Mound Bayou, although perhaps committed to improving the plight of their race, used the town building venture to increase their own personal fortunes. To have expected them to have behaved otherwise would have ruled out the influence of their past socialization in an economic system geared toward individual competition rather than group cooperation. Like Montgomery, who moved from former slave to prosperous planter in a few short years, these men with capital to invest had arrived in each community during its formative stages. For them, economic mobility upward seemed relatively easy. But those who came later found mobility limited by the depth and extent of the local market, and as growth slowed and finally stopped, the black town offered few opportunities for economic advancement. In time, most black-town farmers could only hope that their children would be able to hold onto the land they had struggled to buy. Commenting on Mound Bayou in 1904, a resident of Bolivar County pointed out that by "the time a man gets 160 acres of this swamp land in a good state of cultivation, all the trees, roots and stumps taken up and burnt, he is ready to die."[71]

Utilizing the white belief in black inferiority and appealing to race pride, town promoters asked members of the race to join them in order to gain economic independence and enjoy the benefits of unrestrained freedom while proving to the dominant society that blacks were indeed capable of governing their own affairs. Leaders heralded each town as a practical solution to the race problem in America. Listing a variety of reasons, from the fear of nightriders to the desire to own land, black people flocked to the new towns hoping at long last to find a haven from prejudice where individuals were judged on the basis of actions, not color. Quickly, however, the idea of a great racial experiment was lost in the cheap boosterism of town growth. Economic self-help and racial solidarity gave way to opening a new sub-division, building a canning factory, or speculating in town lots. With vested interests in booming the community, members of the black-town proprietorial class concentrated much of their effort on solidifying their own leadership positions. Those who complained were ridiculed as traitors to the race. In time, the black town became an end in itself, primarily for the economic benefit of a few, rather than a temporary step toward ultimate integration into the mainstream of American life.

Concern with white interference in black-town affairs represented a consistent theme in the early development of each community. On more than one occasion, Montgomery, Banks, and others in Mound Bayou expressed the fear that whites were trying to control the bank or to confiscate the oil mill.[72] Such feelings stemmed in part from a realistic evaluation of race relations in Mississippi at the time. Effectively disenfranchised by the time the town was incorporated, people inside Mound Bayou could behave as they wished, provided of course such behavior had only minimal impact on those living in neighboring white communities. If Mound Bayou had in any way seriously threatened to disrupt the status quo in the Yazoo Delta, whites would have no longer tolerated its existence. Thus, white and black alike clearly understood the limits of acceptable economic, social, and political behavior inside Mound Bayou, and the fact that the community remained unmolested indicates the extent to which leaders there consciously or subconsciously operated according to the dictates of the larger environment. More important, however, the legacy of slavery and the plantation tradition, so familiar to most citizens of the town, acted as a strong force subtly influencing the actions of

Mound Bayou residents. In other words, some of the restraints on people there were no doubt self-imposed. With the town surrounded by white communities who held to a belief that blacks were biologically inferior and thus incapable of caring for themselves, Mound Bayou citizens, very much a product of southern culture, placed more emphasis upon the cultural achievements of community leaders rather than upon the extent to which town growth and development had shown that blacks were capable of self-government. Geographically separated from southern mores, the citizens of Boley, Clearview, and Langston, on the other hand, stressed those events in their towns' histories which proved that race had no impact upon the ability to succeed.

Unlike the other four communities, Nicodemus never experienced complete physical separation from whites. Founded by white Kansas town promoter W. R. Hill, from the beginning Nicodemus contained a few white settlers, such as physician C. H. Newth. In its early years, blacks completely controlled the community, race relations appeared to be cordial, and some intermarriage took place. During its boom period from 1886 to 1888, whites moved in to invest in the town. From that point on, the possibility that Nicodemus would be a haven from white control ceased to be an issue. For a short time, Hill owned and controlled the Nicodemus newspaper, using it primarily for his own political purposes and to boost Hill City for the county seat. While under Hill's ownership, a succession of editors handpicked by him operated the business, and a casual reader of the *Cyclone* would never have detected that Nicodemus in any way differed from a hundred other struggling communities in northwestern Kansas. A. L. McPherson, a white man, opened a bank there in 1887 and whites also operated stores. As the town collapsed following its failure to attract a railroad, whites moved in to buy up surrounding farms. By the 1940's, whites owned a majority of all the sections of land in Nicodemus Township.[73]

Isolation from whites produced both positive and negative results. Long before "black is beautiful" entered the American vernacular, black-town residents exhibited a strong sense of race pride. In home, church, and school, black-town youth were taught self-respect and the glorification of past racial accomplishments. "We are trying here," boasted J. W. Covington, editor of the Mound Bayou *Demonstrator* in 1910, "to saturate them with a realization of the fact that the thrifty, intelligent, well-behaved negro does count."[74] To some extent it worked. Young people living in the three Oklahoma towns held both themselves and their race in much higher esteem than black youth living in mixed communities.[75] To be sure, being proud of the fact you were black constituted the first step toward an identification of self and the fulfillment of individual dignity, but when combined with physical separation from whites it made black-town citizens rigidly hostile and defensive. Some residents seemed highly suspicious that whites were secretly envious of the successes of the community and were quietly laying plans to move in and destroy it at the first opportunity.[76]

To the sensitive, the black town offered a social paradise with freedom to walk the streets without encountering the thousand subtle reminders of membership in a subordinate class. Also one need not fear that a look or gesture might be misinterpreted and bring down the physical wrath of whites. Each day the community blanketed the individual with a sense of well-being, and some who were born and grew up there became addicted to the environment. Within ten miles in any direction lay the outside world, and residents who ventured into it were often shocked and repelled by the realities of American life. Mound Bayou, said Benjamin A. Green, its mayor for twenty years, "gave us kids a sense of security and power and pride that colored kids don't get anywhere else." Outside the town, however, Green found that such feelings were not germane to the real situation. "I don't know which is worse," he wondered, commenting on the ultimate impact of Mound Bayou on its people, "cynicism, apathy, or a false sense of security?"[77] Some who tried

185

to leave the towns recoiled at the prejudice they encountered in other communities and returned. "I have been spoiled since living here," admitted one citizen of an Oklahoma black town, "and I just can't adjust myself when I am around white people."[78] As the dream of community success faded, the black town became a prison without walls for some of its people who had grown distrustful of whites and unable to live and work among them.[79]

The black towns also failed to provide most of their citizens with the skills and industrial discipline necessary to reenter the larger economy. Operating against the trends of the time—the commercialization of agriculture, a rural-urban migration, the growth of large corporations, and a nationalizing market—the black towns struggled against forces which brought thousands of white communities, unburdened with race prejudice, to their knees. Black-town businesses, nearly all oriented toward agricultural service, had to continue to grow in order to provide employment for each new generation of the family or to produce the capital for them to invest in other pursuits. Once black-town farmers could no longer afford to buy more land, the ability to retain their young people was limited by the number of times a farm could be divided and redivided and still provide income for grown children. The town experiment needed enormous amounts of capital, and as members of the race have since discovered, black capitalism required much more than sentimental loyalty and shallow slogans. Some promoters had hoped for the support, or at least the toleration, of whites. Once the towns competed with whites for the exploitation of resources, posed a threat in county politics, or insisted upon an equitable division of public revenue, white patience vanished. At that point, a vicious cycle developed—blacks unified to demand their rights, whites retaliated, prompting more black unity, and on and on.

Before the town-building venture could provide a meaningful and lasting experience, leaders and citizens alike had to come to grips with the basic question of what it meant to be a black person living in America and how their community fit into that relationship. Black pride should have led to a serious search for self-definition. But adopting most of the values and social structures of the larger society created insurmountable contradictions. Promoters committed a serious blunder by using the white belief in black inferiority as a means to attract settlers and to hold them. All minorities face the danger of internalizing the prejudices against them; and blacks, in trying to prove their equality, found themselves in a defensive position that was both self-defeating and psychologically damaging. Each individual failure reinforced white prejudices; each individual success was considered atypical of the race.

Promoters and settlers missed or ignored the inherent contradictions in attempting to remain in the country, withdrawing from the larger society, and yet trying to copy most of its values. Few groups have succeeded by attempting to duplicate the ideas and methods of their oppressor, and the end result had to be a second-rate copy of the original. It was naïve for blacks to believe that isolation from whites represented a viable solution to the race problem in America. Even Isaiah T. Montgomery, the most articulate and idealistic of the promoters, evidently failed to recognize the dichotomy in his own actions. As he supported disenfranchisement of his race on the floor of the Mississippi Constitutional Convention, he apparently never asked himself how blacks could be expected to govern themselves inside Mound Bayou if they were incapable of voting in the state. At Langston, S. Douglas Russell never seemed to comprehend what black vote-splitting between the two major parties really meant. If black votes were divided equally, they had no impact on the election; then going to the polls constituted a meaningless charade.

Not all those who lived in the black town were economically and psychologically trapped. A few leaders practiced leadership roles there and acquired skills that might have been unavailable to them in larger biracial communities.

D. J. Wallace in Langston, Blanche K. Bruce in Mound Bayou, Abram T. Hall in Nicodemus, and others moved on to neighboring communities or to urban areas to become successful doctors, journalists, lawyers, educators, politicians, and businessmen.[80] For a brief period, perhaps only a few years, even those who left penniless and broken took with them worthwhile experiences from their years in a black town. Many had enjoyed freedom and personal dignity for the first time. More important, they had discovered for themselves they could make it on their own without the aid or control of whites. Were they better off to have owned property, voted, and determined their own destiny and lose it all than to have never known the frustration, sorrow, and bitterness of such an experience? "Well, they were better off and didn't know it," argued LuLu Sadler Craig, whose ex-slave parents brought her to Nicodemus at the age of ten. "They were better off because they could rest if they felt like it and they could go to sleep if they wanted to. They were better off and they learned how to find a way of making a living, which had all been planned for them before."[81]

Long after the towns had passed into obscurity, crowds of people, many of whom had traveled from other states, gathered each fall on the streets of Mound Bayou or at Scruggs Grove near Nicodemus to renew old acquaintances, pay tribute to the town's founder, recall a more glorious past, and perhaps to dream of a future in which the promises of American life might some day correspond to its realities. Yes, the black towns died, but dreams die hard, and none harder than those of the poor and downtrodden when they focus on improving their station in life.

Notes

CHAPTER 1

1. As quoted by *Topeka Capital,* August 29, 1937.
2. *Ibid.,* November 22, 1953; *Hill City Times,* February 1, 1968; Smith Center, *Pioneer,* March 21, 1879. Nicodemus was named after an African who was sold into slavery and purchased his freedom in the United States. See *Kansas City Star,* January 26, 1905.
3. Myrtle D. Fesler, *Pioneers of Western Kansas* (New York: Carlton Press, 1962), 191; Arna Bontemps and Jack Conroy, *Anyplace But Here* (New York: Hill and Wang, 1966), 68; *Hill City Times,* July 6, 1961.
4. Fesler, *Pioneers of Western Kansas,* 204; *Hill City Democrat,* February 16, 1888; *Congressional Record, Senate,* 88 Cong., 2 Sess., Vol. 110, Part IV, March 16, 1964, 5352; *Graham County* [Gettysburg] *Lever,* September 4, November 28, 1879. In 1886 Pomeroy built the Boston Cash Store in Hill City, heralded as the largest retail firm of its kind between Topeka and Denver. He later moved to Colorado Springs and invested in the "Lillie" and other gold mines near Cripple Creek. By 1900, his wealth was estimated at $4,000,000. Pomeroy continued his interest in Kansas, establishing an experimental farm near Hill City to test

dry-farming methods, and donated thousands of dollars to various Atchison charities. For some unexplained reason, Hill and Pomeroy feuded, and Hill City remained politically divided until Hill's death in 1905. Pomeroy died two years later. See *Kansas City Star,* February 23, 1900, *Atchison Globe,* February 23, 1900, and *Topeka Capital,* October 4, 1900.

5. For details on the exodus, see John G. Van Deusen, "The Exodus of 1879," *Journal of Negro History* 21 (April, 1936), 111–129, Walter L. Fleming, " 'Pap' Singleton, The Moses of the Colored Exodus," *American Journal of Sociology* 15 (July, 1909), 61–82, Roy Garvin, "Benjamin or 'Pap' Singleton and His Followers," *Journal of Negro History* 33 (January, 1948), 7–23, and Glen Schwendemann, "Wyandotte and the First 'Exodusters' of 1879," *Kansas Historical Quarterly* 26 (Autumn, 1960), 233–249. Van B. Shaw, "Nicodemus, Kansas, A Study in Isolation" (Ph. D. dissertation, University of Missouri, 1951), also found no connection between the exodus and the settlement of Nicodemus.

6. Benjamin Singleton Scrapbook, Manuscripts Division, Kansas State Historical Society, Topeka (hereafter cited KSHS); William J. Balleau, "The Nicodemus Colony of Graham County, Kansas" (M. S. thesis, Fort Hays Kansas State College, 1943), 12; Nell Blythe Waldron, "Colonization in Kansas from 1861–1890" (Ph. D. dissertation, Northwestern University, 1932), 126; *Topeka Journal,* January 7, 1922.

7. *Lawrence Journal,* April 30, 1879; *Kansas City Times,* May 28, 1959; Shaw, "Nicodemus," 100, 103; *Kansas City Star,* January 26, 1905.

8. Federal Writers' Project, *Kansas, A Guide to the Sunflower State* (New York: Viking Press, 1939), 331–332; *Pioneer,* March 24, 1879.

9. Kansas State Census, Graham County, 1885. Microfilm in KSHS.

10. *New York Age,* March 28, 1907; Booker T. Washington, "A Town Owned by Negroes," *The World's Work* 14 (July, 1907), 9126; J. Saunders Redding, *No Day of Triumph* (New York: Harper and Brothers, 1942), 291. In his dis-

cussion, Redding uses fictitious names for the following: River City (Mound Bayou), Calhoun Russ (Eugene P. Booze), Stewart Hall (Charles Banks), Joshua Brockery (Isaiah T. Montgomery), Ten Hamm (Benjamin T. Green), and Tennant Hamm (Benjamin A. Green).

11. Aurelius P. Hood, *The Negro at Mound Bayou* (Nashville: AME Sunday School Union, 1910), 57–58; Maurice E. Jackson, "Mound Bayou: A Study in Social Isolation" (M. S. thesis, University of Alabama, 1937), 88; *Souvenir Program, Mound Bayou Anniversary Celebration,* July, 1962, copy in Mississippi Department of Archives and History, Jackson (hereafter cited MDAH); Day Allen Willey, "Mound Bayou—A Negro Municipality," *Alexander's Magazine* 4 (July 15, 1907), 159–160; Isaiah T. Montgomery to Booker T. Washington, Mound Bayou, November 9, 1905, Booker T. Washington Papers, Library of Congress (hereafter cited BTW).

12. Webb Walton, "All Black: A Unique Negro Community," *Survey Graphic* 27 (January, 1938), 34; "Negro Town," *Newsweek* 14 (July 24, 1939), 14; Redding, *No Day of Triumph,* 294; Montgomery to Charles E. Edgerton, Mound Bayou, December 29, 1904, BTW.

13. *Topeka Commonwealth,* June 28, 1879; *Chicago Tribune,* May 14, 1880; Lee Ella Blake, "The Great Exodus of 1879 and 1880 to Kansas" (M. S. thesis, Kansas State College, 1942), 45; Waldron, "Colonization in Kansas," 129–130.

14. Montgomery to John St. John, Hurricane, Mississippi, May 23, 1879, Papers of Governor John St. John, KSHS.

15. *Ibid.*

16. Hood, *Negro at Mound Bayou,* 58; New York *Age,* April 25, 1912; Charles Banks, *Negro Town and Colony, Mound Bayou, Bolivar Co., Miss., Opportunities Open to Farmers and Settlers* (Mound Bayou: Demonstrator Print, n. d.), 1; Jackson, "Mound Bayou," 28–29.

17. Redding, *No Day of Triumph,* 296.

18. Hiram Tong, "The Pioneers of Mound Bayou," *Century Magazine* 79 (January, 1910), 393; Washington, "Town Owned by Negroes," 9126; Montgomery to Robert Reinhold, Mound Bayou, April 18, 1904, BTW.

19. Montgomery to Edgerton, Mound Bayou, December 29,

1904, BTW; "Mound Bayou," *Time* 30 (July 26, 1937), 14; Walton, "All Black," 35; Hodding Carter, *Lower Mississippi* (New York: Farrar and Rinehart, 1942), 381; B. F. Ousley, "A Town of Colored People in Mississippi," *American Missionary Society Bulletin, 1904,* copy in BTW; Jackson, "Mound Bayou," 45, 64–66.

20. *Souvenir Program of the 50th Anniversary of Mound Bayou, Mississippi, July 11–17, 1937,* 16–22. Copy in MDAH.
21. As quoted in ibid., 22.
22. Green was shot and killed by a local customer in his store in January, 1896, following an altercation over merchandise.
23. Redding, *No Day of Triumph,* 296, 300.
24. Montgomery to Booker T. Washington, Mound Bayou, May 19, 1904, BTW.
25. Ibid.
26. Faye Mathews, "Dream of a Black State," *Sepia* 21 (March, 1972), 67–68; *Topeka Daily Capital,* August 11, 1882.
27. As quoted by Blake, "Great Exodus," 81.
28. William Loren Katz, *The Black West* (New York: Doubleday and Company, 1971), 255; Oklahoma City *Daily Oklahoman,* May 25, 1906; *Topeka Commonwealth,* August 19, 1882; *Hill City Times,* December 27, 1934.
29. Abram T. Hall to Kathryne Henri, Pittsburgh, Pennsylvania, September 6, 1937, KSHS.
30. L. P. Boyd et al., to St. John, Gettsyburg, Kansas, November 8, 1879, St. John Papers, KSHS. The residents of Gettysburg later changed the name of their town to Penokee.
31. *Graham County Lever,* November 28, 1879.
32. John S. Henry to St. John, Topeka, November 8, 1879, St. John Papers, KSHS.
33. Balleau, "Nicodemus Colony," 52.
34. E. P. McCabe, March 1, 1880, Hall and McCabe, March 11, 1879, and John W. Niles et al., February 24, 1880, Nicodemus, to St. John, St. John Papers, KSHS; *Topeka Capital,* November 22, 1953.
35. *Kirwin Chief,* August 17, 1882.
36. *Parsons Eclipse,* August 17, 1882.

37. Nicodemus *Western Cyclone,* July 15, 29, 1886.
38. Ibid., September 9, 1886; *Nicodemus Cyclone,* May 4, 1888.
39. Miscellaneous File, "Langston University," in the Oklahoma Historical Society, Oklahoma City (hereafter cited, OSH); Katz, *Black West,* 257; Mathews, "Dream of a Black State," 68–70; Daniel F. Littlefield, Jr., and Lonnie E. Underhill, "Black Dreams and 'Free' Homes: The Oklahoma Territory, 1891–1894," *Phylon* 34 (December, 1973), 342–357, argue that the town site had previously been owned and plotted by Charles A. Robbins, a white man. McCabe, however, actively promoted the community and took credit for its founding. For more on McCabe and Langston, see: Jere W. Roberson, "Edward P. McCabe and the Langston Experiment," *The Chronicles of Oklahoma* 51 (Fall, 1973), 343–355; Martin Dann, "From Sodom to the Promised Land: E. P. McCabe and the Movement for Oklahoma Colonization," *Kansas Historical Quarterly* 40 (Autumn, 1974), 370–378; and Kenneth M. Hamilton, "The Origin and Early Developments of Langston, Oklahoma," *Journal of Negro History* 62 (July, 1977), 270–282.
40. Mozell C. Hill, "The All-Negro Society in Oklahoma" (Ph. D. dissertation, University of Chicago, 1946), 31; Katz, *Black West,* 256–257; Mathews, "Dream of a Black State," 74.
41. *New York Times,* April 9, 1891; *Topeka Capital,* March 22, 1891; Hill, "All-Negro Society in Oklahoma," 31.
42. For representative examples of the white attitude found in several newspapers, see Kay M. Teall (ed.), *Black History in Oklahoma, A Resource Book* (Oklahoma City: Oklahoma City Public Schools, 1971), 150–161.
43. *San Francisco Examiner,* March 13, 1890; Arthur L. Tolson, "The Negro in Oklahoma Territory, 1889–1907: A Study in Racial Discrimination" (Ph. D. dissertation, University of Oklahoma, 1966), 44–48; McCabe to Benjamin Harrison, Guthrie, December 6, 1889, Benjamin Harrison Papers, Library of Congress.
44. Quotations from various newspapers as cited by Teall, *Black History in Oklahoma,* 152–156.
45. *Norman Transcript,* September 26, 1891.

46. Edwin S. Redkey, *Black Exodus, Black Nationalists and Back-to-Africa, 1890–1910* (New Haven: Yale University Press, 1969), 102; *New York Times,* September 23, 1891.

47. *Langston City Herald,* November 17, 1892, June 15, 1893. Although McCabe sold his interest in the *Herald* sometime during its second year of publication, he continued to promote the town through long real estate advertisements in the newspaper.

48. *Guthrie Daily Leader,* September 27, October 18, 1893; Guthrie, *Daily Oklahoma State Capitol,* September 27, 1893.

49. *Edmond Sun-Democrat,* July 2, 1897; *Daily Oklahoma State Capitol,* February 21, March 19, July 9, 1894; *Daily Leader-Guthrie,* February 10, 1894. For years, the Oklahoma legislature continued this pattern of locating state institutions for black in or near black towns.

50. *Clearview Patriarch,* May 5, 1911.

51. *New York Times,* April 18, 1881. For more on Turner, see Irving Dilliard, "James Milton Turner: A Little Known Benefactor of His People," *Journal of Negro History* 19 (October, 1934), 372–411. A more up-to-date and balanced evaluation of Turner can be found in Lawrence O. Christensen, "J. Milton Turner: An Appraisal," *Missouri Historical Review* 70 (October, 1975), 1–19.

52. As quoted by Sidmund Sameth, "Creek Negroes: A Study of Race Relations" (M. A. thesis, University of Oklahoma, 1940), 56; William E. Bittle and Gilbert Geis, *The Longest Way Home, Chief Alfred Sam's Back-to-Africa Movement* (Detroit: Wayne State University Press, 1964), 21–24; Art Gallaher, Jr., "A Survey of Seminole Freedmen" (M. A. thesis, University of Oklahoma, 1951), contains an excellent discussion of Indian-black relations among the Seminoles.

53. Quotations from Sameth, "Creek Negroes," 45, 54.

54. "Interview with Lemuel Jackson," June 24, 1937, Indian-Pioneer Papers, XXXI, 31–38, OHS.

55. Clearview, *Lincoln Tribune,* September 17, November 19, 1904; *Stillwater Advance,* November 20, 1902. Clearview was originally named Lincoln, but because a town by that name already existed in Oklahoma Territory, federal postal officials designated Clearview as the name of the new post

office there. At a mass meeting in August, 1904, residents voted to accept the new name.

56. *Lincoln Tribune,* August 6, September 17, 1904.

57. Ibid., October 15, 1904; Sameth, "Creek Negroes," 93.

58. *Lincoln Tribune,* October 15, 1904.

59. *Annual Report of the Fifteenth Annual National Negro Business League,* Muskogee, Oklahoma, August 19–21, 1914. Copy in BTW. Typically, Washington packed National Negro Business League convention programs with economically affluent blacks like Thompson who discussed their business acumen and financial success.

60. *Clearview Patriarch,* January 26, 1911, January 18, April 4, 1912.

61. Ibid., January 26, 1911.

62. Ibid., August 1, 1912.

63. *Weleetka American,* August 16, 1907.

64. Ibid., September 20, 1907.

65. *Clearview Patriarch,* July 25, 1912, January 23, 1913.

66. Ralph Tyler to Washington, Muskogee, November 19, 1913, Mound Bayou, December 13, 1913; Emmett Scott to Charles Anderson, Tuskegee, January 24, 1914, BTW.

67. Tyler to Washington, Washington, D.C., September 20, 1913; T. J. Elliott to Scott, Muskogee, November 5, 1913; Tyler to Scott, Guthrie, November 24, 1913, BTW.

68. Tyler to Washington, Boley, December 26, 1913, BTW.

69. Hamilton, "Townsite Speculation and the Origin of Boley, Oklahoma," 181–188; *Boley Progress,* May 17, 1906; John Daniel Bell, "Boley: A Study of a Negro City" (M. A. thesis, University of Kansas, 1928), 9–11; Booker T. Washington, "Boley, A Negro Town in the West," *The Outlook* 88 (January 4, 1908), 30.

70. *Boley Beacon,* February 20, 1908; *Boley Progress,* March 9, 1905; Hazel R. McMahan (ed.), "Stories of Early Oklahoma," manuscript in OHS; Nick Comfort, "Boley," *Oklahoma Journal of Religion* 1 (July, 1944), 11; "Interview with Jay C. Trimble," December 30, 1937, Indian-Pioneer Papers, XCII, 80–85, Western History Collections, University of Oklahoma, Norman; Turner was shot and killed in November, 1932, during the holdup of his bank in Boley. See *Oklahoma City Times,* December 10, 1968.

71. Jay C. Trimble, an early Boley resident, claimed that he established the town's first newspaper, the *Boley Enterprise,* in 1904 and that ten thousand copies of a "booster edition" were published on May 11. No support for Trimble's claim exists nor are there extant copies of the newspaper. See "Interview with Jay C. Trimble."

72. *Boley Progress,* April 27, 1905. With the support of the Fort Smith and Western Railroad, Haynes also developed the town of Vernon, Oklahoma, in September, 1910. Haynes named the community after W. T. Vernon, register of the Treasury and later president of Campbell College, Jackson, Mississippi.

73. Ibid., June 29, 1905; McMahan, "Stories of Early Oklahoma."

74. Bittle and Geis, *Longest Way Home,* 31.

75. *Okemah Ledger,* March 26, 1908.

76. As quoted by McMahan, "Stories of Early Oklahoma."

77. Ibid.

CHAPTER 2

1. *Nicodemus Cyclone,* March 9, 1888; *Langston City Herald,* November 17, 1892, August 10, 1895.

2. Clearview, *Lincoln Tribune,* November 5, 1904.

3. *Clearview Patriarch,* May 9, 1912.

4. *Nicodemus Cyclone,* November 25, 1887, March 30, 1888; *Boley Beacon,* March 12, 1908.

5. *Langston City Herald,* August 11, 1894; *Boley Progress,* February 1, 1906. For an analysis of the black press in general, consult Frederick G. Detweiler, *The Negro Press in the United States* (Chicago: University of Chicago Press, 1922).

6. *Lincoln Tribune,* August 6, September 24, 1906; *Langston City Herald,* June 15, 1893.

7. Nicodemus *Western Cyclone,* March 10, June 2, 1887; *Clearview Patriarch,* May 2, 1912.

8. *Boley Progress,* March 9, 1905; Langston, *Western Age,* April 20, 1906.

9. *Boley Progress,* March 30, April 13, 1905; *Western Age,* January 26, 1906.

10. *Boley Progress,* July 13, 1905, March 17, 1906; Isaiah T. Montgomery to Charles E. Edgerton, Mound Bayou, December 25, 1904; Booker T. Washington Papers, Library of Congress (hereafter cited BTW).

11. Quotations from interviews with black-town residents taken from Mozell C. Hill, "The Negro Society in Oklahoma" (Ph. D. dissertation, University of Chicago, 1946), 22, 63, 69, 125.

12. Ibid., 125, 156–157.

13. As quoted by *Salina Journal,* February 12, 1950.

14. Orval L. McDaniel, "A History of Nicodemus, Graham County, Kansas" (M. S. thesis, Fort Hays Kansas State College, 1950), 65, 131.

15. *Ellis Standard,* September 22, 1877.

16. Van B. Shaw, "Nicodemus, Kansas, A Study in Isolation" (Ph. D. dissertation, University of Missouri, 1951), 368.

17. William E. Bittle and Gilbert Geis, "Racial Self-Fulfillment and the Rise of an All-Negro Community in Oklahoma," *Phylon* 18 (Third Quarter, 1957), 259.

18. *Western Age,* July 24, 1908.

19. William H. and Jane H. Pease, *Black Utopia: Negro Communal Experiments in America* (Madison: State Historical Society of Wisconsin, 1963), also found this to be the case in their study of pre–Civil War black communities in the United States and Canada.

20. *Western Age,* May 8, 1908.

21. Quotation from "Nicodemus," manuscript in the Kansas State Historical Society, Topeka (hereafter cited KSHS).

22. Booker T. Washington, "Law and Order and the Negro," *The Outlook* 93 (November 6, 1909), 552–553; Benjamin Singleton Scrapbook, KSHS; *Western Cyclone,* April 27, 1887; *Graham County* [Gettysburg] *Lever,* December 21, 1879.

23. *Western Cyclone,* July 8, 1886.

24. Ibid., May 13, 1886.

25. *Nicodemus Enterprise,* August 17, 1887.

26. *Boley Progress,* March 11, 1909; Booker T. Washington, "Boley, A Negro Town in the West," *The Outlook* 88 (January 4, 1908), 30.

27. *Nicodemus Cyclone,* July 6, 1888.

28. *St. Louis Globe-Democrat,* February 22, 1913.
29. *Western Age,* October 11, 1907.
30. Washington, "Law and Order and the Negro," 553; Charles Banks, "A Negro Colony, Mound Bayou, Mississippi," typescript copy in BTW. Reliable figures on black-town crime and violence are few, and even the extant records are highly questionable. Leaders seldom mentioned conflict inside their community, and the racial attitudes of some white officials in the county caused them either to exaggerate the extent of such activity there or to ignore it entirely.
31. For an example of this attitude, see *Boley Progress,* July 13, 1905.
32. *Lincoln Tribune,* October 8, 1904.
33. *Western Age,* January 29, 1909.
34. Montgomery to Charles Banks, Mound Bayou, October 20, 1912, and Banks to Booker T. Washington, Mound Bayou, January 20, 1909, BTW.
35. *Boley Progress,* September 21, 1905.
36. Montgomery to Robert Reinhold, Mound Bayou, April 18, 1904, BTW; *Lincoln Tribune,* November 5, 1904.
37. *Langston City Herald,* January 11, February 15, 1886, February 6, 1897; Maurice E. Jackson, "Mound Bayou: A Study in Social Isolation" (M. S. thesis, University of Alabama, 1937), 70–71; Greenville, Mississippi, *Leader,* July 10, 1927; Montgomery to Banks, Mound Bayou, October 2, 1912, BTW.
38. As quoted by Nick Comfort, "Boley," *Oklahoma Journal of Religion* 1 (July, 1944), 10.
39. Ibid.; *Boley Progress,* November 2, 1905, May 17, 1906, January 20, 1910; *Clearview Patriarch,* September 5, October 3, 1914, August 4, 1916; *Guymon Herald,* March 6, 1919; Oklahoma City, *Daily Oklahoman,* March 12, 1912.
40. *Clearview Patriarch,* December 14, 1911.
41. *Boley Progress,* July 20, 1905.
42. *Clearview Patriarch,* July 4, 1912.
43. *Langston City Herald,* April 6, 1895.
44. Comfort, "Boley," 10; Hiram Tong, "The Pioneers of Mound Bayou," *Century Magazine* 79 (January, 1910), 398.
45. *Western Age,* January 17, 1908.

46. *Boley Progress,* January 20, 1910.
47. *Western Age,* November 29, 1907.
48. Hill, "All-Negro Society in Oklahoma," 99.
49. J. Saunders Redding, *No Day of Triumph* (New York: Harper and Brothers, 1942), 302.
50. Hill, "All-Negro Society in Oklahoma," 55.
51. John Daniel Bell, "Boley: A Study of a Negro City" (M. A. thesis, University of Kansas, 1928), 63; Tong, "Pioneers of Mound Bayou," 391; R. Edgar Iles, "Boley: An Exclusively Negro Town in Oklahoma," *Opportunity: The Journal of Negro Life* 3 (August, 1925), 232.
52. As quoted by Hill, "All-Negro Society in Oklahoma," 39.
53. As quoted by Sigmund Sameth, "Creek Negroes: A Study of Race Relations" (M. A. thesis, University of Oklahoma, 1940), 54.
54. Ibid., 58.
55. For discussions of the importance of skin color and hair form in determining status and mobility among blacks in biracial communities, see: Allison Davis, Burleigh B. Gardner, and Mary R. Gardner, *Deep South, A Social Anthropological Study of Caste and Class* (Chicago: University of Chicago Press, 1941), 244; Charles S. Johnson, *Growing Up in the Black Belt, Negro Youth in the Rural South* (Washington, D.C.: American Council of Education, 1941), 256–273; Gunnar Myrdal, *An American Dilemma: The Negro Problem and Modern Democracy* (New York: Harper and Brothers, 1944), 695–700, 1382–1384.
56. As quoted by Hill, "All-Negro Society in Oklahoma," 73–74.
57. *Lincoln Tribune,* October 8, 1904.
58. *Clearview Patriarch,* June 15, 1911.
59. Both Tuskegee Institute in Alabama and the Hampton Institute in Virginia provided a press service for black newspapers. See Detweiler, *The Negro Press in the United States,* 28.
60. *Clearview Patriarch,* April 20, 29, 1911, July 11, November 21, 1912, November 15, 1913, February 14, 1914; *Western Age,* July 10, 1908; *Boley Progress,* December 9, 1909.
61. As quoted by Tong, "Pioneers of Mound Bayou," 398; *Nicodemus Cyclone,* June 15, 1888.

62. For examples, see *Western Age,* July 10, 1908, *Boley Progress,* November 18, 1909–March 3, 1910.
63. As quoted by Tong, "Pioneers of Mound Bayou," 396.
64. Banks to C. C. Buel, Mound Bayou, August 28, 1909, BTW.
65. Comfort, "Boley," 10.
66. As quoted by Hill, "All Negro Society in Oklahoma," 75.
67. *Boley Progress,* January 20, 27, 1910.
68. Redding, *No Day of Triumph,* 302.
69. As quoted by Hodding Carter, *Lower Mississippi* (New York: Farrar and Rinehart, 1942), 383.
70. Redding, *No Day of Triumph,* 302.
71. *Lincoln Tribune,* September 17, 1904.
72. As quoted by Mozell C. Hill and Thelma D. Ackiss, "The 'Insight Interview' Approach to Race Relations," *Journal of Social Psychology* 21 (February, 1945), 202. For a more detailed discussion, see Mozell C. Hill, "Basic Racial Attitudes Toward Whites in the Oklahoma All-Negro Community," *American Journal of Sociology* 49 (May, 1944), 519–523. Hill argues that the black-town attitude toward whites, at least in Oklahoma, depended upon class position and length of residence. Furthermore, people living there did not disapprove of whites quite as strongly as did blacks living in mixed communities.
73. *Boley Progress,* April 19, 1906, July 13, 1905.
74. Tong, "Pioneers of Mound Bayou," 395–396; unidentified newspaper in Clipping Scrapbooks on all-black towns, Hampton Institute, Hampton, Virginia; "Nicodemus," KSHS.
75. *Boley Progress,* November 18, 1909.
76. Iles, "Boley," 234; William Loren Katz, *The Black West* (New York: Doubleday and Company, 1971), 257; *Salina Journal,* February 12, 1950; Tong, "Pioneers of Mound Bayou," 391.
77. *Lincoln Tribune,* September 24, 1904.
78. Ibid., September 24, 1904; *Boley Progress,* November 18, 1909; *Western Age,* June 9, 1905.
79. *Western Age,* April 9, 1909. For another example of the black-town attitude toward Jews, see *Clearview Patriarch,* December 21, 1911.
80. *Western Cyclone,* September 30, 1886.

81. *Clearview Patriarch,* May 30, 1912.
82. Ibid., November 23, 1911; *Nicodemus Cyclone,* December 2, 1887; *Western Age,* August 1, 1907.
83. William H. and Jane H. Pease, "Organized Negro Communities: A North American Experiment," *Journal of Negro History* 47 (January, 1962), 19–34, and Bittle and Geis, "Racial Self-Fulfillment," 248; both support this interpretation.
84. *Clearview Patriarch,* February 28, 1914. For a few examples of the reaction of the black-town press toward Africa, see: *Langston City Herald,* April 20, 1895; *Western Cyclone,* October 28, 1887; *Nicodemus Cyclone,* February 3, 1888; *Boley Beacon,* February 20, 1908.
85. W. E. B. Du Bois, "The Conservation of Races," American Negro Academy *Occasional Papers,* No. 2, 1897, reprinted in Philip S. Foner (ed.), *W. E. B. Du Bois Speaks, Speeches and Addresses, 1890–1919* (New York: Pathfinder Press, 1970), 84.
86. Ibid., 83.
87. Ibid., 79.
88. Du Bois, "Is Race Separation Practicable?," *American Journal of Sociology* 13 (May, 1908), 184, reprinted in Foner, *W. E. B. Du Bois Speaks,* 184.
89. For more on Du Bois, see: Fullinwider, *The Mind and Mood of Black America* (Homewood, Illinois: The Dorsey Press, 1969); Elliott M. Rudwick, *W. E. B. Du Bois, Propagandist of the Negro Protest* (New York: Atheneum, 1969); Francis L. Broderick, *W. E. B. Du Bois, Negro Leader in a Time of Crisis* (Stanford: Stanford University Press, 1959); John Henrik Clarke and others (eds.), *Black Titan, W. E. B. Du Bois* (Boston: Beacon Press, 1970); August Meier, *Negro Thought in America, 1880–1915* (Ann Arbor: University of Michigan Press, 1969).

CHAPTER 3

1. R. Edgar Iles, "Boley, An Exclusively Negro Town in Oklahoma," *Opportunity: The Journal of Negro Life* 3 (August, 1925), 232.
2. Clearview, *Lincoln Tribune,* August 6, 1904; Hiram Tong,

"The Pioneers of Mound Bayou," *Century Magazine* 79 (January, 1910), 397–398.

3. Nicodemus, *Western Cyclone,* June 24, 1886.
4. *Edmond Sun-Democrat,* August 16, 1895; Mozell C. Hill, "The All-Negro Society in Oklahoma" (Ph. D. dissertation, University of Chicago, 1946), 46.
5. *Boley Informer,* May 4, 1911.
6. Emmett Scott to T. J. Elliott, Tuskegee, December 8, 1913, Elliott to Scott, Muskogee, December 11, 1913, January 21, 1913, Booker T. Washington Papers, Library of Congress (hereafter cited BTW).
7. Unidentified newspaper, February 14, 1917, in Clipping Scrapbooks on all-black towns, Hampton Institute, Hampton, Virginia; Bureau of Government Research, University of Mississippi, *Mound Bayou, 1973: City in Transition* (University, Mississippi: University of Mississippi, 1973), 23. For more on Washington's connection with Mound Bayou, see August Meier, "Booker T. Washington and the Town of Mound Bayou," *Phylon* 15 (Fourth Quarter, 1954), 396–401.
8. *Western Cyclone,* March 24, 1887; John Daniel Bell, "Boley: A Study of a Negro City" (M. A. thesis, University of Kansas, 1928), 61.
9. *Boley Beacon,* March 19, 1908.
10. *Boley Progress,* September 28, 1905. Councilmen in Boley received $4.15 per month for their services, the town marshal $10.00 per month plus 2 percent of all the money collected by him; Larrie L. Elahi, "A History of Boley, Oklahoma to 1915" (M. A. thesis, University of Chicago, 1968), 43–56.
11. *Western Cyclone,* September 30, 1886.
12. *Boley Progress,* January 13, 1910.
13. For examples, see: *Lexington Leader,* November 28, 1891; *Edmond Sun-Democrat,* June 28, 1895; *Kingfisher Press,* September 24, 1896; *Stillwater Gazette,* May 27, 1897; Vinita *Indian Chieftain,* August 29, 1901, July 31, 1902; *Krebs Eagle,* December 29, 1899; *Beaver Journal,* April 4, 1903; and *Alva Review,* April 10, 1902.
14. *Western Cyclone,* July 1, 1886.
15. Ibid., August 12, 1887.

16. Stockton, *Rooks County Record,* August 19, 1887; *Nicodemus Enterprise,* August 24, 1887; *Webster Eagle,* August 6, 1887.
17. *Nicodemus Enterprise,* September 7, 1887; Orval L. McDaniel, "A History of Nicodemus, Graham County, Kansas" (M. S. thesis, Fort Hays Kansas State College, 1950), 75.
18. *Nicodemus Enterprise,* August 31, September 28, 1887.
19. Ibid., August 31, October 8, 1887.
20. Ibid., October 8, 26, 1887.
21. *Graham County* [Gettysburg] *Lever,* September 4, November 28, 1879.
22. *Hill City Times,* May 27, 1954.
23. *Lexington Leader,* April 7, 1905.
24. *Mangum Star,* September 28, 1905.
25. William E. Bittle and Gilbert Geis, "Racial Self-Fulfillment and the Rise of an All-Negro Community in Oklahoma," *Phylon* 18 (Third Quarter, 1957), 255.
26. Ibid., 256; *Weleetka American,* February 1, 1907.
27. *Weleetka American,* August 30, 1907.
28. Ibid., September 13, 1907.
29. Ibid.
30. Bittle and Geis, "Racial Self-Fulfillment," 256–257.
31. *Weleetka American,* September 20, 1907.
32. Ibid., October 18, 1907; *Okemah Ledger,* December 26, 1907.
33. *Okemah Ledger,* April 23, 30, 1908.
34. Ibid., May 14, 28, June 4, 1908.
35. Ibid., August 27, 1908. Boley voted: Welettka 184, Okemah 146, and Castle 23.
36. William E. Bittle and Gilbert Geis, "A Dream That Faded," *New York Times Magazine,* December 6, 1964, 52.
37. Bell, "Boley," 49–53; Luther P. Jackson, "Shaped by a Dream, A Town Called Boley," *Life* 65 (November 29, 1968); 74; *Okemah Ledger,* May 25, 1911.
38. *Mound Bayou, Mississippi, Anniversary Diamond Jubilee,* July, 1962, copy in Mississippi Department of Archives and History, Jackson (hereafter cited MDAH); Vernon L. Wharton, *The Negro in Mississippi* (Chapel Hill: University of North Carolina Press, 1947), 211.
39. Wharton, *Negro in Mississippi,* 202–203.

40. Ibid., 206-211.
41. Quotations from a copy of the complete text of Montgomery's speech printed in *Semi-Centennial Celebration, The Founding of Mound Bayou,* July, 1937, copy in MDAH; William Alexander Mabry, "Disenfranchisement of the Negro in Mississippi," *Journal of Southern History* 4 (August, 1938), 329–331.
42. *Raymond* [Mississippi] *Gazette,* September 20, 1890; Louis R. Harlan, *Booker T. Washington, The Making of a Black Leader* (New York: Oxford University Press, 1972), 289; Montgomery to Washington, Mound Bayou, April 5, 1904, BTW; August Meier, *Negro Thought in America, 1880–1915* (Ann Arbor: University of Michigan Press, 1969), 38.
43. C. Vann Woodward, *The Strange Career of Jim Crow* (New York: Oxford University Press, 1966), 101–102.
44. Of the five institutions, three were located in Taft, a black town ten miles west of Muskogee. Boley received the State Training School for Boys, and Langston the Colored Agricultural and Normal University.
45. Arrell M. Gibson, *The Chickasaws* (Norman: University of Oklahoma Press, 1971), 258–264; Angie Debo, *The Rise and Fall of the Choctaw Republic* (Norman: University of Oklahoma Press, 1934), 103–105; also see M. Thomas Bailey, *Reconstruction in Indian Territory* (Port Washington, New York: Kennikat Press, 1972).
46. *Lexington Leader,* November 28, 1891.
47. As quoted by Sigmund Sameth, "Creek Negroes: A Study in Race Relations" (M. A. thesis, University of Oklahoma, 1940), 37.
48. Ibid., 49.
49. *Lincoln Tribune,* September 17, 1904.
50. *Western Age,* December 13, 1907.
51. *Weleetka American,* July 21, 1905.
52. *Graham County Lever,* December 12, 1879.
53. Tong, "Pioneers of Mound Bayou," 394.
54. New Orleans *State,* June 7, 1910.
55. Coyle *Cimarron Valley Clipper,* January 16, 1908; *Western Age,* October 6, 1905, January 23, 1908.
56. *Western Age,* June 9, 1905.
57. Charles Banks, *Negro Town and Colony, Mound Bayou,*

Bolivar Co., Miss., Opportunities Open to Farmers and Settlers (Mound Bayou: Demonstrator Print, n. d.), 11.
58. As quoted by Tong, "Pioneers of Mound Bayou," 398.
59. New Orleans *State,* June 7, 1910.
60. August Meier and Elliott Rudwick, *From Plantation to Ghetto* (New York: Hill and Wang, 1966), 171.
61. *Western Age,* October 11, 1907.
62. Ibid., April 26, May 10, 17, 31, June 24, 1907. Contrary to the Federal Enabling Act, Oklahoma's proposed constitution offered no guarantee against discrimination. In early drafts, the Oklahoma constitution contained a Jim Crow article, but Democrats pushing it were persuaded to drop the provision.
63. Ibid., September 26, 1907.
64. Ibid.; Oklahoma City, *Times-Journal,* August 31, 1907.
65. *Boley Beacon,* February 20, 1908.
66. Rayford W. Logan, *Howard University, The First Hundred Years, 1867–1967* (New York: New York University Press, 1969), 95; *Shawnee Daily-Herald,* February 26, 1908.
67. *Western Age,* February 21, December 4, 1908.
68. Banks to Washington, Mound Bayou, July 9, 1914, BTW.
69. *Western Age,* May 3, 1907, June 5, 1908.
70. *Harlow's Weekly,* June 3, 1916.
71. For examples of this attitude, see *Western Age,* August 15, 1907, May 15, 1908, May 28, 1909; *Boley Beacon,* February 20, 1908; *Clearview Patriarch,* May 15, 1911, September 5, 1912.
72. *Clearview Patriarch,* October 17, 1912.
73. *Western Age,* November 22, 29, 1907, April 3, 1908, January 15, 29, 1909.
74. Ibid., January 15, 1909; *Lexington Leader,* September 24, 1909.
75. *Western Age,* October 2, 1908, March 19, 26, 1909; *Topeka Daily Capital,* November 30, December 1, 1911.
76. As quoted by Hill, "All-Negro Society in Oklahoma," 103.
77. Van B. Shaw, "Nicodemus, Kansas, A Study in Isolation" (Ph. D. dissertation, University of Missouri, 1951), 284.
78. Iles, "Boley," 232.
79. As quoted by Hill, "All-Negro Society in Oklahoma," 103.
80. *Nicodemus Enterprise,* September 21, 1887.

81. For examples, see *Western Age,* October 9, 30, 1908, April 9, 23, 1909.
82. Meier, *Negro Thought in America,* 164–166. Also see James A. Tinsley, "Roosevelt, Foraker, and the Brownsville Affray," *Journal of Negro History* 41 (January, 1956), 43–56, and Lewis N. Wynne, "Brownsville: The Reaction of the Negro Press," *Phylon* 33 (Second Quarter, 1972), 153–160.
83. *Western Age,* January 26, 1906; *Okemah Ledger,* December 14, 1911.
84. *Langston City Herald,* October 19, 1895.
85. Shaw, "Nicodemus," 284.
86. *Clearview Patriarch,* May 16, August 15, October 31, 1912.
87. *Western Age,* October 11, 1907.

CHAPTER 4

1. *Langston City Herald,* September 29, 1895.
2. E. Franklin Frazier, *The Negro in the United States* (New York: The Macmillan Company, 1949), 199; *Clearview Patriarch,* February 6, 13, 1913.
3. *Langston City Herald,* November 9, 1895; *Clearview Patriarch,* February 6, 13, 1913, January 11, 18, May 9, October 24, 1912.
4. *Langston City Herald,* September 28, 1895; *Boley Progress,* August 3, 1905.
5. *Clearview Patriarch,* May 18, 1911. "Third and fourth" was a common sharecropping arrangement, meaning the landlord was to receive one-third of the cotton and one-fourth of the corn for the use of the land. Frequently, the landlord was also the furnishing merchant, in which case the tenant paid one-third of the cotton and one-fourth of the corn, plus what was owed the landlord for furnishing supplies from his store. If the furnishing merchant did not own the land, the tenant had two bills to pay—one for supplies and the other for the use of the land. For a discussion of the furnishing merchants, see Harold D. Woodman, *King Cotton and His Retainers* (Lexington: University of Kentucky Press, 1968), 295–314.
6. *Clearview Patriarch,* July 6, 1911.

7. As quoted by Aurelius P. Hood, *The Negro at Mound Bayou* (Nashville: AME Sunday School Union, 1910), 104–105.
8. *Langston City Herald,* November 17, 1892; *Western Age,* June 19, 1908.
9. Day Allen Willey, "Mound Bayou—A Negro Municipality," *Alexander's Magazine* 4 (June 15, 1907), 162; Transfer Records and Tax Rolls, 1881, 1887, Graham County, Nicodemus Township, Graham County Courthouse, Hill City, Kansas.
10. For examples, see *Lincoln Tribune,* August 6, 1904, *Boley Progress,* January 25, 1906.
11. As quoted by Mozell C. Hill, "The All-Negro Society in Oklahoma" (Ph. D. dissertation, University of Chicago, 1946), 39.
12. As quoted by *Indianapolis Freeman,* February 5, 1910.
13. Charles Banks, "A Negro Colony, Mound Bayou, Mississippi," typescript copy in the Booker T. Washington Papers, Library of Congress (hereafter cited BTW); *Mound Bayou, Mississippi, Anniversary Diamond Jubilee,* July 1962, copy in Mississippi Department of Archives and History, Jackson (hereafter cited MDAH); Banks to Negro Farmers of the Delta, August 31, 1909, T. S. Owens, April 29, 1910, Mound Bayou, BTW.
14. Banks to Dear Sir, August 18, 1909, Attention Farmers, January 12, 1910, and Negro Farmers of the Delta, October, 1911, Mound Bayou, BTW.
15. *Clearview Patriarch,* May 23, 1912.
16. Hiram Tong, "The Pioneers of Mound Bayou," *Century Magazine* 79 (January, 1910), 395.
17. *Langston City Herald,* May 4, 1895; *Boley Progress,* July 13, 1905.
18. Nicodemus, *Western Cyclone,* May 26, 1887; *Clearview Patriarch,* March 28, April 4, 1912.
19. Jane Gottschalk, "The Rhetorical Strategy of Booker T. Washington," *Phylon* 27 (Fourth Quarter, 1966), 390.
20. As quoted by New Orleans *State,* June 7, 1910.
21. *Clearview Patriarch,* January 25, 1912.
22. Banks to Robert W. Taylor, Mound Bayou, June 22, 1908, BTW.

23. As quoted by *Clearview Patriarch,* November 16, 1911.
24. Ibid., December 7, 1911.
25. *Western Age,* June 19, 1908.
26. Ibid., December 15, 1905; *Oakley* [Kansas] *Graphic,* December 4, 1931. A. L. McPherson, a white man, partially alleviated the problem in January, 1887, when he opened the Bank of Nicodemus. See *Western Cyclone,* January 13, 1887, and Glen Schwendemann, "Nicodemus: Negro Haven on the Solomon," *Kansas Historical Quarterly* 34 (Spring, 1968), 29.
27. *Boley Progress,* March 9, 1905, April 8, July 8, 1909; *Clearview Patriarch,* October 3, 1912; *Boley Beacon,* March 19, 1908; John Daniel Bell, "Boley: A Study of a Negro City" (M. A. thesis, University of Kansas, 1928), 13, 21. Thompson's bank for Clearview never materialized.
28. As quoted by Hill, "All-Negro Society in Oklahoma," 40.
29. As quoted by ibid., 62.
30. Charles Banks, *Negro Town and Colony, Mound Bayou, Bolivar Co., Miss., Opportunities Open to Farmers and Settlers* (Mound Bayou, Demonstrator Print, n. d.); Booker T. Washington, "A Town Owned by Negroes," *The World's Work* 14 (July, 1907), 9127–9128; Thomas S. Owen to Booker T. Washington, Cleveland, Mississippi, February 25, 1913, BTW.
31. Much of the information on Banks was taken from various Mound Bayou celebration booklets on deposit in MDAH.
32. Booker T. Washington, *My Larger Education* (New York: Doubleday, Page and Company, 1911), 207–208.
33. Ibid., 209.
34. Booker T. Washington, "Law and Order and the Negro" *The Outlook* 93 (November 6, 1909), 547–555. Also see Washington's comments on Mound Bayou in *The Negro in Business* (Chicago: Afro-American Press, 1968), 69, 91–92.
35. Banks to C. P. Mooney, Mound Bayou, September 23, 1908, BTW.
36. Washington to Banks, Tuskegee, June 27, 1910, BTW.
37. Banks to editor, *New York Sun,* Mound Bayou, December 19, 1910, BTW.

38. Banks to Emmett Scott, Mound Bayou, March 21, 1910, BTW.
39. As quoted in *Mound Bayou, Mississippi Anniversary Diamond Jubilee.*
40. Banks to Theodore Roosevelt, Mound Bayou, December 18, 1915, BTW. Following Washington's death, Banks wrote to Roosevelt to endorse Emmett Scott as the new head of Tuskegee Institute.
41. Washington to Banks, Tuskegee, February 3, 1910, BTW.
42. Banks to Fred R. Moore, Mound Bayou, May 18, 1910; Banks to Scott, Mound Bayou, January 2, 1909, BTW.
43. Banks to Washington, Mound Bayou, October 25, 1915, BTW.
44. Ibid., January 20, April 6, 1909; Scott to Banks, Tuskegee, February 1, 1909, November 21, 1913, BTW.
45. Scott to Banks, Tuskegee, March 17, May 3, November 28, 1910; Banks to Scott, Mound Bayou, January 13, March 23, 1910; Banks to Washington, Mound Bayou, February 27, 1914, BTW.
46. Banks to Scott, Mound Bayou, November 27, 1908, BTW.
47. Scott to Banks, Tuskegee, December 2, 1908, BTW.
48. Banks to Scott, Mound Bayou, February 10, 1910, BTW.
49. Banks to W. L. Park, Mound Bayou, February 9, 1911; Banks to Scott, Mound Bayou, January 13, 1911, BTW.
50. Banks to James H. Dillard, Mound Bayou, February 22, 1909; Banks to Andrew Carnegie, Mound Bayou, December 29, 1908; H. J. Murphy to Banks, New York, December 17, 1908, BTW; August Meier, "Booker T. Washington and the Town of Mound Bayou," *Phylon* 15 (Fourth Quarter, 1954), 398.
51. New York *Age*, November 21, 1907, April 25, 1912; Julius Rosenwald to Banks, Chicago, February 25, 1913, BTW; Meier, "Booker T. Washington and the Town of Mound Bayou," 398.
52. Washington to Banks, Tuskegee, September 5, 1912, BTW.
53. Washington, Tuskegee, February 13, 1913, to French Oil Mill Machinery Company, Carver Cotton Gin Company, D. B. Gamble, BTW.
54. Isaiah T. Montgomery and A. A. Cosey to Investors in the

Mound Bayou Oil Mill and Manufacturing Company, Mound Bayou, copy in BTW.

55. Copy of "Part of the Address Delivered by Booker T. Washington at the Opening of the Cotton Oil Mill . . . ," BTW; Banks to Washington, Mound Bayou, November 2, 1912, BTW.

56. Booker T. Washington, "Boley, A Negro Town in the West," *The Outlook* 88 (January, 1908), 31.

57. Samuel R. Spencer, *Booker T. Washington and the Negro's Place in American Life* (Boston: Little, Brown and Company, 1955), 92; Booker T. Washington, *The Story of the Negro, The Rise of the Race from Slavery* (New York: Doubleday, Page and Company, 1909), II, 252.

58. Galley proof of the Report of the 1914 National Negro Business League, copy in BTW.

59. *Langston City Herald*, July 18, 1896; *Western Age*, November 17, 1905.

60. David J. Turner to Scott, Boley, September 8, 1914, BTW.

61. Washington to J. Harold Coleman, Tuskegee, December 12, 1914; T. J. Elliott to Scott, Muskogee, January 21, 1914, BTW. Black towns sometimes helped to defray the expenses of the national organization. In December, 1913, for example, the Masonic Grand Lodge of Mound Bayou donated a book of railroad tickets good for a thousand miles of travel to cover the transportation costs of Ralph Tyler, the league's national organizer, while Tyler was in Mississippi.

62. Washington to Scott, Castine, Maine, July 6, 1914, BTW.

63. *Clearview Patriarch*, September 5, 1914; *Annual Report of the Fifteenth Annual National Negro Business League*, Muskogee, Oklahoma, August 19–21, 1914, copy in BTW.

64. *Boley Progress*, March 30, September 28, 1905, July 8, 1909; *Nicodemus Cyclone*, March 30, 1888; Tong, "Pioneers of Mound Bayou," 391; Bell, "Boley," 18; Washington, "Law and Order and the Negro," 552; *Cleveland* [Mississippi] *Enterprise*, July 30, 1914.

65. *Boley Progress*, September 28, 1905. In regard to the poll tax, one early resident of Langston felt that "them poll taxes sure made a man feel like he belonged to the town." See Mozell C. Hill and Thelma D. Ackiss, *Culture of a*

Contemporary All-Negro Community (Langston, Oklahoma: Langston University, 1943), 24.

66. *Boley Progress,* March 16, 1905.
67. *Western Age,* June 9, 1905. For other examples, see ibid., July 6, 1905, and *Western Cyclone,* September 23, 1886.
68. *Boley Progress,* March 16, 1905; August N. Meier, *Negro Thought in America, 1880–1915* (Ann Arbor: University of Michigan Press, 1969), 125.
69. *Western Cyclone,* June 6, 1886.
70. *Lincoln Tribune,* November 5, 19, 1904; *Western Age,* December 8, 1905.
71. *Western Cyclone,* August 12, 1887.
72. Lewis Atherton, *Main Street on the Middle Border* (Chicago: Quadrangle Books, 1966), 231–233.
73. *Boley Progress,* November 30, 1905.
74. The money order business at the local post office, to which many black-town boosters pointed with pride as an indication of community prosperity, provided some indication of the amount of capital leaving the town each month. For example, money order sales at the Boley post office during November, 1905, amounted to $8,256.75.
75. *Annual Report of the Fifteenth Annual National Negro Business League.*
76. *Lincoln Tribune,* August 6, September 7, 1904.
77. *Boley Progress,* March 9, August 3, 1905.
78. Ibid., June 8, 1905; "Interview with Jay C. Trimble," December 30, 1937, Indian-Pioneer Papers, XCII, 80–85, Western History Collections, University of Oklahoma, Norman.
79. *Clearview Patriarch,* February 1, 1912.
80. Ibid., October 3, 1912; *Nicodemus Cyclone,* March 9, 1888; *Boley Beacon,* March 19, 1908.
81. For a discussion of class structure in the black section of a mixed community, see St. Clair Drake and Horace R. Cayton, *Black Metropolis* (New York: Harper and Row, 1962), II, 438. Also see August Meier, "Negro Class Structure and Ideology in the Age of Booker T. Washington," *Phylon* 23 (Third Quarter, 1962), 258–266.
82. According to a magazine report, Benjamin A. Green, son of one of the founders of Mound Bayou, and E. P. Booze

finally settled their differences in 1939. See "Negro Town," *Newsweek* 14 (July 24, 1939), 14.

83. *Nicodemus Cyclone,* June 8, 1888; *Clearview Patriarch,* December 7, 1911.
84. *Clearview Patriarch,* November 7, 1912.
85. *Western Cyclone,* October 7, 1887.
86. Ibid.
87. *Langston City Herald,* November 17, 1892.
88. *Boley Progress,* July 27, October 5, 1905; *Boley Informer,* May 18, 1911.
89. *Western Age,* February 14, May 1, 1908; *Clearview Patriarch,* August 1, 1912.
90. *Clearview Patriarch,* June 1, 1911.
91. Ibid., March 14, 1912.
92. *Western Cyclone,* December 30, 1886, January 13, March 24, 1887; Van B. Shaw, "Nicodemus, Kansas, A Study in Isolation" (Ph. D. dissertation, University of Missouri, 1951), 116.
93. *Clearview Patriarch,* June 15, 1911.
94. *Western Age,* July 5, 1907.
95. *Clearview Patriarch,* April 6, 1911.
96. *Nicodemus Cyclone,* March 16, 1888.
97. *Langston City Herald,* May 4, April 20, 1895; *Clearview Patriarch,* July 4, 11, 18, 1912; *Boley Progress,* March 9, 1905.
98. *El Reno News,* January 11, 1900; *Clearview Patriarch,* April 13, October 26, 1911, May 30, 1912; *Boley Beacon,* February 20, 1908; Orval L. McDaniel, "A History of Nicodemus, Graham County, Kansas" (M. S. thesis, Fort Hays Kansas State College, 1950), 76; Joseph Taylor, "Mound Bayou—Past and Present," *Negro History Bulletin* 3 (July, 1940), 109; Nick Comfort, "Boley," *Oklahoma Journal of Religion* 1 (July, 1944), 10.
99. *Boley Progress,* April 27, July 13, August 31, 1905; Shaw, "Nicodemus," 313; R. Edgar Iles, "Boley: An Exclusively Negro Town in Oklahoma," *Opportunity: The Journal of Negro Life* 3 (August, 1925), 235.
100. *Langston City Herald,* June 15, 1893; *Boley Beacon,* March 12, 1908.
101. Iles, "Boley," 235; B. F. Ousley, "A Town of Colored

People in Mississippi," *American Missionary Society Bulletin*, 1904, copy in BTW; *Clearview Patriarch*, September 12, 1912.

102. Hazel R. McMahan (ed.), "Stories of Early Oklahoma," manuscript in the Oklahoma Historical Society; Maurice E. Jackson, "Mound Bayou: A Study in Social Isolation" (M. S. thesis, University of Alabama, 1937), 67.

103. *Clearview Patriarch*, May 23, 1912.

104. Ibid., December 14, 1911.

105. *Boley Progress*, March 1, 1906.

106. Oklahoma City, *Daily Oklahoman*, September 30, 1915.

107. A number of whites living in other states mistakenly thought that black towns even prohibited white visitors. For example, see Philadelphia *Christian Recorder*, November 18, 1909.

108. As quoted by New Orleans *State*, June 7, 1910.

CHAPTER 5

1. Richard Wright, *Black Power, A Record of Reactions in a Land of Pathos* (New York: Harper and Brothers, 1954), 34.

2. As quoted by *St. Louis Globe-Democrat*, February 22, 1913.

3. As quoted by J. Saunders Redding, *No Day of Triumph* (New York: Harper and Brothers, 1942), 300.

4. *Boley Progress*, May 17, 1906.

5. Charles Banks to Dear Friend, Mound Bayou, 1912, Booker T. Washington Papers, Library of Congress (hereafter cited BTW).

6. *Langston City Herald*, September 21, 1895; Banks to Booker T. Washington, Mound Bayou, April 14, 1915, BTW.

7. R. Edgar Iles, "Boley: An Exclusively Negro Town in Oklahoma," *Opportunity: The Journal of Negro Life* 3 (August, 1925), 232–233; Nick Comfort, "Boley," *Oklahoma Journal of Religion* 1 (July, 1944), 11; Mozell C. Hill, "The All-Negro Society in Oklahoma" (Ph. D. dissertation, University of Chicago, 1946), 46.

8. William Loren Katz, *The Black West* (New York: Doubleday and Company, 1971), 196. As one of many examples,

the *Langston City Herald* suspended publication for several months during the spring of 1898.

9. *Western Cyclone*, July 15, 1886.
10. Ibid., November 18, 1886.
11. Deed Record, Abstract of Titles, A, 1897–1939, Second District, Bolivar County Court House, Cleveland, Mississippi.
12. Banks to Washington, Mound Bayou, July 24, 1910, BTW.
13. Ibid., February 20, 1914, BTW.
14. As quoted by August Meier, "Booker T. Washington and the Town of Mound Bayou," *Phylon* 15 (Fourth Quarter, 1954), 399.
15. Ibid., 399–400; Banks to Washington, Mound Bayou, March 11, 1915; telegram, Banks to Washington, Mound Bayou, August 22, 1914, BTW.
16. *Cleveland* [Mississippi] *Enterprise*, September 10, 1914; Banks to Dear Sir, Mound Bayou, November 13, 1914, BTW.
17. Banks to Washington, Mound Bayou, April 14, 1915; Banks to William Graves, Mound Bayou, February 4, 1915, BTW.
18. Banks to Washington, Mound Bayou, September 30, February 15, 1915; Washington to Banks, Tuskegee, October 7, 1915; A. L. Perry to Banks, Greenwood, Mississippi, February 13, 1915; T. S. Owens to William Graves, Mound Bayou, October 4, 1915, BTW.
19. Banks to Fred Moore, Mound Bayou, July 14, 1915; Banks to Washington, Mound Bayou, September 30, 1915; Banks to *The Student* (Tuskegee Institute), Mound Bayou, October 23, 1915, BTW.
20. Emmett Scott to Banks, Tuskegee, October 20, 1915; Banks to Fred Moore, Mound Bayou, July 14, 1915; Banks to Washington, Mound Bayou, March 11, 1915; Banks to Dear Sir, Mound Bayou, December 30, 1914, BTW; Tuskegee Institute, *The Student*, March 6, 1920. Banks estimated his total worth at $100,000 in early 1915.
21. Banks to Washington, Mound Bayou, March 11, 1915, BTW.
22. William E. Bittle and Gilbert Geis, "Racial Self-Fulfillment and the Rise of an All-Negro Community in Okla-

homa," *Phylon* 18 (Third Quarter, 1957), 258.

23. *Souvenir Program of the 50th Anniversary of Mound Bayou, Mississippi, July 11–17, 1937*, copy in Mississippi Department of Archives and History, Jackson (hereafter cited MDAH).

24. Iles, "Boley," 233.

25. *Clearview Patriarch*, February 8, 1912.

26. *Cleveland Enterprise*, July 30, 1914; Montgomery to John P. St. John, Hurricane, Mississippi, May 23, 1879, Papers of Governor John St. John, Archives Division, Kansas State Historical Society, Topeka (hereafter cited KSHS); *Boley Progress*, April 8, 1909.

27. *Boley Progress*, July 8, 1909.

28. H. R. Beale to C. R. Springer, South Bend, Indiana, April 8, 1909, BTW.

29. Banks to Beale, Mound Bayou, April 16, 1909, BTW.

30. As early as April 6, 1907, the editor of the *Paden Times* proposed that no lots inside that community be sold to blacks and that the Paden Townsite Company enforce the prohibition.

31. *Okemah Ledger*, August 31, 1911.

32. As quoted by *Western Age*, September 4, 1908.

33. Destitute, McCabe died in Chicago in February, 1920. Ashamed for her friends to know he died a pauper, McCabe's wife had his body secretly returned to Kansas for a private funeral in Topeka.

34. Harold M. Troper, "The Creek-Negroes of Oklahoma and Canadian Immigration, 1909–11," *Canadian Historical Review* 53 (September, 1972), 272–288; Robin W. Winks, *The Blacks in Canada* (Montreal: McGill-Queen's University Press, 1971), 303–306, 309.

35. *Boley Progress*, January 20, 1910; Vinita *Weekly Chieftain*, March 31, 1911.

36. *Clearview Patriarch*, March 23, April 13, September 21, October 26, 1911.

37. Unless otherwise indicated, material on Chief Sam's movement was taken from William E. Bittle and Gilbert Geis, *The Longest Way Home, Chief Alfred Sam's Back to Africa Movement* (Detroit: Wayne State University Press, 1964). J. Ayo Langley, "Chief Sam's African Movement

and Race Consciousness in Africa," *Phylon* 32 (Second Quarter, 1971), 164–178, deals with the African side of Sam's movement.

38. Katz, *Black West,* 252.
39. This interpretation disagrees with Edwin S. Redkey, *Black Exodus, Black Nationalists and Back to Africa, 1890–1910* (New Haven: Yale University Press, 1969). Redkey argues that the migration of southern blacks to Oklahoma represented an early substitute for an African exodus. Extant records indicate that many Oklahoma blacks considered Africa only after the passage of a Jim Crow law in 1907 and the grandfather clause in 1910. At that point, a number of blacks in the state wrote to the American Colonization Society seeking information on Africa and expressing their desire to leave Oklahoma. For examples of such correspondence, see American Colonization Society Records, Library of Congress, Series 1A, Number 295, Volume 302, Reel 152.
40. Okemah *Independent,* September 4, 1913.
41. Kaye M. Teall (ed.), *Black History in Oklahoma, A Resource Book* (Oklahoma City: Oklahoma City Public Schools, 1971), 287.
42. Okemah *Independent,* August 28, 1913.
43. *Clearview Patriarch,* September 27, 1913.
44. Ibid.
45. Okemah *Independent,* September 4, 1913.
46. *Clearview Patriarch,* October 25, 1913.
47. *Wewoka and Lima Courier,* November 21, 1913.
48. *Clearview Patriarch,* May 30, 1914.
49. *Boley Progress,* July 16, 1915.
50. *Western Cyclone,* February 10, 1887.
51. *Nicodemus Cyclone,* April 1, 1888.
52. Ibid., March 9, 1888.
53. *Kansas City Times,* May 28, 1959; Van B. Shaw, "Nicodemus, Kansas, A Study in Isolation" (Ph. D. dissertation, University of Missouri, 1951), 117–118.
54. *Bogue Signal,* December 20, 1888.
55. *Nicodemus Cyclone,* September 7, 1888.
56. *Bogue Signal,* November 29, 1888; *Kansas City Times,* May 28, 1959; *Salina Journal,* February 12, 1950; Roy

Garvin, "Benjamin or 'Pap' Singleton and His Followers," *Journal of Negro History* 33 (January, 1948), 16–18.

57. Russell became the head of a state institution in the black town of Taft, Oklahoma; Jones moved to Arizona; and Banks mysteriously dropped out of sight in 1918.

58. As quoted by Hill, "All-Negro Society in Oklahoma," 56.

59. As quoted by Joseph Taylor, "Mound Bayou—Past and Present," *Negro History Bulletin* 3 (July, 1940), 110. Green died in 1896, Montgomery in 1924.

60. As quoted by Hill, "All-Negro Society in Oklahoma, 156–157.

61. Population figures for Nicodemus and the other black towns represent approximations. Booster newspapers generally overestimated the number of residents, while state and federal census enumerators sometimes counted the number of people living in the township, the immediate area of the colony, or just those residing inside the town limits.

62. Robert Hackenberg, "A Negro Settlement in Kansas," manuscript in the Kenneth Spencer Research Library, University of Kansas, Lawrence.

63. Federal Writers' Project, *Kansas, A Guide to the Sunflower State* (New York: The Viking Press, 1939), 329.

64. *Hays Daily News*, November 8, 1953; *Salina Journal*, February 12, 1950.

65. Dickson Hartwell and Carol Weld, "Mississippi's Miracle Town," *Coronet* 30 (September, 1951), 125–128; Taylor, "Mound Bayou—Past and Present," 109; Bureau of Government Research, University of Mississippi, *Mound Bayou 1973, City in Transition* (University, Mississippi: University of Mississippi, 1973), 23.

66. As quoted by Redding, *No Day of Triumph*, 292. From 1942 to the present, Mound Bayou citizens have attempted to revitalize the town through the formation of the Mound Bayou Development Corporation and the receipt of over $1,000,000 in grants from private foundations and state and federal governments. Much remains to be done. A report issued by the University of Mississippi Bureau of Government Research in 1973 described dusty streets, abandoned homes and dilapidated houses, inadequate mu-

nicipal services, the relative absence of people with the managerial training necessary to attract industry, a communications gap between leaders and citizens, and a degree of hostility toward the community from a few state officials. A random sample of citizens taken in 1970 indicated that over three-fifths of those interviewed lived at or below the poverty level and that over 90 percent had an annual income of $5,000 or less. In November, 1974, it appeared that the loss of federal funds would close the Delta Community Hospital and Health Center, Inc., at Mound Bayou. See *Mound Bayou 1973, City in Transition*, passim, and "Mound Bayou's Crisis," *Time*, November 25, 1974, 107.

67. Ralph W. Tyler to Washington, Tulsa, November 23, 1913, BTW.
68. *Clearview Patriarch*, January 3, 1914.
69. Iles, "Boley," 232.
70. Ibid., 232–234; John Daniel Bell, "Boley, A Study of a Negro City" (M. S. thesis, University of Kansas, 1928), 36; William E. Bittle and Gilbert Geis, "A Dream That Faded," *New York Times Magazine*, December 6, 1964, 54; Comfort, "Boley," 8–11.
71. As quoted by B. F. Ousley, "A Town of Colored People in Mississippi," *American Missionary Society Bulletin, 1904.*
72. For two of many examples of this attitude, see Montgomery to Washington, Mound Bayou, May 28, 1908, and Banks to Emmett Scott, Mound Bayou, October 29, 1915, BTW.
73. Shaw, "Nicodemus," 105, 108, 123, 304. Perhaps because whites had played such an important role in the town and had later overwhelmed it, Shaw found little expressed concern regarding skin color among residents; Arna Bontemps and Jack Conroy, *Anyplace But Here* (New York: Hill and Wang, 1966), 67; Atchison *Weekly Champion*, July 23, 1881.
74. As quoted by New Orleans *State*, June 7, 1910.
75. Mozell C. Hill, "A Comparative Study of Race Attitudes in the All-Negro Community in Oklahoma," *Phylon* 7 (Third Quarter, 1946), 260–268.
76. Iles, "Boley," 234.

77. As quoted by Redding, *No Day of Triumph*, 300–301.
78. As quoted by Mozell C. Hill, "Basic Racial Attitudes Toward Whites in the Oklahoma All-Negro Community," *American Journal of Sociology* 49 (May, 1944), 522. In *Dark Ghetto, Dilemmas of Social Power* (New York: Harper and Row, 1965), 11–20, Kenneth B. Clark discusses a similar phenomenon in the urban ghetto.
79. Charles S. Johnson, "A Footnote on Isolation," *Survey Graphic* 27 (January, 1938), 36, Edward B. Reuter, *The American Race Problem, A Study of the Negro* (New York: Thomas Y. Crowell Company, 1927), and Richard A. Schermerhorn, *These Our People, Minorities in American Culture* (Boston: D. C. Heath, 1949), contain excellent discussions of the impact of social isolation on individuals and groups.
80. Wallace became the principal of a school in Enid, Oklahoma. After serving as Bolivar County sheriff for three years, Bruce was elected U. S. senator from Mississippi in 1875. Hall moved on to Pittsburg to become a reporter and columnist for a newspaper there.
81. Quotation from the transcript of "A Real Jane Pittman," *CBS 60 Minutes*, VI, Number 17, 9, as broadcast over the CBS Television Network, May 12, 1974.

Bibliography

MANUSCRIPTS

Full citations for the location of all manuscripts are contained in the notes. Since Charles Banks sent Booker T. Washington or Emmett Scott a carbon copy of most of his correspondence concerning Mound Bayou, and because of Washington's interest in the town, the Booker T. Washington Papers in the Library of Congress proved an invaluable source. The Mississippi Department of Archives and History, Jackson, also contains several important items on Mound Bayou. Unfortunately, there are no extant copies of Mound Bayou's newspaper, *The Demonstrator*. In addition to newspapers, much of the information on Boley, Clearview, and Langston was gleaned from the files of the Oklahoma Historical Society. Those interested in Nicodemus should consult the holdings of the Kansas State Historical Society in Topeka. No one studying black history in the period can afford to ignore the fine collection of clipping scrapbooks, some on all-black towns, in the Hampton Institute.

BOOKS AND ARTICLES

Bailey, M. Thomas, *Reconstruction in Indian Territory* (Port Washington, New York: Kennikat Press, 1972).

Bittle, William E., and Gilbert Geis, "A Dream That Faded," *New York Times Magazine*, December 6, 1964, 47–57.

———, "Racial Self-Fulfillment and the Rise of an All-Negro Community in Oklahoma," *Phylon* 18 (Third Quarter, 1957), 247–260.

———, *The Longest Way Home, Chief Alfred Sam's Back-to-Africa Movement* (Detroit: Wayne State University Press, 1964).

Bontemps, Arna, and Jack Conroy, *Anyplace But Here* (New York: Hill and Wang, 1966).

Broderick, Francis L., *W. E. B. Du Bois, Negro Leader in a Time of Crisis* (Stanford: Stanford University Press, 1959).

Carter, Hodding, *Lower Mississippi* (New York: Farrar and Rinehart, 1942).

———, "He's Doing Something About the Race Problem," *Saturday Evening Post,* February 23, 1946, 30–31, 64, 66, 69.

Christensen, Lawrence O., "J. Milton Turner: An Appraisal," *Missouri Historical Review* 70 (October, 1975), 1–19.

Clark, Kenneth B., *Dark Ghetto, Dilemmas of Social Power* (New York: Harper and Row, 1965).

Clarke, John Henrik, and others (eds.), *Black Titan, W. E. B. Du Bois* (Boston: Beacon Press, 1970).

Comfort, Nick, "Boley," *Oklahoma Journal of Religion* 1 (July, 1944), 8–11.

Dann, Martin, "From Sodom to the Promised Land: E. P. McCabe and the Movement for Oklahoma Colonization," *Kansas Historical Quarterly* 40 (Autumn, 1974), 370–378.

Davis, Allison, Burleigh B. Gardner, and Mary R. Gardner, *Deep South, A Social Anthropological Study of Caste and Class* (Chicago: University of Chicago Press, 1941).

Debo, Angie, *The Rise and Fall of the Choctaw Republic* (Norman: University of Oklahoma Press, 1934).

Detweiler, Frederick G., *The Negro Press in the United States* (Chicago: University of Chicago Press, 1922).

Dilliard, Irving, "James Milton Turner: A Little Known Benefactor of His People," *Journal of Negro History* 19 (October, 1934), 372–411.

Drake, St. Clair, and Horace R. Cayton, *Black Metropolis* (New York: Harper and Row, 1962).

Federal Writers' Project, *Kansas, A Guide to the Sunflower State* (New York: Viking Press, 1939).

Fesler, Myrtle D., *Pioneers of Western Kansas* (New York: Carlton Press, 1962).

Fleming, Walter L., " 'Pap' Singleton, The Moses of the Colored Exodus," *American Journal of Sociology* 15 (July, 1909), 61–82.

Foner, Philip S. (ed.), *W. E. B. Du Bois Speaks, Speeches and Addresses, 1890–1919* (New York: Pathfinder Press, 1970).

Frazier, E. Franklin, *The Negro in the United States* (New York: The Macmillan Company, 1949).

Fullinwider, S. P., *The Mind and Mood of Black America* (Homewood, Illinois: The Dorsey Press, 1969).

Garvin, Roy, "Benjamin or 'Pap' Singleton and His Followers," *Journal of Negro History* 33 (January, 1948), 7–23.

Gibson, Arrell M., *The Chickasaws* (Norman: University of Oklahoma Press, 1971).

Gottschalk, Jane, "The Rhetorical Strategy of Booker T. Washington," *Phylon* 27 (Fourth Quarter, 1966), 388–395.

Hamilton, Kenneth M., "The Origin and Early Developments of Langston, Oklahoma," *Journal of Negro History* 62 (July, 1977), 270–282.

———, "Townsite Speculation and the Origin of Boley, Oklahoma," *The Chronicles of Oklahoma* 55 (Summer, 1977), 180–189.

Harlan, Louis R., *Booker T. Washington, The Making of a Black Leader* (New York: Oxford University Press, 1972).

Hartwell, Dickson, and Carol Weld, "Mississippi's Miracle Town," *Coronet* 30 (September, 1951), 125–128.

Hill, Mozell C., "A Comparative Study of Race Attitudes in the All-Negro Community in Oklahoma," *Phylon* 7 (Third Quarter, 1946), 260–268.

———, "Basic Racial Attitudes Toward Whites in the Oklahoma All-Negro Community," *American Journal of Sociology* 49 (May, 1944), 519–523.

———, and Thelma D. Ackiss, "The 'Insight Interview' Approach to Race Relations," *Journal of Social Psychology* 21 (February, 1945), 197–208.

———, *Culture of a Contemporary All-Negro Community* (Langston, Oklahoma: Langston University, 1943).

Iles, R. Edgar, "Boley: An Exclusively Negro Town in Oklahoma," *Opportunity: The Journal of Negro Life* 3 (August, 1925), 231–235.

Jackson, Luther P., "Shaped by a Dream, A Town Called Boley," *Life* 65 (November 29, 1968), 72–74.

Johnson, Charles S., "A Footnote on Isolation," *Survey Graphic* 27 (January, 1938), 36.

———, *Growing Up in the Black Belt, Negro Youth in the Rural South* (Washington, D. C.: American Council of Education, 1941).

Katz, William Loren, *The Black West* (New York: Doubleday and Company, 1971).

Langley, J. Ayo, "Chief Sam's African Movement and Race Consciousness in West Africa," *Phylon* 32 (Second Quarter, 1971), 164–178.

Littlefield, Daniel F., Jr., and Lonnie E. Underhill, "Black Dreams and 'Free' Homes: The Oklahoma Territory, 1891–1894," *Phylon* 34 (December, 1973), 342–357.

Logan, Rayford W., *Howard University, The First Hundred Years, 1867–1967* (New York: New York University Press, 1969).

Mabry, William W., "Disenfranchisement of the Negro in Mississippi," *Journal of Southern History* 4 (August, 1938), 318–333.

Mathews, Faye, "Dream of a Black State," *Sepia* 21 (March, 1972), 66–78.

Meier, August, "Booker T. Washington and the Town of Mound Bayou," *Phylon* 15 (Fourth Quarter, 1954), 396–401.

———, "Negro Class Structure and Ideology in the Age of Booker T. Washington," *Phylon* 23 (Third Quarter, 1962), 258–266.

———, *Negro Thought in America, 1880–1915* (Ann Arbor: University of Michigan Press, 1969).

———, and Elliott Rudwick, *From Plantation to Ghetto* (New York: Hill and Wang, 1966).

"Mound Bayou," *Time* 30 (July 26, 1937), 14.

"Mound Bayou's Crisis," *Time* 104 (November 25, 1974), 107.

Myrdal, Gunnar, *An American Dilemma: The Negro Problem and Modern Democracy* (New York: Harper and Brothers, 1944).

"Negro Town," *Newsweek* 14 (July 24, 1939), 14.

Ousley, B. F., "A Town of Colored People in Mississippi," *American Missionary Society Bulletin, 1904.*

Pease, William H., and Jane H., *Black Utopia: Negro Communal Experiments in America* (Madison: State Historical Society of Wisconsin, 1963).

———, "Organized Negro Communities: A North American Experiment," *Journal of Negro History* 47 (January, 1962), 19–34.

Redding, J. Saunders, *No Day of Triumph* (New York: Harper and Brothers, 1942).

Redkey, Edwin S., *Black Exodus, Black Nationalists and Back to Africa, 1890–1910* (New Haven: Yale University Press, 1969).

Reuter, Edward B., *The American Race Problem, A Study of the Negro* (New York: Thomas Y. Crowell Company, 1927).

Roberson, Jere W., "Edward P. McCabe and the Langston Experiment," *The Chronicles of Oklahoma* 51 (Fall, 1973), 343–355.

Rose, Harold M., "The All-Negro Town: Its Evolution and Function," *Geographic Review* 55 (July, 1965), 362–381.

Rudwick, Elliott M., *W. E. B. Du Bois, Propagandist of the Negro Protest* (New York: Atheneum, 1969).

Schermerhorn, Richard A., *These Our People, Minorities in American Culture* (Boston: D. C. Heath, 1949).

Schwendemann, Glen, "Nicodemus: Negro Haven on the Solomon," *Kansas Historical Quarterly* 34 (Spring, 1968), 10–31.

———, "Wyandotte and the First 'Exodusters' of 1879," *Kansas Historical Quarterly* 26 (Autumn, 1960), 233–249.

Spencer, Samuel R., *Booker T. Washington and the Negro's Place in American Life* (Boston: Little, Brown and Company, 1955).

Taylor, Joseph, "Mound Bayou—Past and Present," *Negro History Bulletin* 3 (July, 1940), 105–111.

Teall, Kaye M. (ed.), *Black History in Oklahoma, A Resource Book* (Oklahoma City: Oklahoma City Public Schools, 1971).

Tong, Hiram, "The Pioneers of Mound Bayou," *Century Magazine* 79 (January, 1910), 390–400.

Troper, Harold M., "The Creek-Negroes of Oklahoma and Canadian Immigration, 1909–11," *Canadian Historical Review* 53 (September, 1972), 272–288.
Van Deusen, John G., "The Exodus of 1879," *Journal of Negro History* 21 (April, 1936), 111–129.
Walton, Webb, "All Black: A Unique Negro Community," *Survey Graphic* 27 (January, 1938), 34–36.
Washington, Booker T., "A Town Owned by Negroes," *The World's Work* 14 (July, 1907), 9125–9134.
———, "Boley, A Negro Town in the West," *The Outlook* 88 (January 4, 1908), 28–31.
———, "Law and Order and the Negro," *The Outlook* 93 (November 6, 1909), 547–555.
———, *My Larger Education* (New York: Doubleday, Page and Company, 1911).
———, *The Negro in Business* (Chicago: Afro-American Press, 1968).
———, *The Story of the Negro, The Rise of the Race From Slavery* (New York: Doubleday, Page and Company, 1909), II.
Wharton, Vernon L., *The Negro in Mississippi, 1865–1890* (Chapel Hill: University of North Carolina Press, 1947).
Willey, Day Allen, "Mound Bayou—A Negro Municipality," *Alexander's Magazine* 4 (July 15, 1907), 159–166.
Winks, Robin W., *The Blacks in Canada* (Montreal: McGill-Queen's University Press, 1971).
Woodman, Harold, *King Cotton and His Retainers* (Lexington: University of Kentucky Press, 1968).
Woodward, C. Vann, *The Strange Career of Jim Crow* (New York: Oxford University Press, 1966).
Wright, Richard, *Black Power, A Record of Reactions in a Land of Pathos* (New York: Harper and Brothers, 1954).
Wynne, Lewis N., "Brownsville, The Reaction of the Negro Press," *Phylon* 38 (Second Quarter, 1972), 153–160.

NEWSPAPERS

Black Town:

   Boley Beacon, 1908.
   Boley Informer, 1911.

Boley News, 1918.
Boley Progress, 1905–1906, 1909–1912, 1915, 1926.
Bookertee [Oklahoma] *Searchlight*, 1919.
Clearview *Lincoln Tribune*, 1904.
Clearview Patriarch, 1911–1914, 1916.
Langston *Church and State*, 1911.
Langston City Herald, 1892–1898.
Langston *Western Age*, 1905–1909.
Nicodemus Cyclone, 1887–1888.
Nicodemus Enterprise, 1887.
Nicodemus *Western Cyclone*, 1886–1887.
Taft [Oklahoma] *Enterprise*, 1911–1912.
Wewoka and Lima [Oklahoma] *Courier*, 1913.

Kansas:

Atchison Globe, 1900.
Atchison *Weekly Champion*, 1881.
Bogue Signal, 1888.
Ellis Standard, 1877.
Graham County [Gettysburg] *Lever*, 1879.
Hays Daily News, 1953.
Hill City Democrat, 1888.
Hill City Times, 1934, 1954, 1961, 1968.
Kirwin Chief, 1882.
Lawrence Journal, 1879.
Oakley Graphic, 1931.
Parsons Eclipse, 1882.
Salina Journal, 1950.
Smith Center *Pioneer*, 1879.
Stockton *Rooks County Record*, 1887.
Topeka Capital, 1891, 1904, 1937, 1953.
Topeka Commonwealth, 1879, 1882.
Topeka Daily Capital, 1911.
Topeka Daily News, 1911.
Topeka Journal, 1922.
Webster Eagle, 1887.

Mississippi:

Cleveland Enterprise, 1914.

Greenville *Leader*, 1927.
Raymond Gazette, 1890.

Oklahoma:

Alva Review, 1902.
Beaver Journal, 1903.
Coyle *Cimarron Valley Clipper*, 1908.
Daily Leader-Guthrie, 1894.
Daily Oklahoman, 1906, 1912, 1915.
Edmond Sun-Democrat, 1895, 1897.
El Reno News, 1900.
Guthrie Daily Leader, 1893.
Guthrie *Daily Oklahoma State Capitol*, 1893, 1894.
Guymon Herald, 1919.
Harlow's Weekly, 1916.
Kingfisher Press, 1896.
Krebs Eagle, 1899.
Lexington Leader, 1891, 1905, 1909.
Mangum Star, 1905.
Norman Transcript, 1891.
Okemah *Independent*, 1913.
Okemah Ledger, 1907, 1908, 1911.
Oklahoma City *Sunday Oklahoman*, 1917.
Oklahoma City Times, 1968.
Oklahoma City *Times Journal*, 1907.
Paden Times, 1907.
Shawnee Daily-Herald, 1908.
Stillwater Advance, 1902.
Stillwater Gazette, 1897.
Vinita *Indian Chieftain*, 1901, 1902.
Vinita *Weekly Chieftain*, 1909, 1911.
Weleetka American, 1905, 1907.

Other:

Chicago Tribune, 1880.
Durham [North Carolina] *Morning Herald*, 1975.
Indianapolis Freeman, 1910.
Kansas City Star, 1900, 1905.
Kansas City Times, 1905, 1959.
New Orleans *State*, 1910.

New York *Age*, 1907, 1912.
New York Times, 1881, 1891.
Philadelphia *Christian Recorder*, 1909.
St. Louis Globe-Democrat, 1913.
San Francisco Examiner, 1890.
Washington Post, 1975.

UNPUBLISHED WORKS

Balleau, William J., "The Nicodemus Colony of Graham County, Kansas" (M. S. thesis, Fort Hays Kansas State College, 1943).

Bell, John Daniel, "Boley: A Study of a Negro City" (M. A. thesis, University of Kansas, 1928).

Blake, Lee Ella, "The Great Exodus of 1879 and 1880 to Kansas" (M. S. thesis, Kansas State College, 1942).

Elahi, Larrie L., "A History of Boley, Oklahoma to 1915" (M. A. thesis, University of Chicago, 1968).

Hackenberg, Robert, "A Negro Settlement in Kansas" (manuscript in the Kenneth Spencer Research Library, University of Kansas).

Hill, Mozell C., "The All-Negro Society in Oklahoma" (Ph. D. dissertation, University of Chicago, 1946).

Jackson, Maurice E., "Mound Bayou: A Study in Social Isolation" (M. S. thesis, University of Alabama, 1937).

McDaniel, Orval L., "A History of Nicodemus, Graham County, Kansas" (M. S. thesis, Fort Hays Kansas State College, 1950)

McMahan, Hazel R. (ed.), "Stories of Early Oklahoma" (manuscript in the Oklahoma Historical Society).

Sameth, Sigmund, "Creek Negroes: A Study of Race Relations" (M. A. thesis, University of Oklahoma, 1940).

Shaw, Van B., "Nicodemus, Kansas, A Study in Isolation" (Ph. D. dissertation, University of Missouri, 1951).

Tolson, Arthur L., "The Negro in Oklahoma Territory, 1889–1907: A Study in Racial Discrimination" (Ph. D. dissertation, University of Oklahoma, 1966).

Waldron, Nell Blythe, "Colonization in Kansas From 1861–1890" (Ph. D. dissertation, Northwestern University, 1932).

OTHER MATERIALS

"A Real Jane Pittman," *CBS 60 Minutes*, Volume VI, No. 17, as broadcast over the CBS Television Network, May 12, 1974.

American Colonization Society Records, Library of Congress, Series 1A, Volume 302, Reel 152.

Annual Report of the Fifteenth Annual National Negro Business League, Muskogee, Oklahoma, August 19–21, 1914.

Banks, Charles, *Negro Town and Colony, Mound Bayou, Bolivar Co., Miss., Opportunities Open to Farmers and Settlers* (Mound Bayou, Mississippi: Demonstrator Print, n. d.).

Benjamin Harrison Papers, Library of Congress.

Boley Commercial Club, *Facts About Boley, Okla., The Largest and Wealthiest Exclusive Negro City in the World* (1911).

Bureau of Government Research, University of Mississippi, *Mound Bayou, 1973, City in Transition* (University, Mississippi: University of Mississippi, 1973).

Congressional Record, Senate, 88 Cong., 2 Sess., Vol. 110, Part IV, March 16, 1964.

Crowell, Arthur, Jr., *The Black Frontier* (Lincoln: University of Nebraska Television, 1970).

Deed Record, Abstract of Titles, A, 1897–1939, Second District, Bolivar County Court House, Cleveland, Mississippi.

Hood, Aurelius P., *The Negro at Mound Bayou* (Nashville, AME Sunday School Union, 1910).

"Interview with Jay C. Trimble," December 30, 1937, Indian-Pioneer Papers, Western History Collections, University of Oklahoma.

"Interview with Lemuel Jackson," June 24, 1937, Indian-Pioneer Papers, Oklahoma Historical Society.

Kansas State Census, Graham County, 1885.

Mound Bayou, Mississippi, Anniversary Diamond Jubilee, July, 1962.

Semi-Centennial Celebration, The Founding of Mound Bayou, July, 1937.

Souvenir Program, Mound Bayou Anniversary Celebration, July, 1962.

Souvenir Program of the 50th Anniversary of Mound Bayou, Mississippi, July 11–17, 1937.

Tax Rolls, 1881, 1887, Nicodemus Township, Graham County Court House, Hill City, Kansas.

Tax Rolls, 1910, 1911, Logan County, Villages, Logan County Court House, Guthrie, Oklahoma.

Index